Church Administration Handbook

Church Administration Handbook

Bruce P. Powers
Editor

BROADMAN PRESS
NASHVILLE, TENNESSEE

4231-12

ISBN: 0-8054-3112-8

Dewey Decimal Classification: 254
Subject Heading: CHURCH ADMINISTRATION

Library of Congress Catalog Card Number: 84-29249
Printed in the United States of America

Scripture quotations marked (GNB) are from the *Good News Bible,* the Bible in Today's English Version. Old Testament: Copyright © American Bible Society 1976; New Testament: Copyright © American Bible Society 1966, 1971, 1976. Used by permission. Those marked (KJV) are from the King James Version of the Bible. Those marked (NEB) are from *The New English Bible.* Copyright © The Delegates of the Oxford University Press and the Syndics of the Cambridge University Press, 1961, 1970. Reprinted by permission. Quotations marked (RSV) are from the Revised Standard Version of the Bible, copyrighted 1946, 1952, © 1971, 1973. Those marked (Phillips) are reprinted with permission of Macmillan Publishing Co., Inc. from J. B. Phillips: *The New Testament in Modern English,* Revised Edition. © J. B. Phillips 1958, 1960, 1972.

Library of Congress Cataloging in Publication Data

Powers, Bruce P.
  Church administration handbook.

  1. Church management—Handbooks, manuals, etc.
I. Title.
BV652.P685 1985   254   84-29249
ISBN 0-8054-3112-8

Preface

Here it is! A comprehensive handbook that gives basic principles and guidelines in the area of general church administration. More specifically, it is a guidebook that brings together theology and the practice of ministry within a framework of concern for

A church being alive and on mission for Christ;

Church growth and discipleship development;

The work being done *and* for those doing it;

Ministers as servant leaders; and

Effective, goal-oriented administration.

This book is designed as a general reference for (1) ministers who desire ready access to information and procedures related to everyday responsibilities, and (2) ministerial students who are studying the work of a minister in a local church.

The content moves sequentially through three broad categories:

1. How a minister relates to organizations and to people (chs. 1-3);
2. How a minister performs administrative functions (chs. 4-15); and
3. How a minister relates to self and colleagues (chs. 16-18).

Each chapter provides basic information, then gives guidelines and procedures related to the topic. At the end of each chapter there is a bibliography of resources for further information or study. The book can be studied sequentially, or can be consulted topically by referring to the expanded table of Contents.

The authors of this volume are well suited to prepare a basic textbook/handbook for church administration. They have served in local churches, in denominational positions, and now as teachers in the field. They are highly respected writers, speakers, and practioners of the type of church administration that undergirds the nature and mission of the church through positive, servant-oriented leadership.

The idea for this book actually began soon after the eager acceptance of an earlier publication, *Christian Education Handbook.* Despite a trend for administrative books to single-issue, specialized publications, the response from many ministers and teachers pinpointed the need for a general, comprehensive handbook that integrates the various functions of ministry. So, here it is.

Just as that earlier book has become a primary reference in the area of educational administration, this book promises to be a standard sourcebook in general church administration.

I would like to express appreciation to the authors—especially for their common commitment to a biblically based, servant-oriented style of leadership in church ministry; to their colleagues and students who have helped refine the concepts, values, and skills presented; and to the many denominational and church leaders who reacted to outlines, previewed the material in conferences, and encouraged the publication of these helps for others.

Personal thanks to my wife, Jean, who assisted with the technical preparation of the manuscript; to Carolyn Bailey, my ever-helpful secretary; and to my colleagues at Southeastern Seminary who have been so helpful and supportive during this project.

BRUCE P. POWERS

Wake Forest, North Carolina

Contents

The Authors

William G. Caldwell, Professor of Church Administration, South-
western Baptist Theological Seminary, Fort Worth, Texas

Robert D. Dale, Professor of Pastoral Leadership and Church Ministries, Southeastern Baptist Theological Seminary, Wake Forest,
North Carolina

J. Ralph Hardee, Associate Professor of Church Administration, The
Southern Baptist Theological Seminary, Louisville, Kentucky

Bob I. Johnson, Associate Professor of Religious Education and
Church Administration, Midwestern Baptist Theological Seminary, Kansas City, Missouri

Bruce P. Powers, Professor of Christian Education, Southeastern
Baptist Theological Seminary, Wake Forest, North Carolina

Mark Short, Associate Professor of Church Administration, New
Orleans Baptist Theological Seminary, New Orleans, Louisiana

1

Managing Christian Institutions

Robert D. Dale

Church administration is ministry, not methods. It's people, not paperwork. It's human processes, not inhumane policies. It's management, not manipulation.

Administration and management refer to an organization's "people processes" and help institutions use their resources well. In the church and other Christian institutions administration is growing people, not simply doing things. Administration is vital if a church is to reach its mission. But "administrivia" is to be avoided if morale for the mission is to remain high.

Administration: Science, Art, Gift

Church administration or management is a science, an art, and a gift. As a science, church management involves procedures and techniques that can be learned by study and by practice. As an art, administration calls for relational sensitivity, intuition, and timing. These artistic people skills are largely natural talents but can be enhanced to some degree by experience and training.

Additionally, the apostle Paul names administration as a spiritual gift (1 Cor. 12:28). Different translations of the New Testament refer to this gift by using a variety of terms such as "governments" (KJV), "administrators" (RSV), "workers of spiritual power" (Phillips), and the "power to guide" (NEB). The Greek term for administration in this passage translates to "helmsman." In the same manner that pilots steer their ships through the rocks and shallows safely to their destinations, ministers guide their congregations toward their missions. Two important observations about steersmen apply also to Christian managers. First, helmsmen are members of the ship's larger crew. Steering is only one vital function in the operation of a ship or an institution. Likewise, ministers serve a congregation's overall needs. Second, helmsmen take orders from the captain. No minister stands above Christ in the management of Christian ministry.

Overview: Choosing, Creating, Catalyzing, Coordinating

Secular business management has become a highly technical field. Since congregations are volunteer, not-for-profit organizations and since ministers generally see themselves as paraprofessional managers, the model which follows is streamlined. Four actions—one personal and three congregational—describe church administration.

Fundamentally, church management calls for choosing, creating, catalyzing, and coordinating personal and institutional resources. The model describes basic processes in congregational management and specifies "what" (a definition of the process), "why" (a theological perspective), "who" (initiators of the processes), and "how" (the applications of the process).

Choosing: Self-Management Actions

Ministers who manage congregations or other Christian institutions make three crucial choices: choose ad-ministry style, choose start-up strategy, choose closure approach. These choices reflect the minister's freedom to choose among options or alternatives.

1. You Can Choose Your Ad-ministry Style.

What? Ad-ministry style describes the process of selecting and using a management pattern consistently.[1] Choosing a personal approach or pattern of managing a congregation's or other Christian institution's resources boils down to how ministers structure their time. Self-management is, after all, largely a matter of stewardship of time and life.

Why? Theologically, administrators can affirm several statements about style and the stewardship of time. (1) God is the God of time and history. God has done His redemptive work through persons and amid history. He is the God of the Exodus, the Exile, the incarnation, and the empty tomb. God's use of time for redemption makes the use of our personal time precious. (2) The Bible speaks of two kinds of time: *chronos* and *kairos*. *Chronos* is the measured, durative time typical of clocks and calendars. All *chronos* belongs to God. *Kairos* smacks of timing and refers to time becoming ripe, full, and overflowing with opportunity (Mark 1:15; Luke 4:21; Matt. 16:3; Luke 12:56). Ministers must use *chronos* well in order to be ready to use *kairos* at all. (3) Jesus had time enough to do God's will. Think of the scope of Jesus' task and the relatively short time He had to accomplish it in. Yet He seemed to manage both the task and the time frame without apparent frustration. Evidently Jesus learned the lesson that God gives persons adequate time to accomplish God's purpose in their lives. (4) Grace frees Christians from yesterday's sin and guilt as well as tomorrow's fears and challenges.

Who? Ministers have numerous resources for selecting a consistent ad-ministry style. Friends and advisors offer feedback. Studying the great biblical leaders provides behavioral models of effective ministry. Biographies of Luther, Wesley, famous evangelists and missionaries, and other denominational and institutional leaders yield insights into management styles. Taking into account that past leaders and current mentors minister in settings that differ from our personal circumstances, only individual ministers make the final choice about their own styles.

How? The basic management challenge for ministers is self-management. Ministers set their own schedules and do eternal work that's always difficult to measure and evaluate. Time use, then, provides the proof of effective style stewardship. Some principles guide ministers in time management.

• Find out how you're using your time now. Keep a time diary of your actual work activities for a week. What do you notice about your stewardship of your professional energies?

• Plan to use your time on priorities. Most effective ministers work from a prioritized "to do" list of daily tasks. They also use a "quiet hour," an uninterrupted time for concentrating on crucial projects. They reserve the times when their biological clocks are at their best for working on their most challenging tasks. They plan before they attempt to complete their work.

• Work on a weekly and daily schedule. Regular structure improves productivity.

• Handle a piece of work once. Use a three-step cycle of action: start, work, stop.

• Delegate to team members. Free yourself for crucial tasks and give others a chance to participate and grow.

• Pace yourself. Move from intense involvement to "sabbath" refreshment.

• Group similar tasks together. For example, think "communication" and write a thank-you note while you're waiting on someone to come to the phone.

• Plan to grow personally and professionally.

• Live one day at a time.

• When uncertain or frustrated, ask yourself the basic time management question: "What's the best use of my time right now?"

2. You Can Choose Your Ministry Start-up Strategy.

What? Ministry start-up generally refers to the first twelve to eighteen months of establishing ministry in a new post. Given average tenures, from 30 to 50 percent of a minister's total professional life is spent in start-up transitions and activities.

Why? Theologically speaking, the Christian view of history provides a foundation for ministry start-up work. (1) Christianity is a historical religion. The Bible is a book of history. For Christians, history really is His-story. (2) Christians believe history has a purpose. History has beginnings, middles, and ends—just like ministry has personal and organizational chapters. In God's plan, history's theme is redemption. (3) Christ is the apex or pivot point of history. Christ stands at the center of all history. Ministers must guard against an attitude of self-importance, especially at the beginning of a ministry when members tend to overestimate abilities.

Who? Personnel committees and pastor selection committees are increasingly serving temporarily as support groups for ministers. They, or another support network, provide encouragement, information about congregational or institutional reactions, advise on relationships and the progress of programs, give feedback, and help evaluate ministries.

How? Start-up is usually conceived as a three-step process: understanding and using the dynamics of the interim period,[2] knowing what to expect in a new ministry setting, and developing a general strategy for establishing yourself in ministry relationships in a new post.[3] Here are some helps in each of the four areas.

Understanding and using the dynamics of the interim period. The interim period actually blends into the next minister's work. How the time between the former minister's resignation, firing, or death has been used determines the beginning point and shapes the climate of ministry start-up. Ordinarily, four issues arise during interim periods.

• The emotions of grief—loss, anger, and guilt—should be recognized and resolved.

• The period creates a management vacuum in which the internal leadership circle shifts as old leaders fade and new leaders emerge.

• Relationships to denominational resources are examined.

• Most important, the interim period allows the basic mission and identity of the church or institution to be evaluated and, if needed, redefined.

Knowing what to expect in a new ministry setting. Checklists of "things to be alert to" during start-up are an important tool.[4] In random order, here are several predictable issues surrounding start-up.

• Most congregations tend to feel the minister is settled in after the moving van is gone and several casseroles have been delivered. More attention is usually paid to physical concerns than to emotional or spiritual issues.

• Generally, the denominational structures expect the new minister "to make things happen."

• The history of a congregation includes more than the statistical and sociological information ordinarily given a new or prospective minister. The congregation's beginnings, heroes, "golden years," conflicts, building programs, and sense of vision shape its present and its future.

• When the self-confidence of the minister or the congregation has eroded during the interim, two perils may develop. The congregation may become overly dependent on the minister as a rescuer. Or the minister may feel the pressure for a "quick win" and fall back on programs that were successful elsewhere.

• First impressions are built on intuitive responses to Are you genuine? and Do you care?

• Watch what surprises you during start-up. Surprises indicate a difference between what you expected and what happened.

• The "honeymoon" is a time when the new minister is given extra leeway. This momentum is precious and should be patiently invested in priority ministries.

• Early in start-up, change only what is needed, wanted, and supported.

• It's easier to follow effective ministers and build on the trust they've accumulated than to inherit the ill will assigned to ministers who have been disappointments.

• Expect to be tested.

• The end to the honeymoon is frightening and calls for clarifying and renegotiating expectations.

• Members with views like the new minister's will tend to move into the centers of power in the church or institution.

• The first conflict in a new ministry helps "set the rules" for future disagreements.

• When the new minister's leadership style exerts more initiative than the congregation expects, overlaps in responsibility occur, and conflict is apt to surface. When the new minister's leadership style takes less initiative than the congregation expects, vacuums in responsibility develop, and frustration results. The new minister is usually more able to sense the differences and adjust levels of leader initiative appropriately than the congregation-at-large.

Developing a general strategy for establishing yourself in ministry relationships in a new post. Broad strategy for start-up lends a structure for establishing ministry.[5] While numerous approaches are available, some guidelines clarify ministry priorities.

• Begin with people and build relationships for ministry and for personal encouragement.

• Help the congregation or institution define its basic purpose or dream.

• Build ministry on mainstream needs.

• Cultivate healthy organizational habits which will facilitate Christian growth.

3. You Can Choose How to Close Out a Ministry.

What? Closure means saying good-bye to a church or institution at the conclusion of a tenure of ministry. Official documents like constitutions and bylaws may specify the mechanics of how the minister terminates, but the minister decides the manner of exiting. Closure flavors ministry and tends to make the minister's impact and reputation better or worse.[6]

Why? Eschatology provides a theological perspective for closure. (1) Christians believe that God will draw history to a close in a purposeful, redemptive, and decisive manner. (2) Human history, like all processes, has an end, and that conclusion is in God's hands.

Who? The minister works with appropriate committees, councils, and task forces to ensure an orderly and productive transition. Official documents may spell out formal procedures for an interim period or tradition may suggest informal approaches.

How? The good-bye saying process is largely a relational one. While proclamation (evangelism, preaching, teaching, and worship) and pastoral care (counseling, family ministry, grief work, and offi- ciating special events) enter into closure strategies, management is the focus here.

Closure involves several attitudes and actions.

• After resigning, ministers immediately become lame ducks and lose their change agent's influence quickly.

• How the members of the congregation or institution react to the minister's resignation is an indication of the minister's overall ad- ministry style. If ministers have encouraged or allowed the congre- gation to become dependent, the members may feel betrayed and panic. If ministers have developed and expanded the leadership base of the church and if administrative processes have been clearly identified and consistently used, the congregation will face interims with more confidence.

• Lame duck leaders should wrap up unfinished projects rather than attempt to launch new ministries.

• An exit interview may be offered by the minister. The experi- ence of working with an overall responsibility for a congregation's ministry can lend insights into the potentials, problems, and charac- teristics of the total group that can serve well the search for a new minister.

• A transition packet containing administrative documents and listings of community and denominational resources is a thoughtful gesture. These materials may assist the next minister's start-up.

Creating: Innovative Congregational Actions

Some management actions are administratively creative: creative dreaming, creative evaluating, creative planning. These administra- tive initiatives focus on originating and producing new ministries and programs.

1. You Can Help Your Congregation Define Its Dream.

What? Dreaming is the process of clarifying, taking ownership of, and communicating forcefully the congregation or institution's re- demptive vision.[7]

Why? Jesus' vision of the kingdom of God formed His core teach- ing. (1) Over eighty times in the Gospels, Jesus spoke of the king- dom He came to introduce and embody. He mentioned the "kingdom of God" or the "kingdom of heaven" more than any other theme. (2) Most of Jesus' parables, the center of His teachings, describe what "the kingdom is like." (3) The kingdom of God calls persons and their institutions to submit to God's rule and provides Christians with the clue to Jesus' dream.

Who? Since every congregation has its own personality and since the Kingdom has a virtually endless variety of local embodiments, the membership at large should shape the congregation's dream of ministry. All leaders in the ministries of the church guide the process of dreaming.

How? Numerous steps can be used in guiding a congregation or institution to focus on its dream.

• Congregations move through a "health cycle" from vigor to disease (Figure 1). The health cycle model can be used to "read" the church, to discover the organization's stage of vitality or illness, and to find ways to renew the congregation.

• Broadly stated, healthy congregations build on and are renewed by their dreams, plan proactively, and minister to others. Unhealthy churches doubt themselves into decline (and, occasionally, death), reactively solve problems, and demand to be ministered to themselves.

• Preaching and teaching Jesus' parables can provide a consciousness-raising experience for a congregation to use when beginning to dream together about what God wants from them here and now.

• One important clue to a congregation's current vision is the dream of the founding group. Not all dreams are of equal value, of course. Negative and narrow visions tend to yield more rigid and ideological congregations. Mission and service-oriented beginnings develop into churches with more positive climates for ministry.

• A balance between leader vision and initiative and broad congregational consensus yields two crucial elements for the dreaming process: sharp focus and general ownership of the vision.

2. You Can Help Your Congregation Evaluate the Effectiveness of Its Ministry Programs.

What? Evaluating is the process of discovering and duplicating the congregation or institution's successes while discovering and eliminating the organization's failures. Evaluation provides an appraisal, feedback, and control mechanism.

Why? Theologically, judgment provides a doctrinal framework for

Figure 1

Health Cycle

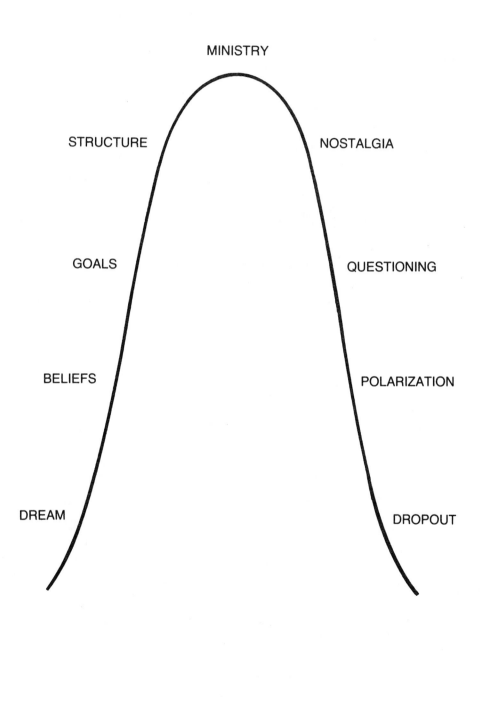

MINISTRY

STRUCTURE   NOSTALGIA

GOALS   QUESTIONING

BELIEFS   POLARIZATION

DREAM   DROPOUT

the administrative process of evaluation. Several affirmations apply. (1) While judgment is built into the fabric of human experience, God is the final judge. Both the New Testament and the creeds of Christian history declare that at the end of history Christ will return gloriously to judge the quick and the dead. (2) Mere humans lack the objectivity to make valid judgments on others' lives. Christ reminds us of our limited perspectives when He observed we may be critical of the specks in others' eyes while we overlook the logs in our own eyes (Matt. 7:3-4). (3) Self-evaluation is an ongoing discipline for every Christian (1 Cor. 9:24-27; 1 Cor. 11:28). (4) In congregational settings, we measure a volunteer worker's service by the goals set earlier by the congregation-at-large. This approach is a type of self-evaluation too. If the original goal-setting process involved the total congregation, then this volunteer has made two commitments to goals—one during the development of the congregation's original goals and another when he or she agreed to serve in the ministry programs of the church. Actions taken toward these goals can be observed and evaluated.

Who? Every group in a congregation with responsibility for ministry actions or for resource management should evaluate its work

Figure 2

Evaluation Cycle

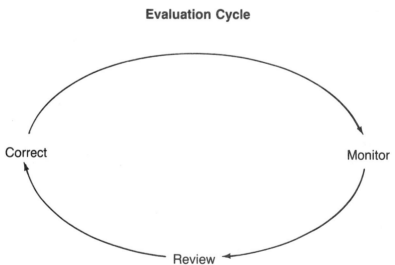

regularly. Most congregations use a representative church council to appraise the total program of the congregation. The evaluation process of monitoring, reviewing, and correcting intends to turn trial and error into trial and success (Figure 2).

How? Evaluation involves five critical elements.

• Evaluating calls us to measure performance against purpose. Good evaluation demands that standards of effectiveness or success be established beforehand. Goals always precede evaluation.

• Evaluating uses both quantitative and qualitative information. More objective information—like statistics, attendance reports, and budget summaries—need to be considered. Additionally, more subjective materials—opinions and other clues to the morale levels of the congregation—need to be included to balance and blend feelings into the factual picture.

• Evaluating uses a range of persons and a variety of methods. Both planners and implementers, along with persons involved in a program *and* those not involved, should be included in the evaluative process. Statistical records, interviews, questionnaires, continua, and pretests and posttests provide a variety of data. Involve as many members as possible and gather only information that will be used. When information is requested, members assume it will be used and are disillusioned if it isn't. Expect persons with negative perspectives to speak up early and loudly; take their opinions seriously without overreacting.

• A model for evaluation should invite both positive and negative perspectives and consider both past and future time frames (Figure 3).

• Evaluation is a continuing cycle. Preevaluation provides status checks before a ministry is launched. Mid-evaluation double-checks progress either to assure that the project is on course or to make mid-course corrections. Postevaluation combines an immediate debriefing after a project is completed as well as more seasoned reflections later on.

3. You Can Help Your Congregation Plan Effective Ministry Programs.

What? Planning is the process of creating your organizational future before it happens. Planning attempts to write history in advance.

Why? Hope provides a theological foundation for planning. (1)

Figure 3

Evaluation Model

Past Plus "In the past, I'm proud that our church has . . ."	Past Minus "In the past, I'm disappointed our church has . . ."
Future Plus "In the future, I hope our church will . . ."	Future Minus "In the future, I fear our church will . . ."

God modeled orderliness and planning in creation and redemption. (2) The future is God's possession. Only God knows the future; only God holds the future. Planning, then, becomes an act of faith that the God who gave us today will also provide a meaningful tomorrow. (3) Ultimately, the Christian's hope is Christ. (4) Christians live between the times. Our planning efforts strive to move our institutions from where we are to where God wants us to be.

Who? The leader team for church planning includes the pastor and other church staff ministers as facilitators and resource persons as well as a specific planning group, like a church council. Remember that people support what they help plan. The participation guideline for planning, then, is: *everyone who will be expected to implement the plan should be involved in planning.*

How? Planning provides congregations and institutions with reasonable targets for fulfilling their dream. Planning processes usually involve several considerations.

• All planning is an abstraction. Project planning, involving concrete acts of ministry, is the least abstract and simplest type of planning. Project planning appeals to smaller organizations and members with more concrete styles of thinking.

• Churches practice two types of planning: operational and directional. Operational planning is usually referred to as annual planning and implements the shorter-range operations of the dream. Directional planning, or long-range planning, forecasts the future needs and wants of your congregation, sets directions, and usually builds on a three- to five-year framework. A variety of computerized planning models are available for church use.

• Ordinarily, a planning sequence begins with the dream or purpose of the congregation or the needs of the church and community and develops goals. Budgeting, then, builds on the goals. New or different organizational structures extend out of budgeted goals. Ministry events and, finally, detailed actions are projected (Figure 4).

• Plan from ends to means and implement your plans from means to ends.

• Set congregational goals high but possible.

Catalyzing: Responsive Congregational Actions

Catalysts in chemistry cause reactions and speed changes. They are change agents: budgeting is catalytic; motivating is catalytic;

Figure 4

Planning Sequence

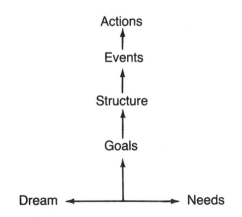

advertising is catalytic. These processes are catalytic management activities for churches.

1. You Can Change Your Congregation Through Your Church Budget.

What? Budgeting is the process of allocating resources toward goals by expressing the church's dream in dollars. An institution's budget is a theological document because it's an expression of the congregation's redemptive dream.

Why? Stewardship to the individual Christian and budgeting to the congregation reflect our response to God as Creator. (1) God calls believers to become His junior partners and trustees in creation. Jesus followed this pattern in His teachings when He made the good steward a key figure in His parables. (2) Our response to God's order of creation demands that Christians use things responsibly, love persons responsibly, and worship God responsibly. (3) The challenge of Christian stewardship is to use things, love persons, and worship God without mixing the verbs and objects. To mismatch the verbs and objects is to sin.

Who? In some smaller churches, an informal group may suggest a budget structure. But most congregations elect a committee (variously called stewardship, budget, or finance) to examine ministry plans, gather information on giving and spending, propose a basic budget structure, and implement an ongoing program of stewardship education.

How? Budgeting is resource management. The budget of an institution provides a stackpole for the coordinated use of the church's four primary resources: *money*—through an adopted, unified budget; *time*—via the church's calendar; *facilities*—by way of the development and maintenance of buildings and properties; and, most important, *people*—through a plan of evangelism, member development, and leader enlistment and training.

The steps in budgeting vary with the philosophy being used. Ministry-action budgeting is the approach outlined here.[8]

• Analyze the congregation's current ministries.

• Request ministry groups to propose ministry actions for the coming year.

• Evaluate the proposals.

• Prepare a budget for congregational discussion.

• Present the revised budget for congregational adoption.

• Fully educate the congregation about the budget and attempt to subscribe it completely.

• Keep the congregation informed throughout the church year about progress toward the ministry actions and the funds involved.

• Begin the review and evaluation process for the next year's budgeting procedures.

2. You Can Help Your Congregation Improve Its Motivational Climate.

What? Motivating is the process of helping members discover, take ownership of, and use their reservoirs of spiritual energy.

Why? Theologically, the Holy Spirit is the Christian's motivator. (1) The Holy Spirit lives within the Christian (John 14:17). This biblical insight favors the internal theories of motivation ("Persons are always motivated on their own to do something.") over the external approaches ("I cause others to act."). Manipulative "carrot-on-a-stick" approaches to motivating others are inconsistent with a reliance on the Spirit of Christ. Motivation in congregational settings, then, becomes largely a matter of setting a motivational climate and helping members channel their energies. (2) The Holy Spirit energizes Christians by encouraging and guiding us (John 14:18; Matt. 28:20). (3) The Holy Spirit ministers actively to our needs (John 14:25-31). The Spirit's internal ministry to our personal concerns is the model of motivational leadership for us to follow.

Who? The leader team for improving the motivational climate includes all organizational directors and leaders. Persons who have other members under their supervision must work to uplift the morale level of their portion of the overall institution.

How? Setting a motivational climate and helping members channel their energies toward the congregation's dream is the challenge of church leaders. Several management actions yield big dividends.

• Create a motivational climate by helping members meet their legitimate needs. People enjoy participating in an organization they can both give to and get from. Legitimate personal needs include our hunger for recognition, structure, and intimacy. Legitimate interpersonal needs involve belonging with others in a meaningful group, influencing our group's life, and being loved by important others.

• Create a motivational climate by building a ministry team. Administrators know that churches thrive on an atmosphere of "we did it" teamwork rather than a self-glorifying "I did it" attitude. Recently, I heard a pastor brag, "I raised three million dollars in a week. I deserve to tell them what to do!" Who does that pastor think contributed the three million? A "we" atmosphere builds a team for long-term, constructive ministry.

• Create a motivational climate by reaching clear agreements with your ministry team. People are motivated by knowing what's expected of them, by negotiating some issues, and by agreeing on their privileges and responsibilities. Groups are held together by promises their members make to each other. These promises or contracts keep us from the demotivating tyranny of undefined expectations. Leaders must build and maintain their credibility if they are to create a motivational climate.

3. You Can Help Your Church Advertise Its Ministries.

What? Advertising is the process of communicating Christ's message and the congregation's image to its community by means of people, print, and other media.

Why? The concept of revelation provides a theological foundation for advertising the congregation's vision. (1) A revelation is an unveiling. For Christians, revelation refers almost exclusively to God and His redemptive actions. (2) God takes the initiative to establish a personal relationship with us. Then, believers become a basic channel for revealing God's kingdom and His work. (3) God's revelation is concrete, direct, intense, and awesome. Christ's incarnation is the highest and most concrete revelation of God's nature and intent. (4) Revelation is dialogic. God reveals Himself to us; we praise and witness to God's mighty acts.

Who? The pastor and church staff usually coordinate communications about the congregation's ministry. Some churches elect a public relations committee to assist the overall congregation and its program groups in telling the stories of their ministry processes and events.

How? Just as God used a variety of approaches to communicate His mighty acts (Heb. 1:1-2), congregations must work strategically to publicize their work. The management of an advertising process incorporates several steps.

• Advertising requires focus. That is, the answers to some questions keep advertising efforts on target. Which message? To whom? For what response? When? Through which media?

• Advertising means putting yourself into the other person's shoes and telling others how your ministry benefits them.

• Advertising uses power words to trigger a positive emotional response to your church and its ministries. Power words are graphic communication tools which make your church attractive and credible.

• Advertising uses images as well as words. A logo and pictures identify your church and its work.

• Advertising uses all available media. Letterheads, bulletin boards, newsletters, and the print and electronic media help your church impact its members and its prospects.

• Advertising shows quality. Attractive material has impact. It sets a mood, creates images, and builds expectations.

• Advertising conveys a clear message. One theme is presented to one audience. The action you hope your reader/hearer will take is specified.

Coordinating: Balancing Congregational Actions

Coordination calls on the church manager to relate the varied elements and activities properly in order that ministry functions harmoniously: coordinating by organizing, coordinating by staffing, coordinating by team building. These processes draw the people and administrative processes together for ministry.

1. You Can Organize Your Congregation's Ministry.

What? Organizing is the process of developing a structure and work plan which helps persons become meaningfully involved in the goals of the congregation.

Why? The product of God's creation provides a theological perspective for the organizing process. (1) God is ultimately responsible for the being of the world. He made it out of nothing. Now creation depends on God to sustain it. (2) God's creation is good. This view argues against religious leaders who claim any organization is bad. (3) Man is a responsible steward of God's creation. Organizational structuring is one congregational application of creation.

Who? The pastor, church staff, church council, program organizational leaders, and finally the entire congregation are responsible for creating new ministry units and pruning away old ones.

How? Organizing the congregation for action is a basic management practice.

• How much organization is necessary? A congregation is under-organized if portions of its dream have no structured work units to implement them. A congregation is overorganized if structured work units exist with no direct connection with the dream. The implicit warning in these two statements is simple: don't create unnecessary organizational units since new units have to be maintained after they are set up.

• Form follows function: that's the *master principle* of organization. The product you want determines the organization you need.

• Most organizing efforts move through a fairly predictable cycle.

(1) Define the congregation's dream.

(2) Define the ministry program you need to organize.

(3) Divide the ministry into manageable units.

(4) Relate the various units of ministry into a workable arrangement.

(5) Enlist workers.

(6) Clarify worker's tasks and train them to do the job.

(7) Empower the workers to do their ministries by delegating authority to them that's equal to their responsibility.

(8) Evaluate the program of ministry in case some reorganization is needed.

2. You Can Coordinate Staffing Your Congregation's Organizations.

What? Staffing is the process of finding, enlisting, training, and encouraging the congregation's volunteer and paid leaders.

Why? Spiritual gifts provide the basis for staffing the church's organization. (1) Every Christian is gifted for service. More than thirty different spiritual gifts are mentioned in the five New Testament listings (1 Cor. 12:4-10; 1 Cor. 12:28-30; Eph. 4:11; Rom. 12:6-8; 1 Pet. 4:10-11). All of these gifts are God-given and are closely tied to the Christian virtue of love (1 Cor. 13). (2) All of the spiritual gifts are significant and are designed to advance the gospel. (3) God provides every congregation with the human resources to implement its Kingdom dream. Members are the most valuable resource in any congregation.

Who? Most churches use a nominating committee to find, enlist, and offer preservice training to workers. Computerized talent searches simplify this committee's work.

How? Several issues are crucial to staffing church organizations.

• The ideal staffing system relates three persons to each job—one person training for the future, one doing the job now, and one experienced worker coaching the other two.

• Persons who are responsible for enlisting workers need to be clear about the motivations, rewards, and morale levels of volunteer workers (and how these factors differ from those of employees).

• Forecast the church's leadership needs.

• Identify future leaders.

• Enlist needed leaders. Link their personal gifts with organizational goals.

• Provide a listing of tasks and expectations and agree on what work will be done.

• Provide training opportunities for the new volunteer leaders.

• Provide supervisory-skills training for directors who will guide the volunteer staff.[9]

3. You Can Build Your Church's Ministry Team.

What? Team building is the process of turning diversity toward unity. Team-building efforts are needed anytime two or more persons depend on each other and work together.

Why? Paul's "body of Christ" image of the church (Rom. 12 and 1 Cor. 12) lends theological substance to the management challenge of team building. (1) The body of Christ has diverse parts. Leadership in team building and coordination are required if congregations are to remain robust (Rom. 12:4,6). (2) All of the diversity is necessary for Christ's body to function well (1 Cor. 12:14-26). (3) Christ is the unifier of the diversity (1 Cor. 12:12-13).

Who? The pastor, church staff, and church council provide the primary resources for team building.

How? Team building holds two congregational concerns in balanced tension: creating a family atmosphere and getting ministry done. (See ch. 3.)

Implications: Act Now

The administrative model of choosing, creating, catalyzing, and coordinating provides church leaders several advantages. First, a framework for conceptualizing and examining your management tasks provides a platform for confident actions. Second, practice and theology are naturally and mutually related in this model. Third, this model helps ministers discover the broad administrative area(s) and/or specific skills they need to develop by further research and education.

These three advantages call for simple actions: think, believe, grow. The helm of the ship is in your hand. Act now as a Christian administrator.

Notes

1. For a full discussion of ministry styles see Robert D. Dale, *Ministers as Leaders* (Nashville: Broadman Press, 1984) and Robert Bolton and Dorothy Grover Bolton, *Social Style/Management Style* (New York: AMACOM, 1984).

2. See William A. Yon, *Prime Time for Renewal* (Washington, D.C.: Alban Institute, 1977).

3. The obvious differences among denominations in which some ministers are "called" and others "appointed" require some adjustments in a minister's start-up work.

4. See Roy M. Oswald, *The Pastor as Newcomer* (Washington, D.C.: Alban Institute, 1977).

5. Robert D. Dale, "Get Ready, Get Set, Get Started in a New Church," *Church Administration,* Mar. 1976, pp. 29-31.

6. Roy M. Oswald, *Running Through the Thistles: Terminating a Ministerial Relationship with a Parish* (Washington, D.C.: Alban Institute, 1978).

7. Robert D. Dale, *To Dream Again* (Nashville: Broadman Press, 1981).

8. For more information, see chapter 7, "Planning and Budgeting."

9. See chapter 3 for information on working with volunteers.

Bibliography

Allred, Thurman, ed. *Basic Small Church Administration.* Nashville: Convention Press, 1981.

Alexander, John W. *Managing Our Work,* rev. ed. Downers Grove, Ill.: Inter-Varsity Press, 1975.

Bolton, Robert and Dorothy Grover Bolton. *Social Style/Management Style.* New York: AMACOM, 1984.

Borst, Diane and Montana, Patrick J. eds. *Managing Nonprofit Organizations.* New York: AMACOM, 1977.

Dale, Robert D. *Ministers as Leaders.* Nashville: Broadman Press, 1984.

_____. "Get Ready, Get Set, Get Started in a New Church." *Church Administration.* March 1976.

_____. *To Dream Again.* Nashville: Broadman Press, 1981. McDonough, Reginald M. *Working with Volunteer Leaders in the Church.* Nashville: Broadman Press, 1976.

Oswald, Roy M. *The Pastor as Newcomer.* Washington, D.C.: Alban Institute, 1977.

_____. *Running Through the Thistles: Terminating a Ministerial Relationship with a Parish.* Washington, D.C.: Alban Institute, 1978.

Rush, Myron. *Management: A Biblical Approach.* Wheaton, Ill.: Victor Books, 1983.

Schaller, Lyle E. and Tidwell, Charles A. *Creative Church Administration.* Nashville: Abingdon Press, 1975.

Stacker, Joe R. and Grubbs, Bruce. *Shared Ministry.* Nashville: Convention Press, 1985.

White, Robert N., ed. *Managing Today's Church.* Valley Forge: Judson Press, 1981.
Wilson, Marlene. *The Effective Management of Volunteer Programs.* Boulder, Col.: Johnson
     Publishing Company, 1976.
Yon, William A. *Prime Time for Renewal.* Washington, D.C.: Alban Institute, 1977.

2

Church Organization

J. Ralph Hardee

Christ came into the world with a mission (John 4:34), and when He returned to His Father He charged the church with this same great mission: "Go forth therefore and make all nations my disciples; baptize men everywhere in the name of the Father and the Son and the Holy Spirit, and teach them to observe all that I have commanded you" (Matt. 28:19-20, NEB). This divinely assigned mission may be called the great co-mission because it is *His* and *ours;* and when a church engages in this mission it has the promise of His presence: "And be assured, I am with you always, to the end of time" (Matt. 28:20, NEB). The success of this co-mission depends upon His best effort and ours. "He told us the *what,*" it has been stated, "but depends on us to provide the *how.* He has declared the purpose, but leaves it to us to provide the organization and the plans; . . . God could do it alone, but apparently he won't."[1]

Christ established the church, but people create and operate its institutional forms. Church leaders serve as "midwives" with God in a church, giving "birth" to an organizational structure that is to be faithful to its mission. Structure can enhance the freedom of church members in using their gifts in the work of a church and become a vehicle for helping a church go into action. However, structure can also impede that freedom and become a hindrance to action. The organizational structure of a church should be of such design that all of the ministry gifts of members can be both individually offered and collectively harmonized for the upbuilding of the body of Christ.

Principles of Church Organization

Organization of a church usually depends on one's interpretation of scriptural teachings about the church. Listed in Figure 1 are some of the basic principles that are considered in this chapter. On the right side of each principle you will see how each might be applied in a local church.

Then, on the following pages, a conceptual model for organizing the work of a New Testament church is described. The model (illustrated in Figure 2) is an outgrowth of the ways in which I have sought to integrate biblical teachings about the church and organizational principles such as those described in Figure 1.

The Nature of a Church's Work

The work of a church must always revolve around the nature and mission of the church. The divinely assigned mission is permanent and unchangeable, as illustrated by the unbroken inner circle in Figure 2. A church has freedom about how to organize its work *around* this mission, but it does not have the freedom to organize its work *apart* from it.

Prior to deciding how a church will *do* its work, members should determine what the church should accomplish *through* its work. In other words, form should follow function, as suggested in the previous chapter. All of the work of a church must be harmonized with its mission.

Other important features in the model include:

• The work of the church is done within a particular environment (represented by the outer circle). While a church's geographic environment is constant, there is a continual interaction among the people, their patterns of living, and the ways in which church and society interface.

• The work of a church is done by its members (the next circle). The mission of a church is accomplished by persons, not programs. As the Holy Spirit empowers members, they interact with their environment, sharing their Christian witness.

• The work of a church is both inward to itself and outward to others (the bidirectional arrows). The inward direction represents work that is done to equip members for ministry and mission. This emphasis is balanced by an outward focus on the work of reconciliation through ministry and mission to others.

Major Areas of Work

The work of a church consists of continuing ministry activities that can be grouped into three major areas.

• Basic ministry programs

Figure 1

Principles of Church Organization

Principle	Application
● A church is an autonomous spiritual body under the leadership of Christ.	● Organization must provide for ascertaining the mind of Christ.
● All members have equal rights and privileges in a church.	● Organization must not obscure the unit of the body of Christ. There cannot be superior/subordinate relationships in the structure.
● Each member ought to be meaningfully involved in the work of his or her church.	● Organization must relate persons to persons and persons to tasks in orderly ways that meet needs, help persons grow, and facilitate achievement of a church's mission.
● The needs of a church are both constant and changing.	● Organization must provide for both long-term activities (to meet recurring, ongoing needs) and short-term activities (to meet temporary, newly emerging needs).
● The mission of a church encompasses both individual and corporate concerns.	● Organization must be judged normatively (that is, Will this structure enhance Christian maturity, Christian community, and Christian ministry and mission through this church?) *and* operationally (that is, What is happening to persons as a result of this structure? Are they growing? What is happening to the church body? Is it healthy?).

Figure 2

**A Model for Organizing the Work
of a New Testament Church**

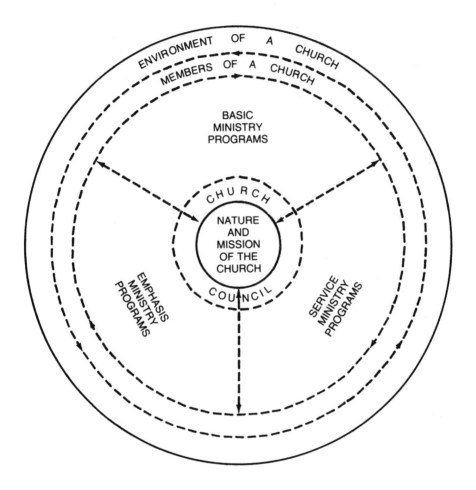

• Service ministry programs
• Emphasis ministry programs

The tasks to be done in each area vary in regard to the number of persons needed to perform them and the organizational structures required. The ministry programs most often found in local churches are listed in Figures 3, 4, and 5, according to the three major areas of work.

Coordination of Programs

The work of a church, if it is to be effective, requires that the structure contain provision for coordinating and correlating these programs. The broken lines between each of the three ministry areas also suggest that the structure is organic. There is a flow of work among and between all of the programs. The programs are interdependent and interrelated and are in continuous interaction.

The central link among all programs/ministries is the Church Council (illustrated around the center in the figures). The capability of a church for accomplishing its mission is increased when all of the ministries in all of the program areas are planned, implemented, and evaluated collaboratively. The creation and effective use of the Church Council provide within the structure a process that helps people work together for the good of the entire body. The Church Council integrates all church ministries, assisting the congregation in effectively responding to the nature and mission of the church.

A Church Organized and Functioning

Every church, regardless of size, has divinely assigned work to do. How much organizational structure is needed by a church must be determined by each local church, depending on its needs and resources. And even the smallest congregation must plan and organize its work.

The variety and extent of program ministries in each of the three areas will vary greatly, depending on a church's size and resources. There is no standard organization, only the principle that there must be a balanced ministry in each of the three major areas of congregational life. For recommendations according to the size of a church, see Figure 6.[2]

In order to function effectively, a church conducts its business primarily in three ways: through church officers, church councils,

Figure 3

The Work of a Church:
Basic Ministry Programs

A Model for Organizing the Work of a New Testament Church

ENVIRONMENT OF A CHURCH
MEMBERS OF A CHURCH
BASIC MINISTRY PROGRAMS

Pastoral Ministries   Educational Ministries

CHURCH COUNCIL

NATURE AND MISSION OF THE CHURCH

Pastoral Ministries
- Lead the church in the accomplishment of its mission.
- Proclaim the gospel to believers and unbelievers.
- Care for the church's members and other persons in the community.
- Interpret and undergird the work of the church and the denomination.

Educational Ministries

Bible Teaching
- Reach persons for Bible study.
- Teach the Bible.
- Witness to persons about Christ and lead persons into church membership.
- Minister to Sunday School members and nonmembers.
- Lead members to worship.
- Interpret and undergird the work of the church and the denomination.

Woman's Missionary Union
- Teach missions.
- Engage in mission action and personal witnessing.
- Support missions.
- Interpret and undergird the work of the church and the denomination.

Music Ministry
- Provide musical experience in congregational services.
- Develop musical skills, attitudes, and understandings.
- Witness and minister through music.
- Interpret and undergird the work of the church and the denomination.

Church Training
- Equip church members for discipleship and personal ministry.
- Teach Christian theology and Baptist doctrine, Christian ethics, Christian history, and church polity and organization.
- Equip church leaders for service.
- Interpret and undergird the work of the church and the denomination.

Brotherhood
- Engage in missions activities.
- Teach missions.
- Pray for and give to missions.
- Develop personal ministry.
- Interpret and undergird the work of the church and the denomination.

Figure 4

The Work of a Church:
Service Ministry Programs

A Model for Organizing the Work of a New Testament Church

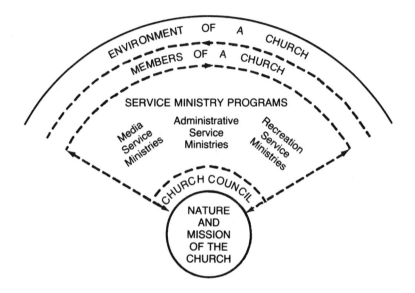

Media Services
- Educate persons in the use of media and provide media and media services to support the church in the achievement of its mission.

Recreation Services
- Provide recreation methods, materials, services, and experiences that will enrich the lives of persons and support the total mission of the church.

Administrative Services
- Assist the church to plan its program, manage its resources, and govern its life and work.

Figure 5

The Work of a Church:
Emphasis Ministry Programs

A Model for Organizing the Work of a New Testament Church

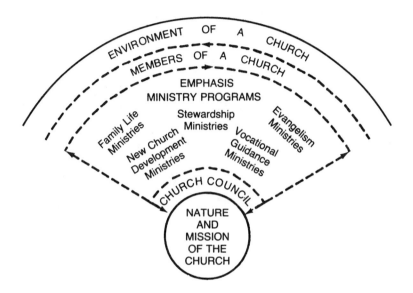

Family Life Ministries
- Minister to the distinctive needs of families, of senior adults, and of single adults.

Stewardship Ministries
- Develop Christian stewards and support Cooperative Program ministries.

Evangelism Ministries
- Develop and implement an effective strategy of evangelism which assists the church to aggressively evangelize the community.

New Church Development Ministries
- Establish new churches.

Vocational Guidance Ministries
- Educate in Christian vocation and guide persons in church occupation and adjustment.

Figure 6

Possibilities for Church Organization

Type of Unit Position	Suggested Units or Positions				
	Churches with Fewer than 150 Members'	Churches with 150 to 399 Members	Churches with 400 to 699 Members	Churches with 700 to 1,499 Members	Churches with 1,500 or more Members
Staff	Pastor Music Director[1]	Pastor Music Director[1] Secretary[2] Custodian[2] Pianist/Organist[1]	Pastor Minister of Music and Education Secretary Custodian Organist[1] Pianist[1]	Pastor Minister of Music Minister of Education Secretaries[3] Custodians[3] Organist[1] Pianist[1] Age-Division Ministers[3]	Pastor Associate Pastor Minister of Education Minister of Music Business Administrator Minister of Recreation Evangelism/Outreach Minister Age-division Ministers Organist-Music Assistant Family Life Minister Secretaries[3] Custodians[3] Hostess Food service personnel[3]
Deacons	Deacons (1 deacon per 15 family units; minimum of 2 deacons)	Deacons (1 deacon per 15 family units)	Deacons (1 deacon per 15 family units)	Deacons (1 deacon per 15 family units)	Deacons (1 deacon per 15 family units)
Church Officers	Moderator (Pastor) Trustees Clerk Treasurer	Moderator Trustees Clerk Treasurer	Moderator Trustees Clerk Treasurer	Moderator Trustees Clerk Treasurer	Moderator Trustees Clerk Treasurer
Church Committees	Nominating Stewardship Missions Evangelism	Nominating Property and Space Stewardship Ushers Missions Preschool[4] Evangelism	Nominating Property and Space Stewardship Personnel Missions Preschool History Ushers Weekday Education[4] Public Relations Evangelism	Nominating Property and Space Stewardship Personnel Missions Preschool Food Service History Ushers Weekday Education[4] Public Relations Evangelism	Nominating Property and Space Stewardship Personnel Missions Preschool Food Service History Ushers Weekday Education[4] Public Relations Evangelism Other committees as needed
Service Programs	Media Services Director	Media Services Director (up to 3 workers) Recreation Director	Media Staff Recreation Staff	Media Staff Recreation Staff	Media Staff Recreation Staff

Special Ministries	Ministry	Ministry	Ministry Singles Ministry	Ministry Singles Ministry	Ministry Singles Ministry	Senior Adult Ministry Singles Ministry Intergenerational Activities
Coordination	Church Council	Church Council, WMU Council, S.S. Council, Brotherhood Council	Church Council, S.S. Council, C.T. Council, WMU Council, Brotherhood Council, Division Coordination Conferences	Church Council, S.S. Council, C.T. Council, Music Council, WMU Council, Brotherhood Council, Division Coordination Conferences	Church Council, S.S. Council, C.T. Council, Music Council, WMU Council, Brotherhood Council, Division Coordination Conferences	Church Council, S.S. Council, C.T. Council, Music Council, WMU Council, Brotherhood Council, Media Services Council, Division Coordination Conferences
Bible Teaching	General officers and organization for each age division	Departments for each age division	Multiple departments as needed	Multiple departments as needed	Multiple departments as needed	Multiple departments as needed
Church Training	Church Training Director, Age-group leaders[4]	Member training groups and departments for each age division, Equipping Centers, New Church Member Training	Member training groups and departments for each age division, Equipping Centers, New Church Member Training	Member training groups and departments for each age division, Equipping Centers, New Church Member Training	Member training groups and departments for each age division, Equipping Centers, New Church Member Training	Member training groups and departments for each age division, Equipping Centers, New Church Member Training
WMU	WMU Director, Age level organizations as needed	Age level organizations as needed	Age level organizations as needed	Age level organizations as needed	Age level organizations as needed	Age level organizations as needed
Brotherhood	Brotherhood Director	Baptist Men, Royal Ambassador groups as needed	Baptist Men, Royal Ambassador groups as needed	Baptist Men, Royal Ambassador groups as needed	Baptist Men, Royal Ambassador groups as needed	Baptist Men, Royal Ambassador groups as needed
Music Ministry	Music Director[5], Pianist, Choir	Music Director[5], Organist, Church Choir or Ensemble, Age-division choirs when possible	Age-division choirs, Instrumental groups as needed	Fully developed Music Ministry	Fully developed Music Ministry	Fully developed Music Ministry

[1] Volunteer or part-time
[2] Part-time
[3] As needed
[4] If needed
[5] Person serves as program leader and staff member

• NOTE: It is important to encourage, in any way possible, churches of 150 members or less to have choir, recreation, and other needed ministries even though directors or other leaders for that activity might not be listed in column one of this chart.

and church committees. The rest of this chapter gives information about and provides basic guidelines for each of these major groups.

Church Officers

Church officers are a part of the administrative services ministries of a church. Officers usually elected by a church include moderator, clerk, treasurer, financial secretary, and trustees.

Persons to serve in these positions should be recommended by the Nominating Committee and elected by the church to serve for a specified time.[3]

On the following pages are job descriptions and other aids related to the work of church officers.

Figure 7

Sample Church Business Meeting Agenda

1. Call to order by Moderator
2. Prayer/Devotional
3. Approval of minutes from previous meeting(s)
4. Church Clerk's report
   - Request for letters
   - Letters received (for new members)
   - Deletions
   - Membership statistics
5. Church Treasurer's report
6. Old business
7. Reports from committees
   - Standing committees
   - Special committees
8. Reports from Church Program Organization directors
   - Bible teaching
   - Training
   - Missions
9. Report from Church Council
10. Report from Deacon Ministry Council
11. Reports from Church Staff
12. New business (from floor)
13. Adjourn with prayer

Moderator

Principal Function: The chief responsibility of the moderator is to make preparation and to preside at church business meetings, that is, to coordinate and facilitate productive business meetings in an orderly, efficient manner. (Many churches require that the pastor serve as moderator.)

Duties

1. Develop church business meeting agenda in cooperation with appropriate persons. Copies should be shared with church staff members, chairperson of deacons, and others included on the agenda prior to each session, if possible. (See sample Church Business Meeting Agenda plan sheet, Figure 7.)
2. Help members stay informed and involved in church business by promoting attendance and participation in business meetings.
3. Preside over all church business meetings.
4. Clarify matters voted for later action and follow up on these.
5. Evaluate each business session and its activities.

Relationships

1. Work with the church clerk in preparation of agenda *before* business meetings and in preparation of minutes *after* meetings.
2. Consult with church staff members, committee chairpersons, church program organization directors and other responsible persons in preparation of the business meeting agenda and in evaluation of each business session and its activities.
3. Follow up after each business meeting with responsible committees, officers, individuals, and others to ensure that decisions are executed.
4. Be in touch with as many members as possible to know the spirit and mood of the congregation.
5. Serve as an active member of the Church Council.

Tips for Moderators

1. Maintain the spirit of Christian love and fellowship while presiding by conducting meetings in an orderly manner. (The Moderator must maintain a neutral position while presiding. If it is necessary to become personally involved in

debate on a question under consideration, ask an assistant to preside.)

2. Be familiar with prescribed parliamentary procedure. Help members to understand parliamentary procedure without embarrassing them.
3. Insist that motions be stated and seconded before discussed.
4. Suggest that a member make a motion by stating: "If a motion is in order, I move . . ."
5. Call on the person who makes a motion to discuss it first.
6. Encourage full and free debate. Lead members to talk through their disagreements.
7. Execute business with dispatch, making certain that all matters are clear and concise. Avoid wasted time on trivialities. Bring together people with differing views and perspectives in the bond of love.
8. Alternate discussions so as to bring out both sides of a question. A member who has not spoken should be given preference over the one who has. Be fair and courteous with all members.
9. Respect the minority. The minority has a right to be heard even though the majority must prevail.
10. Always take the affirmative vote first. Take the negative vote second, but always take it.

Church Clerk

Principal Function: The church clerk is responsible for recording, processing, and maintaining accurate records of all church business meeting transactions. The clerk also is responsible for all official church membership records and communications. (Some responsibilities may be assigned to church staff members.)

Duties
1. Assist in preparation of the agenda for church business meeting(s).
2. Keep an accurate record (in the form of minutes) of all business transactions made and approved in church business meetings.
3. Present the minutes of the prior meeting(s) at each business meeting for official church approval.

4. Provide clerical assistance during the invitation period of the worship services for new members, rededications, and other decisions.
5. Maintain accurate member records. This includes: (a) adding new names and pertinent information to the chronological membership roll and dropping other names as necessary through transfer, inactivity, or death; (b) correcting records for change of address or phone number; and (c) sending a memo as needed to all church personnel keeping separate records to avoid incorrect information.
6. Request letters by transfer from other churches for new members, forward letters to other churches requested by members, and notify persons when their names are removed from the church roll for any reason other than transfer of membership by letter.
7. Prepare and mail all official church correspondence.
8. Preserve records for present and future use.
9. Prepare the annual church letter to the association, submit for church approval, and send to associational office.

Relationships
1. Work with the moderator in preparation of agenda *before* meetings and in preparation of minutes *after* meetings. (It may be necessary at times to consult with appropriate church staff members, church program leaders, committee chairpersons, deacons, and others to be sure that the wording in the minutes is correct as given in the business meetings to avoid confusion either in the next business meeting or at later dates.)
2. Work with the church secretary in getting the minutes prepared for distribution to the members in the next business meeting. (A typed copy of the business meeting minutes should be sent to the church staff members and moderator no later than one week following a business session.)
3. Serve as resource person to the church historian and/or History Committee as requested. (If the church does not have a History Committee, the church clerk should be the church's designated historian.)
4. Provide statistical information on the church membership as requested.

5. Work with appropriate church staff members in official correspondence with other churches.
6. Work with the trustees in preparation of legal documents.
7. Work with various staff members, church program leaders, and committee chairpersons in preparing the annual church letter to the association.
8. Give necessary information about new members to the person in charge of new member orientation as well as other church program leaders and deacons (for Family Ministry Plan) so the new members can be enrolled in these programs.
9. Serve as an active member of the Church Council.

Treasurer

Principal Function: The church treasurer is responsible for the proper receipt, accounting, and disbursement of church funds within policies established by the church for adequate financial control. The treasurer's work focuses primarily on financial records and payment procedures rather than the handling of cash.

Duties
1. Keep accurate records in appropriate financial journals of all monies received and disbursed.
2. Reconcile monthly bank statements and correct ledgers as needed.
3. Sign checks in accordance with church policies and procedures, always verifying supporting data for each check request.
4. Make monthly and annual reports to the Finance Committee and the church.
5. Provide for records of individual contributions to be maintained.
6. Suggest possible investment opportunities; advise about bond(s) purchasing.
7. Keep church staff informed of any trends or changes in fiscal matters.
8. Instill and preserve high financial morale throughout the congregation.

9. Submit accurate financial records for annual audit according to church policy.

Relationships

1. Serve as ex officio member of the Finance Committee. Confer with this committee in:
   a. Recommending and establishing policies related to the receiving, accounting, and disbursing of church monies.
   b. Developing the annual church budget and coordinating the annual stewardship campaign.
   c. Preparing and presenting a monthly financial report to the church business meeting. (Also confer with moderator about presentation of report.)
   d. Providing a continuing program of stewardship education for the church.
2. Receive copy of deposit slip and summary of receipts record from the Counting Committee after each deposit.
3. Work closely with the financial secretary in maintaining records of individual contributions.
4. Confer with the church staff members and deacons to maintain communication in financial matters of the church.
5. Work with staff members, officers, and organizations in administering financial details of church projects, for example, as receipts fall above or below budgeted funds.
6. At the request of the Finance Committee, serve as advisor to various requesting committees in preparing and maintaining their budget.
7. Be available to help individual church members plan their personal and family budget.
8. Serve as an active member of the Church Council. Advise the council and various committee chairpersons about available funds and budgeted funds.

Financial Secretary

Principal Function: The financial secretary is responsible for maintaining accurate records of individual member contributions.

Duties

1. Post offerings weekly to individual accounts; file envelopes.

2. Mail a quarterly and annual statement of giving to each member.
3. Provide statistical financial data as requested by treasurer, Finance Committee, and/or the church staff.

Relationships
1. Receive copy of deposit slip, summary of receipts record, and individual offering envelopes from the Counting Committee after each deposit.
2. Work closely with the treasurer in the posting and reporting of member contributions.
3. Work closely with the church secretary in the mailing of member contribution reports.
4. Serve as resource person to the church staff, church program leaders, officers, and committees to provide needed statistical information about giving records and patterns of giving.
5. Serve as an ex officio member of the Church Council.

Trustees

Principal Function: The trustees serve as legal representatives in all transactions related to the church. They hold legal title to the church property and they sign all documents related to the purchase, sale, mortgaging, or rental of church property after approval by the church in regular business session.

Duties
1. Hold legal title to all church property (as required by state law) and act only as directed by the church in regular business session.
2. Sign all legal documents involving church property, upon direction by the church in regular business session.
3. Maintain an up-to-date inventory of all church property, mortgage loans, and insurance on church property. (Such information should be kept in a safety deposit box with copies filed in the church office for ready reference.)

Relationships
1. Relate to appropriate civil officials in all legal matters involving the church.
2. Keep abreast of latest insurance and legal changes (innovations, programs, etc.), report such changes to the appropriate

church leaders, and advise the church staff and any committee concerning legal matters.

3. Counsel with appropriate church officers and committees in
matters related to church properties, for example, finance
committee, treasurer, property and space committee, deacons, insurance committee, and long-range planning committee.

4. Maintain all church legal documents in conjunction with the
church clerk.

5. If qualified, serve as resource personnel to the church staff
and church families in legal matters.

6. Stay in touch with the Church Council and deacons to report on current plans and ideas as necessary.

7. Report to the church as necessary.

8. Serve as an ex officio member of the Church Council.

The Councils of a Church

The councils of a church exist to plan, coordinate, and evaluate
the work assigned to them by the church. Structurally, councils are
in the area of basic ministry programs. They most often provide
support through the pastoral ministries and educational ministries
programs of a church.

The Church Council

The major functions of the Church Council relate to planning,
coordinating, and evaluating the total work of a church. This body
usually is assigned the following duties on a continuing basis. Actions are performed as required by the planning and administrative
needs of each church.

1. Formulate and recommend to the church suggested church
objectives and goals.

2. Develop and recommend to the church action plans for reaching church goals.

3. Prepare the annual church calendar of activities.

4. Review and coordinate suggested program plans and actions by
the church staff, church officers, organizations, and committees; and
provide for adequate communication among staff, officers, organizations, and committees.

5. Review and report as appropriate to the church the use of

resources in terms of the needs of church programs as they work toward the achievement of the objectives and goals of the church.

6. Evaluate program achievements in terms of church objectives and goals, and report evaluations to the church.

An effectively functioning Church Council helps a church to: (1) determine the focus and scope of its ministry and mission (both now and in the future); (2) use resources wisely; (3) identify priorities; (4) coordinate the church calendar of activities; and (5) enrich fellowship.

Membership.—The membership of the Church Council should include: (1) every church staff member whose responsibility is related to the operation of one or more church programs or services; and (2) all key lay leaders who are responsible for various church programs and services embodying significant work of the church which must be correlated and coordinated so that the church may function as a totality. Some members of the Church Council serve as *active* members, that is, they participate in every meeting of the council. Other members of the Church Council serve as *ex officio* members, that is, they *can* attend any meeting but are *expected* to attend only when the agenda of a meeting includes items which will concern their committee's work. Church staff members, directors of church program organizations, church officers, and chairperson on the Deacon Ministry Council serve as active members. Ex officio members include the chairpersons of all church committees and directors of specialized ministry services, such as media and recreation. The pastor and/or minister of education serves as chairperson of the Church Council.

Meetings.—The work of this body usually is of such significance to the overall life of a church that a monthly meeting is required. Occasionally, the council meets on call. In some churches, every third meeting (once every three months) is an expanded Church Council session that includes all active and ex officio members. For a sample Church Council agenda plan sheet, see Figure 8.4

The Deacon Council

The Deacon Council assists with a church's pastoral ministries program. Its major functions are planning, coordinating, and evaluating the work of the church related to pastoral functions. The concept of deacon comes from the Greek work *diakonein,* which

Figure 8

Church Council Agenda

1. Call to order by chairperson.
2. Scripture/Prayer/Devotional by person enlisted in advance.
3. Approval of/additions to agenda (tentative agenda should be distributed in advance).
4. Approval of minutes of last meeting.
5. Follow-up reports from last meeting, if scheduled.
6. *Review* and *evaluate* church program events and activities conducted since the last meeting. As appropriate, receive reports from the following leaders:
   - Bible teaching
   - Church Training
   - Missions
   - Music
   - Church committees
   - Church officers
   - Church staff
   - Other
7. *Preview* and *coordinate* events and activities planned for the next three months.
8. *Plan* and/or *overview* future events and activities that are more than three months away.
9. Summary of meeting and decisions by chairperson.
10. Preparation of any recommendations.
11. Assignments for follow-up by next meeting (for example, special projects and reports).
12. Brief evaluation of meeting.
13. Adjourn.

means to minister or serve. The personal qualifications of a deacon are found in 1 Timothy 3:8-13.

Each church must determine how many deacons are needed to implement an adequate program of pastoral ministries, and the process by which deacons will be selected. The chairperson of the Deacon Council serves as an active member of the Church Council.

Duties.—The four major functions of deacons include:

1. Proclaim the gospel to believers and unbelievers.
   a. Personal witnessing activities
   b. Preaching as a layperson
   c. Church revival support
2. Care for the church's members and other persons in the community.
   a. Ministering in times of crisis
   b. Listening to burdened persons

    c. Referring persons in need to qualified sources for assis-
tance
    d. Counseling on vocational guidance and family ministry.
3. Build Christian fellowship among church members.
    a. Sharing information about the church's life and work
    b. Assisting in administering ordinances
4. Serve as an exemplary Christian leader.
    a. Set an example in Christian life-style
    b. Set an example in church leadership responsibilities
    c. Give personal support to church activities[5]

Church Program Organization Council(s)

A church should have a council for each of its educational programs, for example, the Sunday School Council. The primary functions of a program council are to plan, coordinate, and evaluate the
work of its organization. This group determines the direction of the
program and coordinates its work with other educational organizations through the Church Council. The directors of major units in
a particular program are members of that program's council and
serve as long as they occupy that position.

Since the Sunday School Council is usually the first program
council to be created in a church, it is used here to illustrate the work
of councils in a church. The Sunday School Council consists of the
general officers of the Sunday School plus the department director
for *each* department of the Sunday School. (For example, each department in the Preschool, Children, Youth, and Adult age group
divisions of the Sunday School will be represented on the Sunday
School Council by the department director.) The director of the
Sunday School serves as chairperson of the Sunday School Council.
To ensure that the work of the Sunday School Council is coordinated with all the other work of a church, the director of the Sunday
School also serves as an active member of the Church Council.[6]

The Work of Church Committees

The committees of a church exist to plan, coordinate, implement,
and evaluate the work asigned to them by the church. A church
committee can study and complete a specialized assignment more
efficiently than can the congregation in business sessions. The committee approach has several distinct benefits for a church.

1. It spreads the administrative load among members of the con-

gregation and broadens participation. This provides the church staff members and deacons more freedom for ministry to the people. Through committees responsibility is delegated, and the church is helped to perform its tasks.

2. It utilizes skills and talents of members of the congregation and makes the church a more efficient and effective ministering body. Through committees the church is assisted in planning.

3. It provides opportunities for differing points of view to be presented and reconciled and produces more harmony among church members. Through committees the church is helped in decision making.

There are two kinds (or types) of work to be done by committees in a church. The first type of work relates to the long-term, ongoing ministries and programs that are basic to the church's life, such as the financial program. For this type of work, the church needs to have committees that are permanent. Such a committee is called a *standing* (or *regular*) committee. The Stewardship Committee, Property and Space Committee, Ushers Committee, and Baptismal Committee are examples of standing committees. The members on these groups should serve on a rotating basis, with a portion of the members being replaced each year.[7]

The second type of committee work in a church relates to the short-term or temporary needs of the church, such as constructing a new sanctuary. For this type of work, a church needs to have some committees that are ad hoc and operate only long enough to accomplish specific tasks. This kind of committee is called a special committee. The Building Committee and Pastor Selection Committee are examples. The members of a special committee should serve as long as the committee exists.

Standing committees carry out very different functions from special committees. The work of standing committees usually revolves primarily around the needs of the church to maintain the best of what it now has. Standing committees give attention to maintaining, operating, and stabilizing already-existing ministries and programs that are ongoing.

Special committees, in contrast, usually focus their work on the needs of the church that are short term, such as for constitutional revision or building an addition. They give attention to creating something new or to revising something old. Special committees are formed and disbanded as needed; they should not continue beyond the time needed to perform their church-assigned task.

In planning an effective committee structure for a church, balanced attention should be given to meeting the need that a church has to maintain both long-term and short-term ministries and programs. Long-term ministries and programs require standing committees. Short-term ministries and programs need special committees.

The work of all church committees should be coordinated by a central coordinating unit such as the Church Council. Thus, the chairpersons of all church committees should serve as ex officio members of the Church Council.

The members of all committees (standing and special) should be recommended by the Nominating Committee and elected by the church. Since the church brings each committee into existence, each committee reports back to the church. There should be a regular time allocated at each church business meeting for church committees to report on work accomplished.

Most of the *new* committees established by a church will be special committees—although it is not unusual for a new standing committee to be created. When it seems desirable to form a new committee:

1. Determine the need for a new committee.
2. Formulate its purpose and duties.
3. Prepare to allocate necessary resources.
4. Present to the church for discussion and vote.
5. Submit personnel needs to the Nominating Committee.
6. Present committee members, with chairperson designated, for church approval.
7. Educate new committee members.

Helping Committees Understand Their Work

One key to effective committee work is the orientation to and training in performance of duties. Chairpersons and committee members need to understand their jobs, and a church is obligated to provide the necessary training.[8] The duties of committee members are listed in Figures 9 and 10.

Figure 9

Duties of a Committee Member

1. Know the purpose, duties, and members of the committee.
2. Be present and on time for meetings.
3. Participate in discussions.
4. Contribute to the planning and achievement of activities/projects.
5. Complete assignments as agreed upon.
6. Keep the committee chairperson informed about progress on assignments; report at committee meetings.

Figure 10

Duties of a Committee Chairperson

1. Know the purpose, duties, and members of the committee.
2. Request and administer committee budgeting.
3. Serve as an ex officio member of the Church Council.
4. Plan the agenda for each meeting of the committee. (See sample of Committee Meeting Agenda, Figure 11.)
5. Conduct meetings.
   a. Each meeting should have a purpose.
   b. Each meeting should have an agenda.
   c. Each meeting needs resources.
   d. Each meeting should plan for follow-up.
   e. Each meeting should be reported.
6. Supervise the work of the committee secretary.
7. Assign responsibility to committee members for follow-through actions.
8. Lead the committee to:
   a. Identify and schedule some activities/projects.
   b. Develop a sequence of actions.
   c. Prepare a timetable.
   d. Determine the resources needed.
   e. Complete activities/projects.
9. Report committee action(s), as appropriate, to the Church Council and/or the church business meeting.
10. Collaborate, as necessary or desirable, with church staff members, church officers, Church Council, Deacon Council, church program directors, and other committees.

Guidelines for Effective Committee Work

This section includes several general guidelines that will contribute to effective committee work. Following these suggestions, specific guidelines are recommended for the four major standing com-

Figure 11

Committee Meeting Agenda

Committee_____ Date of Meeting_____

Time_____ Location _____

Will Attend: _____

_____

Will Not Attend: _____

_____

	Agenda Item	*Time*
1.	Opening Prayer/Devotional	
2.	_____	_____
	_____	
	_____	
3.	_____	_____
	_____	
	_____	
4.	_____	_____
	_____	
	_____	
5.	_____	_____
	_____	
	_____	
6.	_____	_____
	_____	
	_____	
7.	Date for next meeting: _____	_____
	Closing Prayer	

mittees in a church: Nominating (Figure 13), Personnel (Figure 14), Finance (Figure 15), and Property and Space (Figure 16).

1. Maintain rotational membership for all *standing* committees, that is, one third of the members should rotate off each year. (Rotation ensures that two thirds of the membership of a standing committee will have service experience.)

2. Maintain nonrotational membership on all *special* committees, that is, all members serve until the work of the committee is completed or the committee is disbanded by church action.

3. Limit committee membership to only one *standing* committee and, if desirable by the church, to one *special* committee. (Make exceptions only in unusual circumstances.)

4. Have the Nominating Committee recommend members for *all* committees, standing *and* special, to the church. The Nominating Committee should staff newly created committees with at least three members, with one third of the membership rotating off each year. Add additional members (in any quantity) as necessary, but maintain rotational membership for all committees.

5. Usually a committee member should not be reelected to the same standing committee for a period of one year following a three-year term. However, a year of ineligibility should not be mandatory. Need and willingness to serve should be the primary placement criteria.

6. Have the Nominating Committee designate the chairperson of each committee. (This should be done when the committee members are presented to the church for election. Chairpersons of standing committees should be designated to serve one year. Chairpersons of special committees should be designated to serve until the committee completes its work or is disbanded by church action.)

7. Assign a church staff member to each committee to act as an advisor and consultant. (In a single staff church, there should be no more committees than the pastor can counsel and advise adequately.)

8. Be certain each chairperson understands that he or she—not the pastor or any staff member—is to lead the committee and that the committee members—not the pastor or any other staff member—are to do the work.

9. Be certain each chairperson understands that he or she is an ex officio member of the Church Council.

10. Prepare a job description for every committee and provide a copy to every committee member. In preparing job descriptions:

    a. Use available material and information as a guideline (church practice, church bylaws, pamphlets, books, resources from other churches).

    b. Write with *your* church's needs in mind.

    c. Secure committee approval on all parts of each description.

    d. Copy the job descriptions and present them to the church in business meeting for approval.

    e. Make them a part of the bylaws or put them in a handbook to give to each church family.

    f. Update the descriptions periodically as the church situation changes.

11. Provide orientation for new chairpersons and new committee members.

12. Use a Committee Activities Plan Sheet (see sample, Figure 12) to assign and monitor the work of each committee. Meet with the chairperson of each committee periodically to discuss the work of the committee and to coordinate activities. (Both the chairperson of the committee and the church staff advisor for the committee should have an up-to-date copy.)

13. Set aside one night a month (or quarter) as committee meeting night. (For example, the second Wednesday of each month before prayer service. Do not expect committees to have unnecessary meetings. Whether the various committees meet should be left to the discretion of each chairperson. Make the chairperson responsible for seeing that members know whether the committee is to meet.)

14. Instruct committees to report directly to the congregation during a regular business meeting when necessary or upon request. (Every committee should report at least quarterly.) Reports that involve major recommendations or require major decision making by the church should be shared with the church staff/Church Council and Deacon Council for review and/or response prior to the business meeting. Committee reports to the church are beneficial because they:

    a. Inform the church about the work of a committee.

    b. Develop a spirit of achievement.

    c. Provide promotion for the work of a committee.

    d. Serve as an evaluation tool.

Figure 12

Committee Activities Plan Sheet

Committee _____ Chairperson _____
Members _____
_____
_____

Activities/Projects	Beginning Date	Completion Date
1.		
2.		
3.		
4.		
5.		
6.		
7.		
8.		
9.		
10.		

Figure 13

Nominating Committee

Principle Function.—To lead the church in the staffing of all church-elected leadership positions filled by volunteers; to approve all volunteer workers before they are enlisted to serve in church-elected positions.

Relationships and Responsibilities

With Councils
1. Committee chairperson serves as ex officio member of the Church Council, contributing and receiving information related to the work of the Nominating Committee.
2. Study the work responsibilities of the Deacon Council to understand the nature and scope of the work of the deacons.
3. Counsel with the Deacon Council to determine present and/or future leadership needs.
4. Contact and enlist all Deacon Council nominees *prior to* presentation for election.

With Committees
1. Study the work responsibilities of all committees to understand the nature and scope of their work.
2. Counsel with the chairperson of each committee to determine present and/or future leadership needs.
3. Contact and enlist all nominees *prior to* presentation for election.

With Church Officers
1. Study the work responsibilities of all church officers to understand the nature and scope of their work.
2. Contact and enlist all church officer nominees *prior to* presentation for election.
3. Chairperson of committee informs moderator of reports to be made in the church business meeting.
4. Chairperson of committee gives a copy of any reports made during the church business meeting to the church clerk for permanent record in the minutes of the church.

With Church Program Organization Directors
1. Study the work responsibilities of all directors to understand the nature and scope of their work.
2. Contact and enlist all director nominees *prior to* presentation for election.
3. Counsel with each director to determine present and/or future leadership needs.
4. Assist directors in contacting and enlisting nominees *prior to* presentation for election.

Note: Church Program Organization directors should serve on the Nominating Committee.

With Church Staff
1. Counsel with staff members to determine present and future leadership needs in the church and in developing plans to satisfy those needs.
2. Work closely with staff members in discovering potential leaders.

With Church Business Meeting
1. Make periodic reports on the work of the Nominating Committee.
2. Answer questions about the work of the Nominating Committee.
3. Recommend all members of every standing committee.
4. Recommend all members of every special committee.
5. Recommend all members of Deacon Ministry Council.
6. Designate chairperson of each standing committee annually.
7. Designate chairperson of each special committee when committee is elected.
8. Recommend all church-elected leadership for Sunday School, Church Training, Woman's Missionary Union, Brotherhood, and music ministry programs.
9. Recommend all church officers.

Figure 14

Personnel Committee

Principle Function.—To assist the church in administrative matters related to all employed personnel.

Relationships and Responsibilities

With Councils
1. Committee chairperson serves as ex officio member of the Church Council.

With Committees
1. Consult with the Finance Committee in developing and budgeting salaries schedule and benefit provisions for all church staff members *annually.*
2. Consult with the Finance Committee in budgeting for any additional church staff members.

With Church Officers
1. Committee chairperson informs moderator of reports to be made in the church business meeting.
2. Committee chairperson gives a copy of any reports made during the church business meeting to the church clerk for permanent record in the minutes of the church.
3. Committee chairperson keeps the church treasurer informed regarding budgeted salary and benefit provisions for all staff members.

With Church Staff
1. Work with all staff members to:
   a. Prepare and update job descriptions *annually.*
   b. Negotiate a salaries schedule and benefit provisions *annually.*
   c. Develop church policies and procedures relating to church staff personnel.
   d. Discuss needs for additional church staff positions.
2. Consult with appropriate staff member(s) in locating, interviewing, and recommending additional church staff personnel.
3. Assess job performance of each staff member at least *annually* (and be sensitive to job insecurities which may plague them).

With Church Business Meeting
1. Make periodic reports on work of the Personnel Committee.
2. Answer questions about the work of the Personnel Committee.
3. Recommend all employed personnel for every church staff position.
4. Recommend administrative policies and procedures for all employed personnel.

Figure 15

Finance Committee

Principle Function.—To plan and promote stewardship education in all areas of church life and to lead the church in budget planning, promotion, subscription, and administration.

Relationships and Responsibilities

With Councils
1. Committee chairperson serves as ex officio member of the Church Council.
2. Develop and recommend to the Church Council an overall stewardship education/information plan.

With Committees
1. Review with committee chairpersons periodically the expenditures of committees to ensure correspondence with budget allocations and budget adjustments.
2. Consult with the chairperson of each committee annually to determine the financial resources needed by each committee for its work during the following year.

With Church Officers
1. Committee chairperson informs moderator of reports to be made in the church business meeting.
2. Committee chairperson gives to church clerk a copy of any reports made during the church business meeting for permanent record in the minutes of the church.

3. The church treasurer serves as an ex officio member of the Finance Committee.

With Church Program Organization Directors
1. Review with each director periodically the expenditures of the organization in terms of budget allocations and budget adjustments.
2. Consult with each director annually to determine financial resources needed by each organization for its work during the following year.

With Church Staff
1. Consult with appropriate church staff member(s) in the planning, promotion, subscription, and administration of the church budget.
2. At least one church staff minister serves as staff advisor and consultant on the Finance Committee.

With Church Business Meeting
1. Make periodic reports on the work of the Finance Committee.
2. Answer questions about the work of the Finance Committee.
3. Recommend financial policies and procedures to be practiced by the church.
4. Make recommendations concerning proposed expenditures not included in the current budget.
5. Recommend an annual church budget.

Figure 16

Property and Space Committee

Principle Function.—To assist the church in the care of all properties and buildings; to study and recommend the use of space and furnishings as it relates to church programs and activities; to study the need and recommend acquiring property and creating space; and to administer work assigned to it.

Relationships and Responsibilities

With Councils
1. Committee chairperson serves as ex officio member of the Church Council.

With Committees
1. Present an annual budget proposal to the Finance Committee for financial resources needed by the Property and Space Committee to accomplish its assigned work.
2. Recommend to the Personnel Committee the employment, training, and supervision needs of maintenance personnel.
3. Work with the Missions Committee to recommend acquisition and to maintain property and space for mission purposes.
4. Work with the Long Range Planning Committee in determining future property and space needs of the church.

5. Assist other church committees in responsibilities which may relate to the assigned work of the Property and Space Committee.
6. Prepare recommendations to the Finance Committee for additional space and property.

With Church Officers

1. Committee chairperson informs moderator of reports to be made in the church business meeting.
2. Committee chairperson gives the church clerk a copy of any report made during the church business meeting for permanent record in the minutes of the church.
3. Committee chairperson submits purchase order to church treasurer to request finances for budgeted items.

With Church Program Organization Directors

1. Conduct with each director an annual evaluation of space allocations to determine areas needing adjustment and enlargement.
2. Recommend to directors space rearrangement to secure maximum use for education, special activities, and worship.
3. Recommend to directors policies regarding the use of space, equipment, and properties.
4. Assist directors in recommending and maintaining proper and adequate furnishings for programs and activities.

With Church Staff

1. Consult with appropriate staff member(s) in conducting an annual evaluation of space allocations to determine areas needing adjustment and enlargement.
2. Consult with appropriate staff member(s) in determining space rearrangement to ensure maximum use of education, special activities, and worship.
3. Assist the church staff in arranging, equipping, and administering adequate worship space.
4. Work with the staff member responsible for supervision of the maintenance personnel in developing and recommending maintenance policies and procedures.
5. Consult with appropriate staff member(s) regarding the need and process in acquiring new space for continued growth.
6. At least one church staff minister serves as staff advisor/consultant on the Property and Space Committee.

With Church Business Meeting

1. Make periodic reports on work of the Property and Space Committee.
2. Answer questions about the work of the Property and Space Committee.
3. Recommend policies and procedures regarding the use of space, equipment, and properties.
4. Recommend the appointment of a Church Building Survey and Planning Committee when needed and appropriate.

Notes

1. See Alvin Lindgren and Norman Shawchuck, *Management for Your Church* (Nashville: Abingdon, 1977), pp. 14-15.

2. From Bruce P. Powers, editor-compiler, *Christian Education Handbook* (Nashville: Broadman Press, 1981), pp. 130-131.

3. For additional information, see James A. Sheffield, *Church Officer and Committee Guidebook* (Nashville: Convention Press, 1976).

4. A helpful resource for planning and guiding meetings is the *Church Council Handbook* by Truman Brown (Nashville: Convention Press, 1981).

5. For more complete information about the work of the Deacon Council see Henry Webb, *Deacons: Servant Models in the Church,* (Nashville: Convention Press, 1980).

6. For suggestions and guidelines related to the general administration of all educational programs in a local church, see Bruce P. Powers, editor-compiler, *Christian Education Handbook* (Nashville: Broadman Press, 1981).

7. Whenever rotation is recommended, this is to assure that there are always experienced persons serving and that fresh ideas are being considered. Usually persons will serve a term of three years with one third of the group rotating off each year. After a year off, a person may be reelected to the same committee if the church desires.

8. An excellent resource kit that contains study guides and teaching aids is *How to Train Church Committees,* available from Materials Services Department, Nashville, Tenn. 37234. A series of booklets covering most church committees also is available from the same source.

Bibliography

Adams, Arthur M. *Effective Leadership for Today's Church.* Philadelphia: The Westminster Press, 1978.

Bormann, Ernest G. and Bormann, Nancy C. *Effective Committees and Groups in the Church.* Minneapolis: Augsburg, 1973.

Brown, Truman, Jr. *Church Council Handbook.* Nashville: Convention Press, 1981.

Dale, Robert D. *To Dream Again.* Nashville: Broadman Press, 1981.

Dudley, Carl S. *Building Effective Ministry.* San Francisco: Harper and Row, 1983.

Graves, Allen W. *A Church at Work: A Handbook of Church Polity.* Nashville: Convention Press, 1972.

Lindgren, Alvin and Shawchuck, Norman. *Management for Your Church.* Nashville: Abingdon Press, 1977.

McDonough, Reginald M., comp. *A Church on Mission.* Nashville: Convention Press, 1980.

Mosley, Ernest E. *Called to Joy: A Design for Pastoral Ministries.* Nashville: Convention Press, 1973.

Powers, Bruce P., ed./comp. *Christian Education Handbook.* Nashville: Broadman Press, 1981.

Shawchuck, Norman and Perry, Lloyd M. *Revitalizing the Twentieth-Century Church.* Chicago: Moody Press, 1982.

Sheffield, James A. *Church Officer and Committee Guidebook.* Nashville: Convention Press, 1976.

Stacker, Joe R. and Grubbs, Bruce *Shared Ministry.* Nashville: Convention Press, 1985.

Webb, Henry. *Deacons: Servant Models in the Church.* Nashville: Convention Press, 1980.

3

Working with People
Robert D. Dale

Some ministers appear to love humanity but hate people. These folks find themselves uncomfortable in local congregations because those fellowships are just people—all kinds of people.

Interpersonal relationships provide the bridges over which ministry moves. The effective church administrator learns to build one-to-one friendships. Moreover, managers must also expand their skills in relating to work groups, ministry committees, and program councils by learning to function well in one-to-several and one-to-many settings.

Working with church people well involves a variety of administrative challenges.
- Understanding congregations as service organizations
- Ministering through committees
- Paying volunteers
- Building a unified team for ministry
- Solving problems
- Managing ministry meetings
- Chairing decision-making meetings
- Relating to church staffers
- Delegating ministry opportunities
- Supervising fellow church members
- Dealing with difficult people
- Shaping the organizational climate

Working with volunteers in congregations requires keen relational and management skills.

Understanding Congregations as Service Organizations

The management sciences refer to three kinds of organizations: the for-profits, the governmental, and the not-for-profits. Churches and other Christian institutions fit into the not-for-profit category.

Management experts agree that not-for-profits are by far the most challenging organizations to administer. Since the church is both spiritual organism and human organization, congregations are doubly difficult to manage.

What are the factors that make not-for-profits and volunteer organizations so tough to manage?

• Not-for-profits exist to render a service; for-profits exist to show a profit.

• Volunteers relate to their organizations in a somewhat avocational manner.

• Not-for-profits sometimes serve the second-level goals of their members. (Churches, however, should serve ultimate goals.)

• Volunteer organizations often relate to diverse and ill-defined constituencies. Most churches are clear about their formal membership but may be unclear about the various groups of persons in the community they will try to minister to.

• The purpose or dream of the not-for-profit is the most serious challenge for volunteer groups. Objectives are frequently too diffuse to provide a sharp focus for management.

• Not-for-profits are judged by their members' perceptions of effectiveness. Such varied expectations and such imprecise measurements of success create virtually unmanageable work climates.

• Not-for-profits usually produce intangibles.

• The benefits to the members of volunteer organizations are often indirect and sometimes vague.

• Not-for-profits generally function within a high (but occasionally hidden) level of competition. For instance, a small community of 1100 citizens in eastern North Carolina discovered that it had eighty-three volunteer organizations, including seven churches. That's more competition for the allegiance, time, and money of local residents than anyone had recognized before the study.[1]

• The mission of many not-for-profits is often unattainable in the short run.

• Not-for-profits customarily pay their leaders poorly and sometimes recruit their volunteers on an "anybody we can get to take the job" basis.

• Not-for-profit managers must be skilled in consensus building and other political abilities.

• Not-for-profit managers stay caught between an ongoing mission and volunteers who serve part-time or once in a while.

• Volunteer organizations and their committees often find they aren't well served by counting on their informal traditions for formal management clues.[2]

Ministering Through Committees

Committees have taken a bum rap in many churches. You've heard the jokes. "A committee is a group of the unfit trying to lead the unwilling to do the unnecessary." "Keep quiet and be considered dumb; speak up, get put on a committee, and prove what everyone suspected." "The ideal committee consists of four people who don't care and a chairman who wanted to have his own way anyway." "Committees are groups which meet to decide that nothing can be done." "A camel is a horse put together by a committee."

Churches that take the "priesthood of every believer" principle seriously take committee work seriously too. Behind most congregational ministries and services lie the efforts of a committee or committees. This imperfect method of coordinating ministry has a way of working well enough in the end to advance the mission of the congregation.

Keep these things in mind as you work with church committees.[3]

• Committees exist for the church, not vice versa. Committees have no life independent of the congregation. Committees are to help the larger body of believers implement its ministry.

• The congregation sets church policy; committees carry out established policies. Because of a committee's special knowledge of certain congregational needs, that committee may propose new policies or changes in existing policies to the church, however.

• The function of church committees is to help the congregation accomplish tasks that can't be done as well by the congregation acting as a committee-of-the-whole.

• The congregation owes its committees a job description, orientation of its chairperson and members, and a forum for reporting their work to the church.

• Orientation sessions for committees are intended to (1) discuss how committees function in this church, (2) inform committee members of their specific duties, (3) elect any officers whom the church hasn't already specified, and (4) train the committee to complete its planning, implementing, and reporting.

• Regular meetings and special meetings called by committee

chairpersons should be held to ensure the consistent service of the committee for the church.

• Any committee recommendation for congregational consideration should be accompanied by full information, such as, the problem being attacked, the options considered and rejected, the formal recommendation itself, sufficient time to discuss the issue, and the amount of time and/or financial support necessary.

• Some congregations designate a time in their official calendars for committees to meet and do their work.

• Periodically, congregations should evaluate their committee structure in order to cover emerging needs and eliminate any gaps or overlaps in committee duties. Wasted motion is demotivating to all workers, especially volunteers who have less time to invest.

Personal Rewards for Volunteers

Rewards for volunteers? Doesn't that idea fly in the face of the definition of a volunteer as a person who serves freely by personal choice? Not really. It's true that volunteers do not receive wages, fringe benefits, or bonuses. But volunteers do receive psychic and spiritual rewards.[4]

Consider these personal rewards for volunteers. (1) Contributing to a vital cause. Some persons find great satisfaction in being part of a goal-oriented organization. They join with other folks on the same mission and feel the exhilaration of being "on the team." These volunteers are concerned with excellence, production, problem solving, and the achievement of goals. (2) Enjoying the fellowship of like-minded persons. These volunteers relish being with other persons in whose company they feel comfortable. They value warm and friendly relationships and enjoy listening, sharing information and feelings, and giving encouragement to others. (3) Influencing individuals and groups. These volunteers want to be heard, like to have their advice heeded, and enjoy position and prominence. They generally hold strong opinions, are outspoken and fluent, sometimes like to debate issues and win arguments, and intend to change others. Hopefully their major concern at this point is to invest their influence in inspiring and empowering others to reach group goals.

These three categories of volunteers have been called achievers, affiliators, and power people. *Achievers* serve their volunteer organizations best by organizing new projects and programs, by solving challenging problems, and by brainstorming possibilities and options. *Affiliators* nurture and lend support by counseling, greeting, listening, and acting as hosts and hostesses. *Power people* are the movers and shakers who raise money, persuade others to join in, and generally keep the organizational structures moving forward in positive directions or backward in reactionary modes.

In other words, each of these types of volunteers is needed in churches and other volunteer agencies. Additionally, each of these volunteers receives personal rewards. Yes, volunteers are paid—in service, recognition, growth, challenge, results, love, and teamwork.

Building a Unified Team for Ministry

Teamwork is needed in the congregation any time two or more people must work together and depend on each other. (Review the section in chapter 1 on team building.) Think of managing the team-building process as a four-step sequence of (1) sharing personal history in group settings as an ice-breaker and fellowship builder, (2) affirming group members' gifts for and contributions to ministry, (3) goal setting for ministry projects and programs, and (4) celebrating the developing sense of unity (Figure 1). It's important to treat team building as a continuing practice and to use the model as a design factor in every meeting in order to develop and maintain unity.

One key attitude in team building is making ministry results "the captain of the team." That is, group or congregational goals become the focus of team building with individual goals and other concerns becoming secondary. Several ingredients are basic to developing an effective ministry team: (1) a clearly defined congregational dream; (2) settings where people feel free to risk their ideas and opinions; (3) cooperating rather than competing; (4) a commitment to congregational goals.

The team-building model helps workers get acquainted, divide responsibilities, build group cohesion, heighten morale, increase creativity, and deepen loyalty. Independence then becomes interdependence. That's team building!

Solving Problems

Every organization faces problems. Volunteer organizations grapple with tough issues gingerly because these groups are glued

Figure 1

Team-building Model

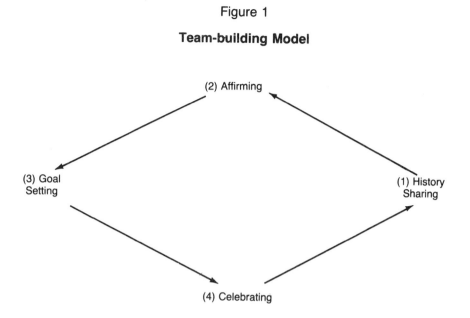

together by a fragile bond called trust. Problem solving, then, involves the entire congregation and demands skilled management.

Problem solving can become a creative instead of a frustrating experience if a good method is used. (1) Begin with a concise and precise statement of the problem under consideration. Include a broad description of an ideal solution too. Both need and hope are identified by this step. (2) Brainstorm possible solutions by "goal wishing." Completing the sentence "I wish that . . ." generates lots of options and lessens our tendency to defend our ideas. After all, anything can be wished for. (3) Take an excursion in your mind. Historically, great inventors and creative thinkers have used ideas and images from unrelated sources to solve their problems. For example, Edwin Land's daughter fretted about the time delay for processing photographs. This complaint stimulated him to invent the Polaroid camera. Thinking deliberately about material or events unrelated to the problem under consideration can provide the key link for solving a problem. (4) Try a force fit. Choose an idea from your excursion, focus on it, return to your problem, and see if something from the excursion idea helps break through to a new solution by examining its positive possibilities first and then its negative potential. If the possibilities outweigh the pitfalls, a solution is available. Personal commitment, group endorsement, and planning the details of implementation complete the problem-solving process.[5]

Managing Ministry Meetings

Business managers complain that they spend as many as 1,000 hours yearly in meetings. While ministers may not spend that much time in meetings, we work with volunteers in our meetings and must guide our meetings well or lose our volunteers.

Extra meetings must be avoided. Meetings are necessary when (1) congregation-wide concerns need to be discussed, (2) consensus building is demanded, (3) verbal reports must be shared, (4) esprit de corps needs to be cultivated, and (5) members need to be trained en masse. Don't call meetings when (1) the same information can be shared as well in writing or over the phone, (2) essential participants will be absent, (3) leaders can't get prepared, and (4) the results will not justify participants' time and energy.

Not all meetings are the same. Basically, the structure of a meeting should match its purpose.

• *Information meetings* convey basic facts and require good communication skills and a variety of methods for sharing data.

• *Problem-solving meetings* focus on difficult questions and demand participative and consensus-building skills.

• *Procedural meetings* announce policies and call for abilities to enhance psychological ownership.[6] Agenda and handouts should be prepared beforehand and, in some cases, circulated in advance.

Most effective-meeting managers have a plan or model they use in guiding the progress of the meeting itself. One helpful meeting management model moves from (1) *evaluating* the group's progress toward its mission, (2) *creating* a range of options and resources for dealing with challenges, (3) *deciding* which alternative to recommend for the congregation's consideration, and (4) *implementing* the congregation's ministry decisions and programs (Figure 2). This approach provides a "picture in the mind" for leaders of conferences and meetings to use during work sessions.

Chairing Decision-Making Meetings

Formal decision-making meetings can be intimidating for the

Figure 2

Meeting Management Model

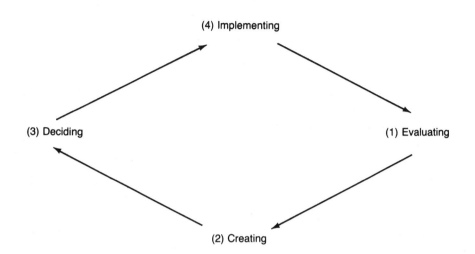

inexperienced or uncertain chairperson. Some straightforward principles can be helpful.

• Limit discussion to one subject at a time.

• Provide every member equal right to speak, offer motions, hold office, and vote.

• Allow for full and free debate.

• Protect the rights of both the majority and the minority.

• Set a climate of teamwork, cooperation, and consideration.

The duties of the chairperson usually include (1) keeping the meetings moving according to agenda, (2) knowing your congregation's formal documents, such as its constitution and bylaws and its adopted parliamentary law, such as *Robert's Rules of Order*, well enough to maintain orderliness, and (3) acting fairly and, if possible, preserving harmony.[7]

Relating to Church Staffers

Every church has a staff. Ninety-nine percent of church staffers nationwide are volunteers. How church leaders treat each other and work together is an important climate setter for congregations. Several principles contribute to good staff relationships.

1. Church staffers are people, not roles. Respect the God-created uniqueness of fellow church leaders. Help them grow, meet their needs, and reach personal and congregational goals.

2. Recognize that there are different kinds of relationships on church staffs. Some staffers' relationships revolve around what sociologists describe as "identity bonds." That is, my personality and gifts for ministry complement your gifts for ministry so that together we form a well-balanced team. Other staffers relate around "task bonds" and, therefore, focus on goals and work to be done.

3. Effective staffs blend specialist and generalist roles. The crucial issue here is that someone—usually the pastor—must maintain a corporate perspective and view the congregation's ministry in its broadest scope. Some church administrators must fill a generalist role for the congregation while others may specialize in particular ministries.

4. The larger the staff, the higher likelihood there is of relational tension. That's not to say that large staffs will inevitably disagree. But relational bonds, or primary interpersonal ties, multiply geometrically and become increasingly complicated as additional staffers are added.[8] Most of us have been led to believe "the more, the merrier" in staff resources. The fact is that where more staffers are involved, there's more potential for complications in staff relationships.

5. Job descriptions provide a formal statement of congregational expectations for employed and volunteer staffers.

6. Adopt a healthy management style with staffers. Provide both freedom and security for workers. A dictatorial management style majors on structure and security while stifling freedom. Managers who use a "path of least resistance" approach supply freedom but no security. Balanced styles are more apt to undergird both freedom and security.

7. Take a developmental stance. Every staffer has some limitations, but most of us can grow with assistance and encouragement.

8. Provide forums for communication and mutual nurture. Structured meetings with friendly atmospheres allow for information sharing, joint learning, teamwork, and supervision.

Delegating Ministry Opportunities

Delegation offers two positive opportunities to church managers.

First, delegation allows ministers to multiply their ministries by involving others. Second, delegation lets others learn by doing.

When is delegation called for?

- When someone else does the job better than you.
- When it saves the church time and/or money.
- When someone can be trained by means of the experience.

Good delegation demands a clear description of the opportunity and its limits, a large enough and complete enough task to challenge the person, a realistic time span for finishing the task, and agreed-upon checkpoints for reporting on progress. When delegating, let the task go; don't breathe down someone's neck while he is trying to share your work burden.

Supervising Fellow Church Members

Directly observing good supervision isn't a common experience. But several years ago I saw a first-rate example of supervision, and I was the guinea pig for the entire process. I had gone to the teaching hospital at Nashville's Vanderbilt Hospital for an eye examination. There I was treated by an ophthalmologist and a young intern on his first day of rotation in the eye clinic. The doctor would carefully explain what he was going to do and what he'd be looking for. After checking me himself, he would turn me over to the trainee and ask, "What do you see?" Sometimes the doctor would say, "See that? If his eyes were abnormal, they would . . ." and he'd proceed to describe what a diseased eye would look like. The step-by-step process and the careful instructions kept my usual "doctor's office anxieties" at a minimum. Suddenly, I became very worried. The doctor announced that he was ready to dilate my eyes and asked the intern, "Will his pupils get larger or smaller?" I was horrified when the intern answered incorrectly. I knew more about this process than the young doctor-to-be! Then my lesson in good supervision emerged. The ophthalmologist patiently and gently explained the physiological reaction that would take place. His attitude calmed me as well as teaching the young intern without embarrassing him. Good supervision combines gentleness with firmness.

This experience demonstrated supervision for me. Supervision, especially in a volunteer organization, is a supportive relationship. In other words, supervision calls for a comfortable but structured relationship. Typically, we have thought of supervision as a boss-employee tie with authority as the lever for change. Supervision is actually more of a mentor-novice relationship. The mentor serves as sponsor, guide, guru, model, and cheerleader. The novice, on the other hand, receives encouragement, nourishment, guidance, and proven ways of working. Supervision is a reciprocal relationship—like a two-person rail cart that requires both persons' efforts to move it down the track. The end result of supervision is growth for both the novice and the mentor.

Supervision blends learning by example, practice, and feedback. (1) Pastors and other church staff ministers who supervise volunteer leaders and workers must be willing to put their ministry on display and allow others to look over their shoulders. The opportunity for novices to observe and question is an invaluable learning experience. (2) The practice of ministry is learning by doing. Much of it is "on-the-job" training. What's second nature to the veteran in ministry can be broken down into bite-sized hunks for the less experienced. (3) Feedback extends self-evaluation into objective, behavior-based change. Feedback allows failure to become a base for learning. Effective supervisors affirm first and then confront with caring directness.

Several mistakes are common to supervision in the church.

• Trying to become supervisors without having been supervised
• Making hasty selections of workers
• Allowing jobs to expand without planning
• Failing to keep work assignments clear
• Bossing rather than coaching
• Avoiding necessary discipline
• Neglecting to train workers

These mistakes can be deadly for congregational health whether the supervisees are church staff ministers or volunteer teachers, officers, and committee workers.

Dealing with Difficult People

Every church has members who are abrasive to the larger congregation. They aren't emotionally unbalanced; they're just relationally out of step with the mainstream of the church. *These folks may become a threat to congregational health if they try to take control of the congregation's atmosphere and mission. In fact, controlling behavior is the mark of the difficult person.*[9]

Difficult people fall into two broad categories: *aggressives* and *passives*. Aggressive controllers include hostile persons, cliques, and noncommunicating "crazymakers." Passive controllers count in their numbers apathetic persons, lonely people, and traditionalists. Aggressives try to dominate the agenda of their congregations; passives place a drag on the mission and momentum of their congregations.

Which of these six difficult types is hardest to work with in ministry? All are tough to deal with, but the most difficult depends on you. Generally, the most offensive persons to us reflect the darker, more shadowy sides of our own personalities. We often have difficulty with the same aspect of the behavior of others that we fear in ourselves.

A general strategy for coping effectively with difficult persons must be broad based and constructive. Consider these actions.

• Pinpoint the problem. What exactly is the issue that's calling out the controller(s) and creating the tension in the congregation?

• Rate the relationship. How strong are the ties between the controller(s) and the leaders of the congregation?

• Count the costs of negative behavior within the congregation. Can the controlling actions be ignored, or must they be confronted?

• Search for a solution. What options are available for dealing with controlling behaviors?

• Covenant for continuity. Can an agreement be reached that will allow the congregation to advance toward its ultimate mission?

Each of the difficult persons mentioned above displays controlling actions differently. For instance, hostiles control their groups by daring to "be bad" in an institution that has a "nice" self-image. Their belligerence and demanding confrontiveness sets the emotional tone for relating. If we avoid conflict or naively assume the hostiles will ease the tension, we give the hostile an important measure of control.

Cliques control a congregation's atmosphere for good or ill. Negatively, cliques gather for protection, revenge, or warfare. Positively, cliques lend status or share information with their members.

Crazymakers control communication processes by changing the subject, overloading the conversation with multiple issues, and contradicting. When we try to communicate with crazymakers, we are thrown off balance and feel "crazy." Crazymakers cause us to feel uncertain, therefore, they maintain leverage over us.

Apathetics exercise control in two passive modes. They withhold energy from the congregation's goals. They divide a congregation's focus between internal ministry to the apathetics themselves and outreach to others.

Lonelies control the attempts of others to build relationships by seeming to invite friendship and then holding others at arm's length. Additionally, they control many well-meaning helpers who develop a guilty conscience when their relationship building efforts don't work.

Traditionalists worship the past so much they try to control a congregation's future. They seek to preserve by resisting all but emergency changes.

Several attitudes and actions provide a repertoire for reinvolving difficult persons in the congregation. (1) Accept difficult persons as worthy of attention without approving their attempts to control. (2) Build and maintain an open and up-to-date relationship with difficult persons. (3) Try to look at the church through difficult persons' eyes. Anticipate their behavior patterns. (4) Spare the entire congregation unnecessary strife by working behind the scenes with difficult persons. (5) Use Christian love as an antidote for controlling behavior. Remember that love also includes firmness.

Shaping the Organizational Climate

Every congregation and institution takes on its own personality, aura, or atmosphere. This climate is apparent to the discerning eye. Some church climates are sunny, others stormy. Some are pleasant, others ominous and threatening. Climate, variously referred to as the informal organization, norms, the organizational unconscious, and the intangible congregation, sets the tone of congregational life and ministry.[10] Climate is the organization's internal religion, its beliefs binding it together, and the molding force of its unique character.[11]

Leaders develop the congregation's climate by articulating its dream, building trust and teamwork, keeping lines of communication open, developing positive ceremonies of recognition and rites of passage, and valuing the membership. The larger and more diverse the congregation becomes, the more challenging—and more important, shaping—the organizational climate becomes.

Notes

1. Lyle E. Schaller, *Understanding Tomorrow* (Nashville: Abingdon Press, 1976), pp. 96-97.
2. For helpful perspectives on not-for-profits, their characteristics, and their management, see Richard L. Lesher, "Management of Not-For-Profit Organizations," in *Encyclopedia of Professional Management*, ed. Lester R. Bittel (New York: McGraw-Hill Book Company, 1978), pp. 778-780 and Robert N. Anthony, "Can Nonprofit Organizations Be Well Managed?" in *Managing Nonprofit Organizations*, eds. Diane Borst and Patrick J. Montana (New York: AMA-COM, 1977), pp. 7-15.
3. Organizational details are given in chapter 2.
4. Marlene Wilson, *How to Mobilize Church Volunteers* (Minneapolis: Augsburg Publishing House, 1983), pp. 28-36.
5. For a full discussion of the "synectic" problem-solving method, see W. J. J. Gordon, *Synectics—the Development of Creative Capacity* (New York: Harper & Row, 1961) and George Prince, *The Practice of Creativity* (New York: Harper & Row, 1970).
6. For a more complete exploration of managing meetings, see Robert D. Dale, *Ministers as Leaders* (Nashville: Broadman Press, 1984), especially chapter 8.
7. For helpful information on parliamentary rule and its applications, see Edmund Haugen, *Mister/Madam Chairman* (Minneapolis: Augsburg Publishing House, 1963) and O. Garfield Jones, *Parliamentary Procedure at a Glance* (New York: Hawthorn Books, 1971).
8. Here's a formula for specifying the number of relational bonds in a work group: (the number of staffers) times (the number of staffers minus one) divided by two equals the total bonds. For example, a staff of two contains only 1 bond, a staff of four has 6 bonds, a staff of ten involves 45 bonds, and a staff of fifty consists of 1225 bonds.
9. For a complete discussion of how controlling actions impact congregations negatively, see Robert D. Dale, *Surviving Difficult Church Members* (Nashville: Abingdon Press, 1984).
10. For discussions of organizational climate, see Robert D. Dale, *To Dream Again* (Nashville: Broadman Press, 1981), pp. 83-85 and 91-95; Robert F. Allen and Charlotte Kraft, *The Organizational Unconscious* (Englewood Cliffs, N.J.: Prentice-Hall, Inc., 1982); and Robert D. Dale, *Ministers as Leaders* (Nashville: Broadman Press, 1984), especially chapter 9.
11. Edwin L. Baker, "Managing Organizational Culture," *Management Review*, July 1980, p. 8.

Bibliography

Allen, Robert F. and Kraft, Charlotte. *The Organizational Unconscious.* Englewood Cliffs: Prentice-Hall, Inc., 1982.

Anthony, Robert N. "Can Nonprofit Organizations Be Well Managed?" *Managing Nonprofit Organizations.* Eds. Diane Borst and Patrick J. Montana. New York: AMA-COM, 1977.

Baker, Edwin L. "Managing Organizational Culture." *Management Review,* July 1980.

Dale, Robert D. *Ministers as Leaders.* Nashville: Broadman Press, 1984.

————. *Surviving Difficult Church Members.* Nashville: Abingdon Press, 1984.

————. *To Dream Again.* Nashville: Broadman Press, 1981.

Gordon, W. J. J. *Synectics—The Development of Creative Capacity.* New York: Harper and Row, 1961.

Haugen, Edmund. *Mister, Madam Chairman.* Minneapolis: Augsburg Publishing House, 1963.

Jones, O. Garfield. *Parliamentary Procedure at a Glance.* New York: Hawthorn Books, 1971.

Lesher, Richard L. "Management of Not-for-Profit Organizations." *Encyclopedia of Professional Management.* Ed. Lester A. Bittel. New York: McGraw-Hill Book Company, 1978.

Prince, George. *The Practice of Creativity.* New York: Harper and Row, 1970.

Schaller, Lyle E. *Understanding Tomorrow.* Nashville: Abingdon Press, 1976.

Stacker, Joe R. and Grubbs, Bruce. *Shared Ministry.* Nashville: Convention Press, 1985.

Wilson, Marlene. *How to Mobilize Church Volunteers.* Minneapolis: Augsburg Publishing House, 1983.

4

Personnel Administration

Mark Short

A careful analysis of church budgets indicates that many congregations in the middle to large range in membership are budgeting in excess of 50 percent in annual income to paid staff. These costs are found in several places in the budget, rarely in one general account. When searching for the total amount of staff compensation, one should include salaries, wages, total benefits package, worker's compensation, Christmas bonuses, and Social Security.

This computation should include the ministers, support personnel, secretaries, custodians, engineer, food service personnel, accompanists, and child care staff. Only when all salaries and benefits are totaled does one get a true picture of the amount of the budget going to personnel.

When confronted with financial reports that indicate this sizable percentage of church income is going to the maintenance of the church staff, it becomes imperative that the church understand the dynamics of personnel management. In fact, in the business world that term *personnel management* has been replaced by the term *human resources development.* That seems to lend a spiritual responsibility to the church not only to use God's money wisely but to be a partner in the development of each staff member regardless of his or her task.

Personnel Committee

The first step in this partnership of human resources development is the establishment of a Personnel Committee to study the staff needs of the church, develop a personnel policy, and administer that policy in behalf of the church. The Personnel Committee should rotate a third of its membership each year. It is recommended that the committee be made up of no more than six church members with the pastor serving ex officio.

A task description might follow this form.

Personnel Committee

The Personnel Committee is responsible to the church for locating, interviewing, and recommending qualified persons for all paid staff positions with the exception of the pastor. The term of office is three years.

Duties

1. Study the needs for future personnel.

2. Develop and keep current all position descriptions.

3. Develop and maintain an organization chart and personnel policy.

4. Locate, interview, and recommend to the church all employed staff personnel.

5. Recommend to the church a salary and benefit plan.

The Personnel Committee fills a significant place of service in the church. Its members should be spiritually mature, sensitive to the needs of persons, and willing to become knowledgeable in human resources development.

Personnel Policy

Every church, regardless of size, should have a personnel policy. In the small church with a bivocational pastor, the policy can become an article in the bylaws. Larger churches will want to develop a personnel policy manual to assure productivity and to avoid organizational and legal problems.

Here is a suggested format for a personnel policy in a middle-size church.

Personnel Policy General Information

Offer of employment to new staff members will be made by the personal committee in writing, outlining the duties of the office, its compensation, and all the conditions set forth in this personnel policy. Acceptance of the offer must be presented in writing to the committee.

All resignations from the staff must be presented to the Personnel Committee in writing.

Coverage in the retirement plan under the Annuity Board is available to all eligible staff members. Hospitalization insurance is provided for each employee and dependents.

All employees except the ordained ministers are covered under Federal Social Security. All employees are covered by Worker's Compensation.

It shall be the responsibility of the Personnel Committee to implement this personnel policy.

Paid Vacations

Within each calendar year, vacations are regularly scheduled for all employees. Unused vacation time cannot be carried over into the next year, nor will employees receive additional pay for vacation time not taken.

Vacation time is allotted according to the following policy.

1. An employee beginning service between January 1 and June 16 will, after six months of continuous service, receive one week (five work days).

2. An employee beginning service between January 1 and June 16 and taking one week (five work days) before the end of the calendar year will, after twelve months of continuous service, be eligible for two weeks (ten work days) during the ensuing calendar year.

3. After ten years of continuous service, an employee will receive three weeks (fifteen work days) vacation.

Holidays

The church facilities will be closed for one day to observe New Year's Day, Memorial Day, Independence Day, and Labor Day, and for two days to observe Thanksgiving and Christmas. When any of these holidays occur on the weekend, employee-selected weekday(s) will be observed.

Paid Leave

The following policy will be adhered to regarding paid leave for each calendar year.

1. Leave will be granted due to: personal illness; illness of a member of the immediate family which requires hospitalization; a death in the family. The immediate family includes mate, child, parent, and sibling.

2. Prior to the completion of one year of service, leave will be prorated on the basis of one day for each month employed. Leave is not to exceed ten work days.

3. After one year of continuous service, two weeks leave (ten work days) will be granted.

4. After five years of continuous service, four weeks leave (twenty work days) will be granted.

5. Three days leave will be granted for the death of a member of the immediate family. One day will be granted for the death of grandparent, aunt, uncle, niece, nephew, and first cousin. Leave will be granted whether deceased person was related by blood or marriage.

6. Deductions from salary will be made for leave extending beyond above stated policies unless an extension of leave has been granted by the Personnel Committee.

7. A request for extension of leave should be made to the Personnel Committee.

8. Leave is not cumulative, nor will employee be paid for unused leave upon termination of employment.

Time Off

The ministerial staff shall be allowed to be away for two weeks of revival, conferences, and/or educational meetings in which they serve as guest minister or clinician. In addition, they are granted two weeks away from the church for conventions and conferences such as Ridgecrest and Glorieta.

Retirement

1. Retirement at age seventy is required for all employees.

2. Employees shall have an amount equal to 10 percent of their salary paid into a retirement plan.

3. The employee is fully vested from the first month of payment.

5. All accrued rights to benefits provided by total contribution to date of termination may be retained by employee and received as benefit at retirement age or earlier disability or death.

5. The Finance Committee of the church will be advised by the Personnel Committee of any proposed supplement as each annual budget is planned.

Study Leave

The ministers shall be granted a leave every five years, with full pay, to engage in study. This leave is in addition to other time off.

After the completion of five years service .... 2 months

After the completion of ten years service .... 3 months

After the completion of fifteen years service .... 4 months

After the completion of twenty years service .... 4 months

The church shall consider assisting in paying costs of room, board, tuition, and conference fees for the ministers.

Staff Inventory

Full-time - Forty hours per week		4 Employees
Part-time - Less than forty hours per week		7 Employees

Full-time		*Part-time*	
Pastor	1	Accompanist	2
Minister of Music		Preschool Employee	3
and Education	1	Youth & Recreation	1
Church Secretary	1	Cook	1
Custodian	1		———
			7
	———		
	4		

Organization Chart and Job Descriptions

The remainder of the policy guidelines would specify the organizational structure of the staff and supervisory responsibilities. An organizational chart listing job titles should be included, followed by a job description for each position. Sample job descriptions are at the end of this chapter.[1]

After the Personnel Committee has completed the big task of writing the personnel policy manual, it should be approved by the church and put into effect at an agreed-upon date. Each year the policy will need an annual evaluation to determine if it still meets the needs of staff and congregation.

Filling Staff Vacancies

Staff vacancies are filled primarily in two ways: through an *application* and *hiring* process and through a *search* and *call* process. The former is used to fill nonministerial positions, while the latter is the way vacancies for pastors, ministers of education, ministers of music, and other ministers are filled.

Figure 1

Application Form

_____ Church

Date _____

I. *PERSONAL DATA*

Name (last) _____ (first) _____ (middle) _____

Address (street) _____

(city) _____ (state) _____ (zip code) _____

Phone Number _____ Social Security Number _____

Birth Date (month) _____ (day) _____ (year) _____

Marital Status: Single____ Married____ Divorced____ Separated____ Widow____

II. *EDUCATION*

High School Diploma: yes_____ no_____; if yes, when? _____

Business College: yes_____ no_____; if yes, where located? _____

University or College: yes_____ no_____; if yes, did you graduate? _____

What was your major? _____ Minor? _____

Name and location of college _____

School or college activities in which you engaged? _____

III. *EMPLOYMENT HISTORY* (Start with present or most recent job)

1. Name of Employer _____

   Address _____

   Worked from _____ to _____

   Monthly salary or hourly rate _____

   Type of work performed _____

   Reason for leaving _____

2. Name of Employer _____

   Address _____

   Worked from _____ to _____

   Monthly salary or hourly rate _____

   Type of work performed _____

   Reason for leaving _____

3. Name of Employer _____

   Address _____

   Worked from _____ to _____

   Monthly salary or hourly rate _____

   Type of work performed _____

   Reason for leaving _____

IV. *JOB DATA* (Check areas in which you have had experience or training)
    _____ Typing (Speed _____ WPM)   _____ Receptionist
    _____ Word Processor   _____ Writing and Editing
    _____ Transcribing Machine   _____ Supervisor
    _____ Bookkeeping   _____ Custodian
    _____ Duplicating Machine   _____
    _____ Addressograph Machine   _____

V. *CHURCH LIFE*
Denomination _____
Name of Church (Where you hold membership) _____
    Location _____
    What church activities did (do) you participate in? _____
_____

VI. *HEALTH*
How would you describe your general health? _____
Hearing? _____ Eyesight? _____
Physical defects, if any? _____
Date of last physical examination _____

VII. *CHARACTER REFERENCES* (Do not list relatives or former employers)
    1. Name _____ Address _____
        Occupation _____ Years Known _____
    2. Name _____ Address _____
        Occupation _____ Years Known _____
    3. Name _____ Address _____
        Occupation _____ Years Known _____

VIII. *ADDITIONAL INFORMATION*
Please give us any additional information you desire about your education and experience (include any special talents).

Please Sign Your Name _____

Figure 2

Employment Reference Check   First Church

Request for Reference

Name of Applicant _____

Position under consideration _____

Person contacted for reference_____

  Firm _____ Phone _____

Employment period covered:

  From _____ to _____ Firm (if different) _____

- -

The above person has given your name as a reference. Please complete the confidential questions below and return in the enclosed, postage-paid envelope. *Thank you!*

1. In what capacity did you know the applicant and for how long?_____
_____

2. What was his/her title? _____
   What specifically did he/she do?_____

3. How would you rate his/her (a) Performance? _____
                                 (b) Supervisory abilities?_____
                                   (c) Independent work? _____
                                   (d) Creativity? _____

4. How does he/she get along with others? _____

5. Any unusual work habits? _____

6. What were the circumstances surrounding his/her leaving? _____
_____

   Would you rehire him/her? Yes _____ Any qualifications? _____
                                 No _____ Why? _____

7. What are his/her strong points? General _____
   Technical _____

8. Are there any negative aspects or weaknesses? _____

9. Any additional comments:

Signed _____ Title _____ Date _____

These two processes require different procedures. First, the steps for application and hiring:

- Prepare/update job description and qualifications.
- Prepare an application form and solicit applicants. (See Figure 1.)
- Conduct interviews with promising applicants.
- Test for job skills if appropriate.
- Prepare reference follow-up form; secure references on most promising applicants. (See Figure 2.)
- Choose best prospect(s) and conduct an in-depth interview to follow-up on references, discuss details of the job, review salary and benefits, and determine whether or not to offer the job. In small to medium-size churches, the person to whom the worker will report usually conducts the interviews and approves hiring. In larger situations, the screening process to this point may be done by someone else. Either way, the supervisor(s) of the new worker *must be involved* in the final screening, interview(s), and choice of the worker.
- Review all information and make a choice. See the information in Figure 3, "Evaluating Potential Employees."

The search and call of staff *ministers* is a more complicated process. Procedures vary from denomination to denomination and even from church to church. The following information describes typical procedures.[2]

Finding Staff Ministers

The Personnel Committee will begin the search for the approved staff member. There is the possibility that the committee will ask that a special ad hoc search committee be appointed to assist in seeking the new staff member.[3]

Where are prospective staff members found today? Word of mouth still seems to be the biggest supplier of future staff members in today's church.

The "Church Employment Agency" has been at work for many years. It has no board of trustees, no executive director, no office, and no letterhead. There is never a referral fee paid by employer or employee. And yet, there is a vast amount of business carried on each day among religious leaders using the key phrases: "Do you know where I can find a good music minister?" or "I'm calling to

Figure 3

Evaluating Potential Employees

1. Is the applicant a Christian? Does he or she participate in a local church? Live and act responsibly? Have good character and reputation?
2. Is the applicant neat? Alert? Does he or she have good posture? Good facial expression?
3. Is the applicant tactful? Courteous? Confident? Warm? Enthusiastic? Cheerful? Optimistic? Animated? Humorous?
4. Does the applicant have good pronunciation? Enunciation? Vocabulary? Grammar? Does the applicant express himself or herself freely? With clarity? In an organized manner?
5. Does the applicant have good educational and professional backgrounds? Can he or she do the job at an acceptable level now? Or with training?
6. Has the applicant exhibited mental effectiveness? Good personality? Skill in getting along with people? Insight?
7. In short, beginning with your initial contact did you immediately sense that this person would fit in well and is qualified for the job?

recommend a top-notch minister of education to your church." This is the style many churches currently use in locating staff members, and it seems to work quite well. There doesn't seem to be any movement to change this time-honored method of staff selection.

If you don't believe the agency is in full operation, just ask state convention workers and directors of missions how many calls they get per week relative to this agency's work. Or better still, just listen as you stand in the exhibit hall at the next state convention. Pastors and Personnel Committee members are fervently searching out the best people possible for their churches.

Some religious organizations have minister relations departments that assist churches with prospective workers. Résumés are kept current and on file to provide personnel committees with helpful information.

Even better than calling friends and denominational workers for prospect lists is the plan to find people *before* you need them. It is important that pastor and Personnel Committee be observant of those who are doing a good job in another place of service. Encourage the membership to share names of people who have impressed them.

Obviously, church staff members will be found in churches most of the time. However, don't overlook faculty and staff members from seminaries and colleges. Frequently, staff members from denominational agencies will feel God's call to return to the local church. These people make excellent workers in the church.

Smaller churches should not hesitate to interview and call recent graduates from seminaries. Many of these well-trained and highly motivated young people are ready to make a lasting contribution to God's work in the local church. If the graduating seminarian has had church staff responsibilities during school days, his or her possible contribution is greatly enhanced in the first full-time church.

Generally speaking, the prospective staff members will be observed and called out of other local church situations, drawn from recent seminary graduates, or secured through recommendations from denominational offices.

Initiate the Search

There is disagreement over how to begin the search for new staff members. Some feel that the prospective staff member should be thoroughly investigated prior to any formal contact. Some prefer the plan of an informal, get-acquainted visit in the home or office of the prospect. It seems best to have consent from the person before beginning any formal investigation.

In the conferences which follow, great care should be given in describing the church, other staff members, the people, prospects for growth, and how the prospective staff member can aid the church. Leave off the rose-colored glasses for this interview. Show negative as well as positive factors in the church. If God leads the church and the prospect to each other, this honesty and openness will have long-term dividends. This is no time to pull punches about the task, its rewards, and possible difficulties. Above all, don't make promises that can't be kept. This is always counterproductive in future relationships.

The square peg in the round hole can be detrimental to the fellowship, future growth, ministry, and financial program of the church. Churches need God-called men and women to work. The Personnel Committee and church will be called to prayer in seeking the leadership of the Holy Spirit in this strategic matter. Don't rush the process until there is a strong consensus that God is leading.

Here are specific questions that the prospective minister and the

Personnel, or Search, Committee should ask themselves in the evaluation process.

1. Does the prospect display leadership skills? Today's churches demand people who can lead. Is the prospect too slow to keep up with the people or so visionary so as to be too far in front? Does the staff member have basic traits of leadership such as truthfulness, honesty, willingness to work, interest in people?

2. Is there an overwhelming sense of God's call evident in the prospect? The dynamic church in today's society demands a high calling from God.

3. Is there a strong commitment to teaching and preaching God's Word? This is absolutely imperative in the life of a prospective leader.

4. Is the person flexible? "Rolling with the punches" seems to be a necessary trait of church leaders. Amending programs to meet needs is most helpful in today's churches.

5. Is the prospective staff member a generalist? This trait is helpful in local churches. A staff member who is interested in and helpful toward all church programs is important.

6. Are there indicators of continued growth in the individual? Staff members need an ongoing program of education and updating of knowledge. This is a key point of leadership in progressive churches.

7. Is there an evident love for people and their needs? The staff member who stays secluded day after day will have a difficult time in relating to the real-life needs of people.

After the Personnel Committee members come to the conclusion that the prospect may be the person God would have in their church, they are ready to take the final step in the search process. This step is twofold.

1. The prospect must come to the same conclusion. He or she must be willing to show enough interest to make a visit, meet the people and—along with the church—consider the possibility of an invitation to join the staff. After this has been done, the prospective staff member will need to seek God's will in the matter.

2. The church members should have an opportunity to meet the prospective staff member. The leaders with whom the staff member would have the most exposure should assuredly have dialogue with the prospect. The future effectiveness of the staff person can be

harmed or enhanced by the way this get-acquainted visit is conducted.

At the conclusion of the visit, the church also will need to seek God's will and move accordingly. Compensation should be stated clearly to both church and future employee. There should be a general agreement as to the position expectations and performance standards. If the church approves and the staff member accepts, both parties begin to establish a productive and enjoyable relationship.

Creating a New Staff Position

As the church grows, a need will arise to add one or more staff members. Since there will be a substantial increase in budget costs, especially a full-time position on the ministerial staff, the Personnel Committee will ask some serious questions before approaching the church with a request. Some questions that will be asked include:

1. What task is to be accomplished with this new staff member? Does the task match our objective? Do we have adequate resources?

2. Why is it important to the church? Is this position really needed?

3. Where will the new staff member work? Is office space currently available?

4. When will the staff member begin work?

5. What skills will this person need?

6. What methods will he or she use?

When these questions have been answered to the satisfaction of the Personnel Committee and the congregation, a job description has been prepared, and the church has given formal approval, the process for filling the position can start. If the position is nonministerial, follow the application and hiring procedures listed above. If the position is for a new minister, follow the search and call procedures given.

Orientation of a New Employee

There are few self-starters who on their own are willing to ask all the necessary questions to complete a self-orientation. That really isn't the task of the new worker. The staff member needs a knowledgeable person to acquaint him or her in the new post.

Here are the things you should include when orienting a new staff member.[4] Naturally, you will want to make adjustments depending on the level of experience and background of the individual, and you may spread this over several days.

- Introduce staff members and tour the church facilities.
- Tell how the staff is organized to carry out the church's programs and ministries.
- Describe the church's programs, ministries, calendar of events, schedule of services, and interpret the *personality* of the congregation; review the church's history.
- Review how the church operates through its deacons, Church Council, committees, and so forth.
- Explain employee benefits, personnel policies, salary plan, pay dates, work hours, holidays, and other pertinent items.
- Review and explain job duties.
- Tour the community; introduce the new person to important business contacts with whom he or she will work, such as the postmaster, printer, bank officials, and social service representatives.
- Visit the church's mission(s), if any.

Working as a Team

As recently as the early part of this century, the word *team* was associated primarily with beasts of burden. Until recently, we would never have visualized a team as a group of people working together on a church staff. Current research indicates that "unity of purpose" is the chief distinguishing feature of an outstanding church staff.

If a church staff is to be effective, it should have the same characteristics that a competitive sports team has. The members will form a cohesive whole which is greater than the sum of its parts. Staff members will be interdependent with each person supporting others on the staff. This interaction is stimulating and enjoyable to all those who are involved.

In most team sports each member of the team relates to every other member of the team. Instead of hierarchy, as one would have in a military structure, there should be a broad-based equality on a church staff. Even though at a given time one member of the team may be more important to the outcome of the contest, there is general recognition of equality. *Relationships* is a key word in the team effort of the church staff.

Today's most productive church staff teams seem to have a general set of characteristics that mark their effectiveness.

1. There is recognition for the individual staff member. One pastor's response indicated that there was enough love and appreciation in his church for every staff member. This churchwide love and appreciation leads to staff security in work and in relationships. This security leads to an enhanced team effort.

2. There is responsibility but also freedom: freedom to be creative; freedom to innovate; freedom to pioneer; and freedom to fail. A loving congregation will understand that the staff leader may indeed miss projections, fail in the development of an organization, or misread the needs of the people.

3. There is understanding. Staff members grow through an understanding of themselves, others on the staff, and the people they lead. They grow as they understand the objective of the church and its goals. They grow by playing on the team to achieve those goals.

4. There is cooperation. All staff members pull together in support of each other's work as well as the total life of the church. It is this type of cooperative spirit that nurtures staff members in their own sense of purposefulness and fulfillment as servant leaders.

Figure 4

Pastor

Principle Function.—The pastor is responsible to the church to proclaim the gospel of Jesus Christ, to teach the biblical revelation, to engage in pastoral care ministries, to provide administrative leadership in all areas of church life, and to act as the chief administrator of the paid staff.

Responsibilities
1. Plan and conduct the worship services; prepare and deliver sermons; lead in observance of ordinances.
2. Lead the church in an effective program of witnessing and in a caring ministry for persons in the church and community.
3. Visit members and prospects.
4. Conduct counseling sessions; perform wedding ceremonies; conduct funerals.
5. Serve as chairman of the Church Council to lead in planning, organizing, directing, coordinating, and evaluating the total program of the church.
6. Work with deacons, church officers, and committees as they perform their assigned responsibilities; train and lead the deacons in a program of family ministries.
7. Act as moderator of church business meetings.
8. Cooperate with associational, state, and denominational leaders in matters of mutual interest and concern; keep the church informed of denominational development; represent the church in civic matters.
9. Serve as chief administrator of the paid church staff; supervise the work of assigned paid staff workers.

Figure 5

Minister of Education

Principle Function.—The minister of education is responsible to the pastor for providing staff leadership to the entire church educational program. This involves assisting church program leaders in planning, conducting, and evaluating a comprehensive ministry of Christian education in support of the mission and objectives of the church.

Responsibilities

1. Lead the church in planning, conducting, and evaluating a comprehensive program of Christian education.
2. Serve as educational resource person and advisor to the leaders of church program and service organizations such as Sunday School, Church Training, Woman's Missionary Union, Brotherhood, church library, and church recreation.
3. Serve as educational resource person and advisor to the committees of the church as requested.
4. Work with the church Nominating Committee to select, enlist, and train qualified leaders.
5. Coordinate the production of informational and public relations materials such as church publications and news releases.
6. Develop special educational and training projects such as camps, retreats, and study seminars for various age groups within the congregation.
7. Lead the church to be aware of the educational and curriculum materials available and lead the church to choose the most suitable.
8. Assist the pastor in planning, conducting, and evaluating congregational services as requested.
9. Serve on the Church Council.
10. Supervise appropriate church staff members, such as age-group directors, recreation leaders, educational secretary, and custodian.
11. Keep informed on methods, materials, principles, procedures, promotion, and administration as related to the education program.

Figure 6

Minister of Music

Principle Function.—The minister of music is responsible to the pastor for the development and promotion of the music program of the church.

Responsibilities
1. Direct the planning, organizing, conducting, and evaluating of a comprehensive music program including choirs, vocal and/or instrumental ensembles.
2. Supervise the work of assigned paid staff workers.
3. Cooperate with the church Nominating Committee to enlist and train leaders for the church music ministry including graded choir workers, song leaders, and accompanists for the church education organizations.
4. Lead in planning and promoting a graded choir program; direct and coordinate the work of lay choir directors; direct adult, youth, and other choirs as needed.
5. Serve as a member of the Church Council; coordinate the music program with the organizational calendar and emphases of the church.
6. Assist the pastor in planning all services of worship.
7. Give direction to a music ministry plan of visitation.
8. Arrange and provide music for weddings, funerals, special projects, ministries, and other church-related activities upon request.
9. Plan, organize, and promote choir tours, mission trips, camps, festivals, workshops, clinics, and programs for the various choirs.
10. Maintain music library, materials, supplies, musical instruments, and other equipment.
11. Keep informed on music methods, materials, promotion, and administration.
12. Prepare an annual music budget for approval; administer the approved budget.
13. Cooperate with associational and state leaders in promoting activities of mutual interest.

Figure 7

Business Administrator

Principle Function.—The business administrator is responsible to the pastor for administering the business affairs of the church.

Responsibilities

1. Work with paid staff and church members to achieve the goals of the church.
2. Establish and operate an efficient plan of financial record keeping and reporting; develop bookkeeping procedures.
3. Prepare financial information for the Finance and Budget Committees and treasurer of the church.
4. Serve as resource person regarding legal and business matters of the church; study annually the insurance program and make recommendations, if any.
5. Maintain records on church staff personnel; establish and maintain records of equipment and facilities; approve and process requisitions and purchase orders.
6. Administer church-adopted policies and procedures concerning the use of all church properties and facilities.
7. Assist Building Committee in its relationships with architect, contractors, and others in building, remodeling, and equipping church buildings.
8. Serve on the Church Council; serve as ex officio member of the deacons and church committees.
9. Work with the Property and Space Committee in preparing an annual budget of maintenance and equipment needs.
10. Supervise workers in the maintenance and repair of all physical properties; establish and implement cleaning, painting, renovating schedules; operate within approved budget.
11. Supervise the operation of food services.
12. Supervise assigned office personnel.
13. Perform other duties as assigned by the pastor.

Several of the duties are usually included in the minister of education's position description when the church does not have a business administrator.

Figure 8

Minister of Youth/Director of Youth Education

Principal Function.—The director of youth work is responsible to the minister of education for assisting church program organizations to develop a comprehensive program of youth education. He or she consults with other staff members concerning activities, policies and procedures that relate to their areas of responsibility.

Responsibilities
1. Counsel with church program organization leaders in planning, conducting, and evaluating a youth education ministry and in enlisting appropriate youth workers.
2. Conduct special training projects for youth workers in proper relationship to the Church Training program.
3. Advise in the use of program materials, equipment, supplies and space by youth groups in all church program organizations.
4. Work with the director of library services and the director of the recreation service to provide needed services.
5. Assist with planning and conducting special projects (such as camps and retreats) for youth program organization groups.
6. Work with organization leaders to coordinate visitation for the Youth Division and lead workers to visit prospects and absentees.
7. Work with program leaders and teachers and appropriate staff members to resolve philosophical, procedural, and scheduling problems in the Youth Division.

Note: This description could be used for any age-group specialist; simply substitute the appropriate age group for "youth."

Figure 9

Secretary

Principal Function.—Perform general office work in relieving supervisor of minor executive and clerical duties.

Regular Duties
1. Transcribe dictation; type sermons; use word processing equipment as required.
2. Perform general office work; maintain supplies and various files; keep records and compile these into periodic or occasional reports.
3. Review, open, and distribute mail; prepare routine answers without direction for approval and signature; answer routine letters in absence of the supervisor.
4. Act as required during supervisor's absence in making decisions or taking any necessary action not requiring supervisory approval.
5. Exercise tact, courtesy, and diplomacy in receiving callers, personal or telephone; keep calendar of appointments.
6. Notify committee members of meeting dates.

Other Duties
7. May edit and prepare bulletin copy.
8. May order literature and office supplies.
9. May assist in training new office workers.

Figure 10

Organist and Music Assistant

Principal Function.—The organist and music assistant is responsible to the minister of music for serving as organist of the church and assisting in the music ministry.

Responsibilities
1. Play for all services of the church, both regular and special.
2. Serve as accompanist for choirs, ensembles, and soloists in regular and special rehearsals and performances, as assigned.
3. Play for weddings and funerals, as requested, and with the approval of the minister of music.
4. Assist in planning worship services, choir rehearsals, and special music events.
5. Plan and give direction to a training program designed for developing organists and pianists in the church.
6. Maintain a regular schedule of organ practice and study.
7. Serve as secretary to the minister of music; take and transcribe dictation; and maintain music ministry files, library and equipment inventories.
8. Prepare workbooks and study materials for the graded choirs as assigned.
9. Perform other related responsibilities as assigned.

Figure 11

Minister of Education and Music

Principal Function.—The minister of education and music is responsible to the pastor for the development and promotion of the educational and music programs of the church.

Responsibilities

1. Direct the planning, coordinating, conducting, and evaluating of comprehensive educational and music programs based on program tasks.
2. Supervise the work of assigned paid staff members.
3. Serve as a member of the Church Council.
4. Lead in enlisting and training volunteer workers in cooperation with the church Nominating Committee and Church Training.
5. Organize and direct a churchwide visitation program.
6. Assist the pastor in planning all services of worship; arrange and provide music for weddings, funerals, special projects, ministries, and other church-related activities upon request.
7. Maintain personnel records of all paid staff workers; maintain music library, materials, supplies, musical instruments, and other equipment.
8. Serve as the purchasing agent for the church as assigned.
9. Develop projects such as mission trips, festivals, youth camps, retreats; plan activities for senior adults.
10. Edit church publications as assigned.
11. Assist the chairpersons of the various church committees; serve as ex officio member of church committees.
12. Prepare an annual program ministry budget for approval; administer the approved budget.
13. Keep informed on educational and music methods, materials, promotions, and administration.
14. Cooperate with association and state leaders in promoting activities of mutual interest.

Figure 12

Minister of Activities/Director of Recreation

Principal Function.—The minister of activities/director of recreation is responsible to the minister of education for leading the church in planning, conducting, and evaluating a program of recreation for church members and other persons in the community.

Responsibilities
1. Direct the planning, coordination, conducting, and evaluation of recreation activities in the church.
2. Coordinate and administer activities in the church's recreation center, as assigned by the church.
3. Work with the church Nominating Committee to recruit and enlist workers for the church's recreation program.
4. Plan and coordinate training for all volunteer recreation workers in proper relationship to the Church Training program.
5. Serve as ex officio member of the Church Council and coordinate the recreation activities with the calendar and emphases of the church.
6. Serve as recreation resource person and advisor to organizations of the church as requested.
7. Lead the church to provide equipment and supplies needed in the recreation activities.
8. Supervise the inventory, care, repair, and storage of recreation equipment and supplies.
9. Provide representation for the church in planning, conducting, and evaluating recreation activities that involve other churches and groups.

Figure 13

Financial Secretary

Principal Function.—Maintain the church financial records and prepare financial reports.

Regular Duties
1. Receive, count, and deposit all church offerings.
2. Post receipts and disbursements of all accounts according to financial system.
3. Post offerings weekly to individual accounts; file envelopes.
4. Prepare bank reconciliation statements monthly.
5. Prepare monthly and annual financial reports for Finance Committee, deacons, and church business meetings.
6. Prepare quarterly and annual government reports.
7. Check and total all invoices when approved; inform responsible persons of their budget expenditures.
8. Receive and answer queries concerning financial matters; maintain file of invoices, correspondence, and reports.
9. Prepare and issue checks to staff members, designations, and organizations in accordance with church policy.
10. Mail pledge cards, stewardship letters, and envelopes to new members.

Other Duties
11. Requisition and prepare all forms and records for the annual stewardship emphasis.
12. Serve in related office duties, as assigned.

Figure 14

Stenographer

Principal Function.—Transcribe dictation and perform general office work. Take dictation and/or use word processing equipment as required.

Regular Duties
1. Transcribe dictation; use word processing equipment.
2. Perform general office work; maintain files and supplies; keep records and compile these into periodic reports.
3. Type copy for reproduction.
4. Receive visitors; arrange appointments and keep calendar of appointments.
5. Receive and distribute incoming mail.
6. Answer the telephone.

Other Duties
7. May assist in mailing out the bulletin.
8. Assist in clerical work as assigned.

Figure 15

Clerk-Typist

Principal Function.—Maintain office files, records, and schedules; make requisitions, prepare reports, and type copy.

Regular Duties
1. Maintain office files, program records, and schedules.
2. Fill out requisition forms.
3. Prepare reports periodically or as directed.
4. Do routine typing and compose routine letters.
5. Correct addressograph mailing lists; operate addressograph.
6. Operate duplicating machine.

Other Duties
7. May take and transcribe dictation.
8. May answer telephone and serve as receptionist.
9. Assist in clerical work as assigned.

Figure 16

Typist

Principal Function.—Type routine copy; address envelopes. Use word processing equipment as required.

Regular Duties
1. Type routine form letters, copy, records, record cards, and reproduction masters.
2. Address and stuff envelopes.
3. Perform routine clerical work as assigned.

Other Duties
4. May answer the telephone.
5. May sort and deliver incoming mail.
6. May maintain addressograph file.

Figure 17

Church Hostess

Principal Function.—Oversee the operation of the kitchen and dining areas for all food services.

Regular Duties
1. Plan meals; purchase, prepare, and serve food for all scheduled meals and snacks and for social functions as requested.
2. Supervise assigned personnel; enlist and direct volunteer workers; train workers in proper food preparation and service.
3. Maintain high standards of sanitation in cleanliness of cooking utensils, dishes, glasses, silverware, and in food handling, preparation, service, storage, and so forth, to assure compliance with local health and sanitation laws; maintain clean work areas, storage bins, and so forth.
4. Maintain accurate records in cost and operation.
5. Maintain up-to-date inventory of food supplies.
6. Arrange for the servicing, repairing, and replacement of equipment in the kitchen as needed.
7. Work with the building superintendent on table and room arrangements for all meals and social functions.
8. Assist as requested in other food services.

Figure 18

Custodian

Principal Function.—Maintain clean buildings and grounds; make minor repairs.

Regular Duties
1. Sweep, mop, buff, clean, and wax floors according to schedule; dust furniture and equipment; wash walls and windows and vacuum carpets as scheduled.
2. Maintain clean rest rooms; replenish tissue and towels; empty waste cans.
3. Request cleaning and maintenance supplies and equipment as needed.
4. Operate heating and cooling equipment according to schedule and instructions.
5. Prepare baptistry for use as directed and clean following use.
6. Open and close building daily as scheduled.
7. Mow grass; trim shrubbery, maintain clean church entrance, sidewalk, and parking areas.
8. Check with church office or supervisor daily for special assignments.
9. Move furniture, set up tables and chairs for suppers, banquets, and other similar occasions; set up assembly and classroom areas for regular activities.

Other Duties
10. Make minor electrical, plumbing, and equipment repairs as requested.
11. Paint walls, furniture, and equipment.
12. Perform messenger service.
13. Perform other duties as assigned.

Notes

1. Job descriptions and other items adapted from Leonard E. Wedel, *Church Staff Administration* (Nashville: Broadman Press, 1978), pp. 195 *ff.*
2. If you are unsure about the specific procedures for your church, consult the denominational office in your association, region, or state.
3. This practice varies from denomination to denomination. The focus in this chapter is on churches with a congregational-style polity.
4. Adapted from Leonard E. Wedel, *Church Staff Administration* (Nashville: Broadman Press, 1978), p. 32.

Bibliography

Anderson, James D. and Jones, Ezra Earl. *The Management of Ministry*. New York: Harper and Row, 1978.

Bender, Henry E. and Eichel, Evelyn. *Performance Appraisal*. New York: AMACOM, 1984.

Bingham, Robert E. and Loessner, Ernest J. *Serving with the Saints*. Nashville: Broadman Press, 1970.

Brown, Jerry. *Church Staff Teams that Win*. Nashville: Convention Press, 1979.

Cribbin, James L. *Leadership*. New York: AMACOM, 1981.

Eims, Leroy. *Be a Motivational Leader*. Wheaton, Ill.: Victor, 1981.

Stacker, Joe R. and Grubbs, Bruce. *Shared Ministry*. Nashville: Convention Press, 1985.

Stanton, Erwin W. *Reality-Centered People Management*. New York: AMACOM, 1982.

Sweet, Herman J. *The Multiple Staff in the Local Church*. Philadelphia: Westminster, 1963.

Terry, George R. *Supervisory Management*. Homewood, Ill.: Irwin, Inc., 1971.

Wedel, Leonard E. *Church Staff Administration*. Nashville: Broadman Press, 1978.

Williamson, Gerald M. *Pastor Search Committee Primer*. Nashville: Broadman Press, 1981.

5

Office Administration

Bruce P. Powers

A church office is the nerve center of a congregation's life. It is a support system for church staff members and volunteer leaders, a communication center for church life, and a business location for transacting church affairs. It is at the center of support services for church administration.

Purpose of the Church Office

The purpose of the church office is to provide support services that assist the congregation in achieving church-approved goals. Under the guidance of designated leaders, tasks will be organized and performed in such a manner as to enable a church and its leadership to function effectively and efficiently.

The church office is the administrative center for the congregation as well as the major contact point for members throughout the week.

Checkpoints for Office Administration

There are five major areas to consider: location, environment, facilities, equipment, and work systems. General guidelines for each of these will be given. Keep in mind, however, that you will have to determine specific ways to apply these in your situation. The number of church staff members, the availability of facilities, and financial considerations influence the extent to which a church can provide centralized support services.

Location

Where is your church office? It should easily be accessible by church members *and* by persons not familiar with your facilities. Parking should be nearby, access by young and elderly should be easy, directional signs should point the way, and the area should be convenient to other offices and workrooms.

Pretend you are a newcomer to town and that you are going to the church office to get information about worship services. Drive up to your church and approach it as a newcomer would. What would you see? Where would you park? What entrance would you use? What signs would tell you where to go? What would you think of the church before even reaching the office?

Environment

As you walk into your church office, what impresses you? Does it appear orderly? And would you know where to stand or sit, or where to get information if you were a stranger? How would you be greeted, and by whom?

The personality of an office is just as important in relating to people as your personality is to you. It elicits a positive or negative feeling, it gives confidence or doubt, it can inspire trust or encourage suspicion about the quality of administrative leadership in a church. Just by the *impressions* of the environment in your church office.

Most often mentioned in office manuals are the following.

• Clean and uncluttered work areas
• Clean and attractive reception/waiting area
• Clean and well-maintained furnishings
• Clean and well-maintained floors, walls, and ceilings
• Adherence to published office hours
• Warm, personal greeting when a guest enters

Office consultants would tell many of us: clean up, throw away, paint, and spend a little money on attractive furnishings.

Facilities

An office can be a corner of a room, or it can be a suite of offices, workrooms, and storage areas. One basic principle overrides all others: everything must be functional—it must help you do your job! The church office must not be a catchall for old literature, storage place for athletic equipment, and place to retire used furniture that some well-meaning member donates.

An old administrative guideline says, *A Place for Everything, and Everything in Its Place.* That is pretty good advice. You need a reception area, work stations (desks or tables), walkways, work areas, and storage facilities. Each of these requires decisions about what is needed, where it should be located, and how best to manage the work flow.

Reception Area

This area should be immediately inside the entrance to the office and should be separated from the work area by a reception desk, counter, planter, or some other device. Items needed: at least two comfortable chairs, a table, lamp (or good overhead lighting), and a small trash can. Keep some current church literature and brochures about your church on the table.

The secretary or receptionist should have line-of-sight vision of the entrance in order to greet immediately any visitor. Seats in the reception area should be arranged so that persons waiting are not looking directly at the work areas; this way jobs can be continued without office workers appearing rude.

Guidelines

1. Greet each visitor and determine what he or she needs.

2. If the visitor has an appointment, ask the guest to be seated while you notify the appropriate person.

3. If the person has an information or work request, determine immediately whether you can handle the request or need to refer it. Most requests will be routine, and you can handle according to established procedures. If you are not sure how to handle a request, write down the information and inform the person when and to whom you will channel the request.

4. When a visitor is kept waiting, tell the person you are sorry and give a reason if appropriate. Don't let a person sit and wonder why the delay.

5. Keep a record of visitors, requests, and work you perform on a drop-in basis. Use a daily calendar or appointment sheet. This is invaluable if you are asked to tell about something that was said or done, if you need to assess the work flow in the church office, or if you need to recall the details later when you are doing some work that someone had requested.

6. Keep the area fresh and clean. Live plants, up-to-date reading materials, a box of tissues, and attractive furnishings will make a good impression for your church.

Work Stations

Desks, tables, and chairs should be at a comfortable height: desks, 29-30 inches; typing or keyboard tables, about 26 1/2 inches; and chairs, adjustable from 17 to 21 inches. Chairs *must* be comfortable in size and in design. It is unwise to use cheap chairs to save a little bit of money and lose efficiency due to poor back support.

The size and design of furniture should be appropriate for the work to be performed. Consider the size and number of machines and other devices that must regularly be within reach of the person working at a particular place. If you are outfitting a new office, consult with an office supplier to determine what might be appropriate in your situation. If you are evaluating a current arrangement, discuss needs with those who use the equipment. Be sensitive to expressions of back and shoulder discomfort, eye fatigue, and inability to concentrate for extended periods—signs often related to design of work areas.

Guidelines

1. Determine what needs to be done at a work station, the appropriate furniture, necessary equipment, and the resources that need to be nearby.

2. Design each work area so that all major items (phone, primary work machines, and other equipment) are within a radius of about three feet from the worker. A swivel chair with rollers is preferable for many situations; this allows quick, easy access to secondary resources (file cabinet, supply shelf) within about about six feet. The distance from the floor should range between 6 and 54 inches, with ideal being within 12 inches of the desk top.

3. Locate large and/or noisy operations away from the central office. In a small church, this may be in the next room. In a big church, locations most appropriate for the operations should be selected. Be sure to check the lighting, power, heating/cooling, and communications needs for remote office functions such as printing, addressing and mailing, literature processing, and such before making any final decisions.

4. Storage areas of often-used supplies should be in the immediate area where they are used. For example, word processing supplies should be at or near the desks and typing machines or terminals, printing supplies in the printing/duplicating area, and financial materials in the area or office where such matters are handled. In a

small church, obviously, there may be a main storage cabinet; this would be located so that a secretary could secure paper or a typing ribbon without leaving the phone or reception area unattended. Label the location on each shelf or in each drawer for all items kept on hand. When the supply of a certain item is low, it will be easy to determine what is needed and reorder. A storage rack for coats, umbrellas, lunches, and other items belonging to workers should be provided in a convenient but out-of-sight location.

5. Arrange work stations so that there is a minimum of distraction to a worker when someone walks by. In general, arrange a walkway on one side of a work area rather than through it. Whenever possible, arrange a divider at least 54 inches high between work stations to provide privacy, control the noise level, and to avoid distractions. Make sure that all areas have good overhead lighting, preferably fluorescent, and adequate ventilation.

6. Evaluate your office arrangement whenever new workers come, or there is a change in work assignments, equipment, or quality/quantity of work. Experiment with various arrangements by using graph paper to sketch out the possibilities.

Equipment

The administrator's concern with equipment primarily is at the point of how best to speed up the work. An office *could* function without any mechanical assistance, but how nice it is to have labor-saving devices that improve efficiency. Each church has to determine what it is willing to invest in order to make its work easier, get it done faster, or do more of it.

One caution: the concern for improved efficiency through the use of machines must not result in a loss of the personal touch of ministry extended to people through the church office.

Church office equipment generally helps us to do one of the following.

Word processing
Financial reporting
Data filing and sorting
Duplicating
Communicating

In each of these areas, there is a great variety of equipment ranging from simple, cheap, and slow to complex, expensive, and fast. In general, the least expensive—and most widely used—machines are those that have been around for years and are mechanical in operation, such as the nonelectric typewriter. The more expensive options—and the devices that are revolutionizing the way office work is done—are *electronic* in operation, such as the "memory" typewriter and personal computer.

The work can be done well at a number of levels, for example word processing: by hand, mechanical typewriter, electric typewriter, "memory" typewriter, word-processing computer. Price range, about 19 cents to about $2,500. Personnel time, ten minutes per letter versus about three minutes; a second or slightly revised copy, ten minutes versus thirty seconds. A typed bulletin that takes one hour to complete a perfect master on a mechanical typewriter takes twelve to fifteen minutes on a computer.

Consider the following options in making decisions.

Word Processing

As a general guideline, ten hours devoted to typing by an efficient worker with a manual typewriter can be reduced to eight hours with a good electric typewriter and to three to five hours with a word-processing computer and printer. The real value of the computer is that corrections and changes can be made on a screen and fresh, original copies typed in a few seconds.

New and revised copies typed on a manual machine can be typed at 50 to 70 words per minute; a computer types the same material error free at 400 to 600 words per minute. If a high-quality, carbon-ribbon image is not needed, a dot-matrix printer can be used that will type more than 1,400 words per minute. Visit a computer dealer to compare work speed, typing quality, and price ranges for various options.

Another consideration is the memory that is available with electronic machines. After items are typed the first time, they can be stored until you need them again, desire to revise them, or choose to delete them—all with very little time and trouble. Take the church bulletin, for example. Type it one time, and store it in memory; the next week push a button, and it will appear on a screen. Type over the incorrect parts with the new date, hymns, sermon title, and announcements; press a button, and a perfect master is printed. You just saved three fourths of the time it would have taken with a manual typewriter.

Financial Reporting

The same examples given for word processing could be given for financial reporting. The only difference is that *much more time* can be saved. Rather than using a journal, making entries by hand, performing calculations with a machine, and entering the results, a computer works this way.

1. A spread sheet or budget form is displayed on the screen.

2. Figures are entered using the calculating keys on the computer keyboard.

3. Push a key and all of the entries are automatically calculated or readjusted in a matter of seconds.

4. Push a key and an accurate report is typed at 50 to 180 characters *per second.*

Data Filing and Sorting

Two types of filing cabinets are in general use in church offices. One is the traditional stacked-drawers model that files materials front to back. A newer style—called a lateral file—opens on the side, and file folders are placed side by side as if on a shelf. This design makes it easy to get to a large number of files without pulling and pushing drawers. If you wish, you can pull down a sliding cover over the materials.

Sorting devices for information are rather rare. Usually, materials will be sorted before filing, as in the case of a prospect list sorted by age groups, then left in that form in a notebook, card file, or folder. One of the first sorting devices used punched cards and a long pin that looks like a knitting needle. Information on the card was coded by punching out positions around the edge of the card. When a particular type of information is needed, one sticks the pin through the cards in the right hole and gently lift; the cards are in one stack with the desired information.

To help with this task, most administrators have used codes like colors or symbols to facilitate what basically has been a manual operation.

The computer has revolutionized filing and sorting. With any information that must continually be updated, combined, sorted into parts, or in any way rearranged, a filing program on a computer will prove invaluable. Computer files can be used for membership rolls, financial records, sermons, ideas, prospects, visitation records, pastoral calls, sick lists, appointment schedules, in fact for anything that you might normally write on paper and stick in a file folder. All of this is encoded by typing the information on a screen, then recording it in an electronic file system. The most useful systems place the information on a disk, usually no larger than a phonograph record. For example, a 5 1/4-inch flexible diskette might hold 320,000 characters, more than 250 typed, double-spaced pages.

A membership record could be keyed to print out names sorted by zip code, age, vocation, and so forth. A talent file could within seconds list prospects for a vacant position. A sermon file could display a message preached in the past; it could be updated, added to, parts deleted, and a fresh *new* sermon produced in a short period of time. Do you need to list new members in an alphabetical file? Simple. Type the information and tell the computer to insert it in the correct places. The insertations are made, and *all* material is automatically re-sorted to produce an accurate, up-to-date list. Want a new typed copy? Press a button.

Duplicating

Three forms of duplication are widely used in churches: mimeograph, offset printing, and photocopying. For many copies, mimeograph machines and offset presses provide the best results for the cost. For less than twenty-five copies, a photocopy machine often is the best choice. Equipment for all three methods ranges in cost and quality from very low to very high. You usually get what you pay for. In order to make a decision about quality, costs, and additional possibilities for duplicating in your office, list the items and the number of copies that need to be made during a typical month. Then discuss your needs with an office supply specialist.

Communicating

The basic equipment for communication is the telephone. However, the traditional use of one line with several extensions has been replaced by several options that are more efficient and very cost effective.

Of course, there is still the need for that basic telephone service line to the church office. This is provided through your local telephone company. But once the line is installed, you may make whatever decisions you wish since all equipment now can be purchased or leased from any source.

Consider the following options.

1. Invest in a tone-dial (touch-tone) system. All equipment eventually will operate by using tones.

2. In a small office, consider one desk phone and extensions as needed. If a private extension is needed, such as in a minister's study, arrange for an intercom on the phone system.

3. In larger offices that have several rooms and/or private working areas, you must have a switchboard to direct calls. Switchboards no longer are large and unsightly; they may take little more space than the phone and a large box of tissues. Discuss options for this with several vendors; secure proposals with specific bids. Consider leasing *and* purchasing.

4. Buy at least one good cordless phone, with a range of at least 700 feet and an intercom feature. This can be plugged right into a phone plug and used as an extension phone. Whenever someone has to work away from the office, the portable handset can be carried. The church phone can be answered from this handset, or the person can be paged from the location of the phone's base. Some models offer multiple handsets that can operate from the same base.

5. Consider installing an answering and message machine. This device can be used very effectively to "tend the office" and to provide information about the church and scheduled activities when the office is closed. Callers can be greeted curteously by a recorded message, then asked, if they would, to leave a message for someone. *Note:* Make your recorded messages short and personable, then tell callers how to leave a message. Always check the recorded message file as soon as possible after returning to the office and *respond promptly to messages.*

6. Consider placing answer-only phones and/or pay phones in locations where a phone is needed but use cannot be monitored, such as in a fellowship hall or in a gym.

Audit of Equipment Needs

Whenever there are questions about the efficiency and effectiveness of office functions, an audit can help to determine what equipment is appropriate for the job. The forms in Figures 1 and 2 can be used to evaluate either proposed or existing equipment needs.

Guidelines

1. Determine:
   • What needs to be done.

Figure 1

Audit of Equipment Needs

WHAT NEEDS TO BE DONE? (What results do you expect?)	BY WHOM? (Name the person or position)	HOW FAST? (Rate from 1-10) Now	Needed	QUALITY LEVEL NEEDED (Rate from 1-10) Now	Needed	TOTAL POINT DIFFERENCE
1.						
2.						
3.						
4.						
5.						
6.						
7.						

Instructions

Complete the above information for each specific job function that requires equipment. Rate the pesent speed and quality on a scale between 1 and 10 with 1 the lowest. Then rate the *needed* performance level from 1 to 10. Substract the *now* score from the *needed* score on each line; add these two numbers and enter the sum under *Total Point Difference*.

PRIORITY ITEMS (List the above needs in order from the highest score to the lowest.)

1.
2.
3.
4.
5.
6.
7.

Figure 2

Evaluation of Equipment or Software

EVALUATION OF EQUIPMENT OR SOFTWARE FOR: _____(job)
NAME OF EQUIPMENT OR SOFTWARE: _____
VENDOR OR SUPPLIER: _____

REQUIREMENTS FOR THIS ITEM	EVALUATION USE A SCALE FROM 1-10			COMMENTS FOR OR AGAINST
	References From Users	Vendor Literature	Demonstrations You Have Seen	
SPEED				
QUALITY				
EASE OF USE				
EASE OF LEARNING				
EASE OF MAINTENANCE				

POINT AVERAGE_____   ESTIMATE THE VALUE OF THIS ITEM
                            BASED ON THE COST: ___ SUPERIOR
COST_____   ___ GOOD
RECOMMENDATION: ___ FAIR
                                           ___ POOR

SIGNED _____ POSITION _____

- Who will do it.
- How fast does it need to be done.
- What level of quality is necessary.

2. According to the availability of resources, choose the most efficient equipment for the work that needs to be done. Consult with several vendors (such as office equipment, computer supply, and phone stores) to get acquainted with equipment options and to secure recommendations. Meanwhile, discuss needs with knowledgeable business persons in your church.

3. Evaluate possibilities with workers who would be affected.

4. Work through the normal decision-making channels in your church to secure and/or replace equipment.

5. Use only reputable dealers that have a reputation for service and attention *after* a sale. Avoid trading after-the-sale assistance to save a few dollars; the best price must be determined over the life of the equipment.

6. As you convert to computers, keep at least one typewriter in service. Short-work items like addressing an envelope can be done much easier this way, volunteers helping out in the office can use it, and you will have a backup machine for typing when the other equipment is being serviced.

7. When considering computer applications, keep in mind:

- No computer can replace poor manual procedures. It operates best when the information systems of the office are well designed and understood.

- A computer will not fit exactly your present methods; adjustments in work flow and duties will be necessary.

- Computers help *good* workers. They can only extend and enhance the skills of those using them. Don't count on a computer to make up for poor performance of a worker.

- While your office is adjusting to a computer, demands will be greater for those learning how to operate the equipment and use the system. Be patient.

- Evaluate the specific needs of your office. Then, if you desire to move toward computer applications, evaluate the programs (software) that are available. Find those that best meet your needs, then consider the equipment (hardware) that will operate the programs.

Work Systems

On the following pages you will see a variety of work systems that could be used in your office. Each of them obviously must be part of a larger operation; everyone and everything in an office must work together for the benefit of the church.

Review these ideas, consider your existing systems, then determine what you might want to revise. In some cases you can take the suggestions and use them with very little adaptation. In others, you will want to consult the suggested resources and then work out your own version. Either way, good administrative practice requires that those who are involved in doing the work be involved in making decisions about how to improve.

Office Protocol

Review and/or determine the items in Figure 3 for your situation. Write in the general expectations. Discuss them with those involved; then prepare a final copy that can be distributed and used as a set of guidelines for office protocol.

Telephone/Communications

1. If possible, the same person should do all the answering, forwarding of calls, and message taking. In case this person is unable to answer, agree that anyone in the office will answer after three rings. Be sure *all* personnel are trained in how to answer the phone and what to say. Few things are worse for your image than a gruff "Hello!" followed in a few seconds by "I don't know."

2. Identify the church, then yourself, and ask: "May I help you?"

3. Do not keep a person waiting. If a caller cannot be helped or connected right away, arrange to take a message or to call the person back. Avoid placing a person on "hold."

4. Use a standard form such as illustrated in Figure 4 to record all messages.

5. If there are several people who work in your office, use a sign-in and sign-out sheet so that the phone attendant will know who is available. Also, persons in conference must notify the attendant when they desire not to be disturbed.

6. Maintain a log for all long-distance calls. This will serve as a checklist when the bill comes.

7. Develop a policy regarding the use of church phones for

Figure 3

Guidelines for Office Protocol

Office Hours
Dress Code
Reception Duties
How to Greet Callers
  On the phone
  In person
When to Use What Titles (Mr., Mrs., Dr., Rev., etc.)
  In reference to ministerial staff
  Church members
  Outsiders
How to Handle Requests
Message Taking Procedure
How to Handle Emergencies
What to Do When Someone Is Angry or Demanding
  Member
  Visitor
  Business or civic representative
  Vagrant
What to Do When You
  Are sick
  Are angry
  Have a conflict with a co-worker
Expectations About Supervision
Expectations About Confidentiality

private purposes by workers or by members. What local and what long distance calls are appropriate to receive? to make?

8. If your church has a cordless phone, this can be taken when someone is on an errand in the building. If there is only one worker, the phone can be answered in the normal way without anyone being aware where the person is. If there are several workers, the person with the cordless phone can be paged if necessary.

9. Consider the use of one of the long distance phone services in your area. Many of them provide savings of up to 40 percent over traditional rates.

10. Limit personal calls, both incoming and outgoing, to necessary messages. Also, be careful about letting business calls turn into pleasure calls.

11. Use an answering and message telephone when there is no one

Figure 4

Office Message Form

TO		DATE	TIME
FROM		TELEPHONE NO.	EXT. NO.

WHILE YOU WERE GONE, THE ABOVE PERSON
☐ TELEPHONED   ☐ CALLED IN PERSON
☐ RETURNED YOUR CALL
☐ WILL CALL AGAIN
☐ PLEASE CALL   ☐ IMMEDIATELY

MESSAGE TAKEN BY

☐ YOUR INFORMATION   ☐ HANDLE   ☐ PREPARE REPLY
☐ AS YOU REQUESTED   ☐ CALL ME   ☐ RETURN
☐ PER CONVERSATION   ☐ SEE ME   ☐ FOR APPROVAL
☐ TYPE_____COPIES   ☐ COMMENT   ☐ SIGNATURE
   ☐ SINGLE SPACE   ☐ SUPPLY INFORMATION   ☐ FILE
   ☐ DOUBLE SPACE   ☐ RECOMMEND   ☐ DESTROY
☐ MAKE_____COPIES

☐ THANK YOU!   DATE NEEDED   TIME NEEDED

COMMENTS

in the office. Listen and respond to messages first thing upon returning.

12. Publish your church office telephone number along with the name of the church in all membership publications. List the church's name and number in the yellow pages of the phone book as well as in the white pages. In a large church, you may wish to provide and publish a separate number for the pastor or senior minister's office and/or home.

Filing and Storing Records

1. Keep ready-reference materials—those items that need to be stored and used in the church office—in sturdy folders or file cabinets/containers within easy reach of workers. Categories of materials and possible filing options are given in Figure 5.

Figure 5

Ready Reference Materials

ITEM	FILING OPTIONS		
	Journal or Notebook	File Drawer or Similar Device	Computer*
To-Do List	X		
Correspondence		X	
Purchasing Records		X	
Leadership List	X		X
Organizational Records		X	X
Membership Records	X	X	X
Record of Contributions	X		X
Financial Reports	X	X	X
Prospect List		X	X
Sick List		X	X
Visitation List		X	X
Business Meeting Minutes	X	X	X
Inventory of Equipment	X	X	X
Personnel Records—Individuals		X	
Employment/Personnel Data		X	
Business Contracts		X	
Legal Data		X	

* The use of a computer compresses significantly the amount of space required as well as making the information easy to recall, tabulate, and revise. However, items recorded on a disk or cassette should *always* be backed up with a spare copy. You can, of course, have the computer type copies of the information whenever desired.

2. Records that must be retained either for the benefit of the church or to fulfill legal obligations often are not in the ready-reference category. They must be filed and stored but may be placed in a secure location adjacent to or near the work areas. These are materials such as bank records, historical documents, deeds, and business contracts. The usual rule is: keep all valuable and/or historical materials in a vault or safe box and all other records either in or near the church office. A Record Retention Schedule in Figure 6 gives an approximate time to keep different types of materials.

3. Code all materials that come to the church office as soon as practicable. Work out a system for someone to determine what information needs to be saved and for how long. Place a code in the upper right corner, "File: _____." Items that come in bulk, such as

supplies and literature, should be labeled with the person's name and location to which the items are to go.

Figure 6

Record Retention Schedule

Keep at Least Three Years
　　Deposit Records, Bank Statements, and Processed Checks
　　General Correspondence
　　Inventory of Equipment (after new one is prepared)
　　Purchasing Records
　　Financial Statements/Reports to the Congregation
　　Organizational Records (A summary should be included in the church minutes
　　　　at least once a year, and in an annual denominational report.)
Keep at Least Five Years
　　Insurance Policies (after expiration date)
　　Record of Individual Contributions
　　Individual Personnel Records (after person has left employment)
　　Tax Records—Employees
　　Business Contracts (maintenance and supply items/services)
Keep Permanently
　　Historical Items (charter, constitution and bylaws, pictures, etc.)
　　Legal Items (deeds, contracts, bonds, incorporation documents, tax records,
　　　　and other related items)
　　Church Business Meeting Minutes
　　Audit and Financial Reports
　　Master Membership Record
　　Employment/Personnel Records
　　Annual Report of Church Activities

————

Some denominations provide a microfilm service to preserve church records. Contact your denominational office to inquire.

4. Separate mail into categories: personal, church, and "to whom it may concern" items, such as catalogs and sales brochures. Handle the personal, send the church items to the appropriate person for action, and make an immediate decision whether to save or discard the junk mail.

5. If items will not be saved, use or circulate them as appropriate then discard.

6. Attach copies of correspondence sent from your office to the letter being answered or copy of order sent. Retain correspondence

copies in two file folders: mark one "Letters Inside" for communications within the membership and one "Letters Outside" for others; write the beginning date underneath. When one of the files becomes bulky, remove them *both;* write the ending date on each folder and place them among the files not needed for ready reference. Prepare new file folders.

7. Keep records of decisions made, instructions received, actions taken, and *any* significant or unusual activities in which you are involved. *This is a must for effective administration.* Do not count on remembering the facts when something goes wrong, when someone wants to know exactly what is happening and why, or when a business sends an order and no one knows exactly what leader requested the items. For general records, write notes in your datebook or desk diary. For major actions, write notes on a sheet of paper and file in your personal records.

8. For expenditure of church funds, always follow a church-approved financial plan. Maintain either a purchase order system or a journal in which all transactions are recorded, along with person approving. For petty cash disbursements, require a cash receipt for the item signed by the person being reimbursed. For additional guidelines related to financial matters, see chapter 6.

Mailing Services

1. Establish a routine for receiving and processing incoming mail. Determine whether or not all mail except that marked personal will be opened and sorted by the assigned person. All mail addressed to a specific person should be placed in an agreed upon spot. Financial items such as bills and statements should be placed together for the treasurer. Nonspecific mail should be processed according to established procedures.

2. If incoming mail is centrally processed, open all mail first, attach any enclosures to the enclosed letter, check to see that the letterhead has the return address information that is on the envelope (if not, staple it to the letter), stamp the first-class mail with date received, sort it, and then handle as agreed upon.

3. When there are several workers in an office, consider having a mail and message pickup point. There should be slots or boxes for each person that can be seen easily when passing by. Normally, this location would be near the phone attendent so that messages could

easily be placed in the appropriate place. Additional boxes and/or locations could be arranged for key church leaders and for employees who may work in other locations.

4. A pickup point also is a good location for a collection box for all outgoing items. Determine the mail pickup time(s) in your area and post the time(s) by which mail must be in the box to be picked up and/or delivered to the post office.

5. Consult either with the postmaster or the customer service office of your local post office. Secure information about rates and specifications for the various classes of mail. Discuss the types and frequency of mailings from your church, and get recommendations for how best to secure good service at the least cost. Record all information and place it along with pamphlets from the post office in a file folder.

6. Arrange the writing, editing, printing, and addressing activities for each major item mailed on a regular basis. Set the schedule so that everyone knows exactly what must be done, when, and by whom in order to get the mailing to the post office at the appointed time. A sample preparation schedule is included in chapter 10.

7. A postal scale will be of great assistance in determining the amount of postage to affix to letters and packages. This often saves a trip to the post office or allows mail to be posted sooner.

8. In most churches it is a simple matter to keep a roll of first-class and a variety of other stamps in a box, replenishing when necessary. However, when there are many letters and packages mailed, a postage meter is preferable. The actual cost can be determined and the postage printed on a label, just like at the post office. The amount is subtracted automatically from the amount of credit in your machine. You can even include your church's imprint on the label, if you wish. Consult your postmaster about the companies in your area offering this service.

9. Make a file for "Mail Services—Special." Secure information about special handling and next-day delivery from the post office. Get a small supply of certified and registered mail materials so that they can be prepared at your office. Find out if next-day delivery is available to and from your post office. Also call some of the other overnight air services to determine if they pick up and deliver in your area and the costs for letters and packages. Request a small supply of mailing envelopes. Contact a parcel service and request rates, pickup/delivery points, and schedules. Prepare the folder so

that information and procedures are readily available. Make sure the person who handles the church's mail is thoroughly familiar with all mailing options.

Communications Within the Office

Effective interoffice communications make work easier. When personal contact is important, call or talk with persons directly. When this is not possible or necessary, choose one of the following methods.

1. Use an interoffice message form such as the one shown earlier in Figure 4. Similar forms are available from any office supply store.

2. Arrange for a central mail and/or message pickup point, such as described in the section on Mailing Services. The simplest device is a wooden block or triangle with notches that will hold messages or envelopes. Each notch is labeled with a person's name. The best location for this is where office workers often pass and within easy reach of the person who answers the phone.

3. Whenever you send an outside letter that includes information needed elsewhere in the office, instruct that a copy go to the appropriate person. This can either be indicated in the letter (c: name of recipient of copy), or it can be a blind copy (bc: name of recipient; type on office copies only).

4. Use NCR (no carbon required) pads for quick handwritten or typed notes. These can be standard memo forms or can be forms printed especially for your church. Remove the number of sheets desired, write or type on the top sheet, and you have an original and the number of copies desired. No mess, and it is fast.

5. Dictation is easier and more efficient if a recording device is used. Very rarely is dictation given personally anymore. New devices make it easier and more convenient for the person who sends information and for the person who transcribes. Devices are available that can be carried easily from office to car to home, offering a timesaving option for busy church workers. The recorded information can then be left for dictation, with the typist being able to start and stop the tape as necessary in order to prepare the desired material.

6. When asked to give a verbal message to someone in your office, especially from a member of the congregation, write it down. Then place it on the message board and forget it.

7. When preparing committee meeting minutes and other such

reports, make enough extra copies to send to key staff persons. This will keep them informed with little extra effort.

8. Purchase standard office forms or develop your own for all regular information recorded and/or distributed in your office. If a suitable form is not available from an office supply store, type the form as you wish it to look; leave lines and spaces where the desired information can be inserted. This form can be duplicated in your office, or it can be sent to a printer. If desired, pads of your custom-designed form can be made either by the printer or in your office. Inquire at your office supply about the way to bind forms in a tear-off pad.

9. Memos and forms that will be filed in a notebook should be duplicated on *punched* paper. Paper can be bought by the ream with holes already punched for very little extra cost.

10. All church staff members must tell the receptionist/phone attendent when they will be out or unavailable during office hours. Keep this information next to the phone.

Minutes of Business Meetings

The following procedures are helpful in maintaining an accurate accounting of important information in the life of the church. While these steps are specifically for business meeting minutes, the same process could be used for processing any records for which the church office is responsible.

1. The clerk or other authorized person should take the minutes.

2. The minutes should be prepared, typed, and reviewed for accuracy.

3. Send a copy to the presiding officer/pastor for review.

4. Minutes of the previous meeting should be read, corrected as necessary, and approved at the next regular business meeting.

5. An official copy and two photocopies should then be distributed as follows: the original to a chronological file of church business meeting records; a copy for the clerk's file; and a copy to be retained for ready-reference in the church office.

6. Store *official* minutes in a secure, preferably fireproof location, under the care of an appointed staff member. Use them only for official purposes such as a church audit. Minutes should be permanently bound either by the year or by several years, depending on the number of pages.

7. Keep the office copy of minutes in a notebook for easy use.

Retain these copies on a reference shelf in the office for three years, or longer if there appears to be a need.

Membership and Organizational Records

1. Determine a scheduled time each week when all regular files are updated. Here is a sample plan.

Monday	Compilation of Sunday Visitors
	Sick List
	Church Membership Requests (sent and received)
Tuesday	Organizational Files (attendance records, visitors, new members, drops, etc.)
Wednesday	Prospect File and Visitation List
Thursday	Master Membership File
	Specialized Files (newcomers list, newsletter mailing list, college students away, etc.)

2. Whenever possible, combine other tasks with the above activities. For example, when processing requests for church membership, also fill out a form that will add the person to the church mailing list; place the person's name on the prospect list for church organizations; give the pastor pertinent information; notify the new member committee.

3. Evaluate the present system for handling these routine tasks. If there are not established procedures, write the exact steps that are to be completed and review them with those who are involved. Look for ways to cut and combine steps. Then adopt the procedures that will best serve your office. Once this has been done, work can be delegated or shared with other workers or with volunteers. The procedures become the basis for training and for determining the exact duties to be done.

4. Maintenance of membership and organizational records requires the use of standard forms and other supplies. One person should be responsible for determining the materials used regularly and keeping an adequate supply on hand.

5. Consult with your denominational book store or an office supply store to determine the best binders, holders, files, and other supplies to manage these materials. Often there are specialized devices that save much time and effort.

6. A definite advantage in record maintenance will come as computer applications are made in church offices. Several resources are

mentioned in the bibliography that will acquaint you with the possibilities. You might also want to contact your denominational office or seminary to see what information and assistance are available.

Bibliography

Bedell, Kenneth and Parker Rossman. *Computers: New Opportunities for Personalized Ministry.* Valley Forge: Judson Press, 1984.

Dilday, Russell H., Jr. *Personal Computer: A New Tool for Ministers.* Nashville: Broadman Press, 1985.

Eckersley-Johnson, Anna L., ed. *Webster's Secretarial Handbook.* Springfield, Mass.: G. & C. Merriam Co., 1976.

Hoskins, Lucy R., comp. *A Church Office Style Manual.* Nashville: Convention Press, 1978.

_____. *Shortcuts for Church Office Workers.* Nashville: Convention Press, 1979.

_____. *The Work of the Church Secretary.* Nashville: Convention Press, 1981.

Myers, Marvin, author/comp. *Managing the Business Affairs of a Church.* Nashville: Convention Press, 1981.

Powers, Bruce P., ed./comp. *Christian Education Handbook.* Nashville: Broadman Press, 1981.

Smith, Harold T. *The Office Revolution: Strategies for Managing Tomorrow's Workforce.* Willow Grove, Pa.: Administrative Management Society Foundation, 1983.

Wedel, Leonard E. *Church Staff Administration.* Nashville: Broadman Press, 1978.

6

Financial Procedures

Mark Short

The church has two limited resources: money and the leadership of the people. It is incumbent on the local church to use both of these limited assets wisely. This chapter will address the need to budget, subscribe the budget, and use the funds from this limited resource in keeping with the wishes of the congregation.

A pastor recently did research in the giving patterns of his membership. He discovered that 59 percent of the membership gave 100 percent of the budget and that 41 percent gave nothing during a twelve month period. Estimates indicate that in most evangelical churches 20 percent of the people give 80 percent of the money.

The church, through its leadership, has a keen responsibility in planning, raising, and spending the tithes and offerings of the people. The highest level of integrity is called for when caring for God's money as given through a local church.

Mission efforts and worthy programs suffer from lack of adequate funding. Through the absence of financial planning, churches are strapped with unrealistic debt, ballooning personnel costs, and rising maintenance and utility charges.

Train the Stewardship Committee

In organizing for action in providing funding for the work of the church, a Stewardship Committee will be selected and trained to give vital leadership in financial matters. The committee will seek to develop distinctive Christian stewards through all areas of the church's life and work. It will endeavor to permeate all teaching, preaching, training, and mission work with biblical concepts of stewardship. It is obvious that church members do not automatically become distinctive Christian stewards when they come to know Christ; but they do become learners, disciples. This committee can help a church give attention to this aspect of discipleship.

Members of the church Stewardship Committee should give evidence of being dedicated Christian stewards. They should also reflect a growing commitment to Christ. The characteristics of a distinctive steward have been described as one who makes Christ Lord, acknowledges God as owner of everything, and accepts responsibility as a trustee of God's bountiful blessings. A member of the Stewardship Committee will demonstrate a redeemed life in giving.

Committee members should also be concerned with the growth of the church, its needs and opportunities. They should be adept at informing others of these facts. Committee members should be spiritually mature persons who have the confidence of other church members. They should participate fully in the activities of the committee as well as in all stewardship functions of the church. Members of the church Stewardship Committee should be carefully selected and elected according to the procedures of the church.

Develop a Budget

Zero-based budgeting simply means that you start each year and develop a budget based on fixed costs with variables being assigned funds in order of their priority. In a local church this plan of assessing needs and resources is called ministry-action budgeting. This is a process by which a church plans its spending around the ministry it conceives as God's will for its life. And since budgeting is an evidence of our interpretation of that will, we carefully study its processes.

Ministry-action budgeting is based on people. The size of a church has little to do with the ministries it performs—planning does. This process may be used by a church of a hundred members as easily as it can be used by a church of a thousand members. What it asks in the final analysis is:

1. What are the ministries our church will be engaged in next year to accomplish the mission God has given us?

2. How much will these ministries cost?

3. Is there a better way to get the job done?

In essence, each church needs to rediscover what it is to do, and find ways of getting that job done. Ministry-action budgeting is one effective way of doing the job. It is a process by which a church plans its spending around the ministries it conceives as God's will for its life. Guidelines for developing a budget are given in chapter 7.

Presenting the Budget for Church Approval

Methods of presenting the budget can be changed from year to year. The use of audiovisuals, panel discussion, and congregational discussion can heighten interest in the budget. Major changes in budget format, additional staff, or new buildings should be thoroughly explained and discussed until all questions have been answered. Save enough time for a discussion period.

Some churches adopt the report of the Stewardship Committee and the new church budget at the end of the discussion period. Other fellowships wait several days before the vote is taken in the morning worship service.

Pledging the Budget

From the time of budget adoption and the pledging which will underwrite the budget, there is a time of prayer, education, and promotion. Many varied and productive plans are available to assist the Stewardship Committee in this significant task.[1] Sermons will be preached, stewardship lessons will be taught in Sunday School, and tithing testimonies will be featured in the worship services. An individual commitment will be sought from each church and Sunday School member.

The Accounting of the Budget

A procedure for receiving and expending funds is critical to the integrity of the church's financial plan. Anytime money is received, at least two church members should be present to assume responsibility for these monies! The counting of funds should be done in a place where reasonable security can be maintained. Again, two members should be present during the counting of the money. As soon as possible it should be deposited in the church's bank account. Under no circumstances should money remain in the church or in a home overnight.

A procedure for the accounting of church funds should follow this schedule.
- Receive monies from all sources within the church.
- Count the money, and fill out appropriate records (see Figure 1).

Figure 1

Contribution Report

SUNDAY SCHOOL		CHURCH SERVICE
_____	Amount Loose	_____
_____	in Envelopes	_____
	Designated Items:	
_____	_____	_____
_____	_____	_____
_____	_____	_____
_____	_____	_____
_____	_____	_____
_____	_____	_____
_____	_____	_____
$ _____	Total Cash	$ _____
$ _____	Total Checks	$ _____

GRAND TOTAL $ _____

- -

CASH COUNT

Currency:

	$50.00	_____	_____
	20.00	_____	_____
	10.00	_____	_____
	5.00	_____	_____
	1.00	_____	_____

Change:

	.50	_____	_____
	.25	_____	_____
	.10	_____	_____
	.05	_____	_____
	.01	_____	_____
Total	$	_____	$ _____

Approved by _____ Date _____

- Deposit all money.
- Post member contributions and record all financial transactions.
- Make a monthly report to the church.

A current practice among some churches is to secure a bond for each person who has fiduciary responsibility. This is a prudent business decision that all churches should follow. In no way does bonding question the honesty of the person who handles church funds. It is simply good business practice.

Using Purchase Orders

Some churches control spending by using a purchase order system. For purchases less than a specified amount, authorized persons can buy needed items and receive reimbursement from a petty cash fund (see Figure 2).

For more costly items and things that must be ordered, a request is given to the financial secretary or the fiscal representative of the Stewardship Committee. This request may be oral or written according to church policy. (For a purchase requisition form, see Figure 3). After a request is received and approved, a purchase order form (Figure 4) is prepared and delivered. The number on the purchase order must then appear on the invoice before payment is made.

Preprinted forms similar to those illustrated in this chapter are available from office supply stores. They can also be ordered with the name of your church or organization imprinted.

Checks will be drawn against the general bank account of the church when a check requesition like the sample in Figure 5 has been completed and authorized. Normally, payroll checks are not drawn with a check requisition. All other checks, however, should have this approval safeguard before being issued.

In many churches two signatures are required on each church check. Usually the treasurer and one other member of the Stewardship Committee are authorized to sign checks.

The Annual Audit

There is a growing trend toward securing an annual audit conducted by an independent firm of public accountants. There are several benefits.

- Credibility of the financial statement

Figure 2

Petty Cash Slip

No. _____

RECEIVED OF PETTY CASH $ _____

For _____

_____

Charge to _____

_____

Signed _____

Approved _____

Figure 3

Purchase Requisition

PURCHASE REQUISITION

Requisition No. _____

Date _____

Please purchase for:

Name _____

Committee or program to be charged _____

Purpose or use _____

_____

Deliver to _____

Notify _____

Date needed _____

Preferred vendor _____

Remarks _____

_____

Quantity	Description	Unit	Total
		Total	

Signed _____

Approved _____

Received by _____

Figure 4

Purchase Order

PURCHASE ORDER

No. _____

This number must appear on all correspondence, invoices, shipping papers and packages.

TO

SHIP TO

DELIVERY

Date	Req. No.	Terms	Ship via	F.O.B. Point

Quantity	Please enter our order in accordance with prices, delivery and specifications given	Price

By _____

Figure 5

Date_____

Check Requisition
Name of Church

Address   Phone

Make Check to_____

Address_____City_____State_____Zip_____

Amount of Check $_____

Purpose of Check_____

Budget Account Number_____

Approved by_____

• Assistance in developing good and meaningful financial statements and reports

• Professional advice on controls and other administrative matters

• Compliance with legal requirements

In addition, an experienced accountant can provide the technical assistance for establishing suitable record systems which reflect the needs of specialized church activities and simplify treasury functions. The audit is a procedure that establishes in-depth information provided in the financial statement.

If the church has never had an audit, the initial cost will be greater than subsequent audit costs. A base for assets and liabilities will be established and future audits will be constructed from that base.

Designated Accounts

The majority of churches do not have any fiscal problem with designated accounts. Major difficulties can be avoided by having a policy drawn by the Stewardship Committee and adopted by the church. One of the problems often faced in the absence of a policy is the giving of a gift for a specified purpose that does not fit into the church's priorities. Then the church risks losing the gift or changing its priorities. Designated accounts should be handled with integrity.

Chart of Accounts

A simple but extremely helpful device for proper budget coding is called a chart of accounts. Each line item in the budget should have a corresponding descriptive paragraph telling what items are to be charged to that particular budget number. The Stewardship Committee prepares, evaluates, and updates the chart of accounts. See sample in Figure 6.

Special Gifts

The Stewardship Committee will possibly have a subcommittee to seek and encourage special gifts. Many church members are unaware of tax advantages that are available to the giver. The Stewardship Committee should plan to inform the membership of these advantages toward the end of each year. Gifts that are to be sought are:

Real Estate: Opportunities for giving homes, farms, or other property will allow a federal income tax deduction for its full value,

Figure 6

Chart of Accounts

Assets and Fund Balance 100
101   Cash in Bank A
102   Cash in Bank B
110   Petty Cash
120   Transfers to (from) Other Funds
190   Fund Balance
Designated Receipts 200
210   Missions
215   Organ Gifts
225   Debt Retirement
230   Other
Designated Disbursements 300
310   Missions
315   Organ Gifts
325   Debt Retirement
330   Other
Undesignated Receitps 400
410   Budget Receipts
412   Loose Offerings
Undesignated Disbursements
Missions 500
510   Cooperative Program
520   Associational Missions
530   Other Missions
Educational Ministry 600
610   Sunday School
613   Church Training
615   Music
619   Denominational Literature
621   Vacation Bible School
625   Woman's Missionary Union (In-
        cluding Related Youth Groups)
627   Brotherhood (Including Related
        Youth Groups)
630   Youth
644   Honoraria

648   Conventions and Conferences
651   Library
655   Scouts
660   Kindergarten
General Operations 700
706   Public Relations
712   Denominational Retirement
718   Insurance—Property
721   Kitchen
728   Office Supplies
735   Postage
738   Hospitality
745   Payroll Taxes
750   Utilities
756   Laundry
759   Ordinances
764   Altar and Flowers
769   Employee Hospital Insurance
772   Miscellaneous
Property and Debt Retirement 800
810   Building Equipment
820   Building Maintenance
825   Office Equipment and Main-
        tenance
830   Grounds
840   Debt Retirement
Personnel Salaries and Allowances 900
910   Pastor
915   Minister of Education
920   Minister of Youth
925   Church Secretary
930   Education Secretary
935   Organist
940   Nursery Coordinator
945   Nursery Assistants
950   Janitor

and avoid capital gains tax if the property's value has increased. Property can also be used to fund a trust which returns regular income for the life of the donor.

Memorial Gifts: Often families, respecting the wishes of deceased loved ones, request that memorials be sent to a favorite charitable cause.

Gifts in Kind: Gifts in kind (jewelry, crops, livestock, works of art, coin collections, antiques, royalties, etc.) can be the perfect answer to giving interests. Mortgages, leases, or notes can be donated to the church.

Cash: If deductions are itemized on a federal income tax return, all gifts of cash up to 50 percent of adjusted gross income can generally be deducted. If more than 50 percent of adjusted gross income is donated one year, the excess amount can be carried over into as many as the next five tax years.

Securities (stocks, bonds, mutual funds): There are three ways generally recommended for giving securities so that the gift benefits the charitable organization as well as the giver.

1. Give a security that has appreciated and qualifies for long-term, capital gains status.
2. Give the capital gains portion of an appreciated security and retain the amount of original cost.
3. Sell a depreciated security, deduct the loss, and donate the proceeds from the sale.

Life Insurance: Many people do not realize that life insurance policies or dividends paid on the policies make practical gifts. There are several ways to donate life insurance:

- Give policies no longer needed for their original purposes.
- Give a fully paid-up policy, and deduct its replacement cost.
- Give a policy on which premiums are being paid and deduct the approximate cash value, plus all future premiums paid.

A Systems Approach to Financial Record Keeping

Churches of all sizes are moving rapidly toward a systems approach to all record keeping, especially financial records. Personal computers are being used in smaller churches while large churches are going to more sophisticated hardware.

Several companies are producing softwear to meet the financial record-keeping needs of a church. Included in the program should be the capability to do all bookkeeping functions, individual member contributions, payroll, and monthly statements.

In addition to financial records, the computer should have the capacity to accommodate all educational organization records, membership rolls, and master prospect file.[2]

Notes

1. Request information from your denominational office or book store.

2. Many private publishers and several denominations have developed software packages for use in a church. For information and recommendations, contact your denominational office, book store, or seminary.

Bibliography

Bedell, Kenneth. *Using Personal Computers in the Church.* Valley Forge: Judson Press, 1981.

Bedell, Kenneth and Parker Rossman. *Computers: New Opportunities for Personalized Ministry.* Valley Forge: Judson Press, 1984.

Davis, Lee E. *In Charge: Managing Money for Christian Living.* Nashville: Broadman Press, 1984.

Davis, Lee E. and Standerfer, Ernest D. *Christian Stewardship in Action.* Nashville: Convention Press, 1983.

Eischen, Martha. *Does Your Small Business Need a Computer?* Blue Ridge Summit, Pa.: Tab Books, 1983.

Ellis, Loudell W. *Church Treasurer's Handbook.* Valley Forge: Judson Press, 1978.

Gray, Robert N. *Managing the Church,* Volumes I and II. Enid, Okla.: National Institute on Church Management, 1977, 1979.

Gurin, Maurice G. *What Volunteers Should Know for Successful Fund Raising.* Briar Cliff Manor, N.Y.: Scarborough House, 1982.

Haller, Leon. *Financial Resource Management for Nonprofit Organizations.* Englewood Cliffs, N.J.: Spectrum Books, 1982.

Holck, Manfred. *Church Finances in a Complex Society.* Nashville: Abingdon Press, 1983.

Johnson, Douglas W. *The Tithe: Challenge or Legalism.* Nashville: Abingdon Press, 1984.

Midgett, Elwin W. *An Accounting Primer,* rev. ed. New York: New American Library, 1978.

Myers, Marvin, author/compiler. *Managing the Business Affairs of a Church.* Nashville: Convention Press, 1981.

Seymour, John. *Coping with Computer Egos.* New York: AMACOM, 1984.

7

Planning and Budgeting

Bob I. Johnson

Jesus promised, "On this rock I will build my church, and the powers of death shall not prevail against it (Matt. 16:18, RSV). In moving a church toward knowing and claiming this mind-boggling promise, planning and budgeting play strategic roles. All business and service organizations engage in these two functions. The church, however, is unique in all of the world and thus needs a specific word about how it projects its future and utilizes its resources.

In planning and budgeting, the church will be saying something significant to itself, its community, its larger world, and ultimately to God who birthed and sustains the church. This chapter is designed to offer you practical help in planning and budgeting. It will also seek to emphasize the impact you can have through these functions on the story which your church is telling.

Planning

Nothing takes the place of a good beginning in any effort, large or small. The approach you take to planning is the most significant factor in determining the outcome of such planning. For example, if you rely solely on the planning model which studies the congregation, the geographical communities surrounding the meeting place, the resources available to that congregation for ministry, then the results will probably highlight the weaknesses, liabilities, and shortcomings of the congregation. It isn't that these things don't need to be done; however, if this is the sole approach, then the effect may be rather negative. Planning ought to help the church enhance its statement about what it wants to be under God.

In the first chapter, planning is described as the process of creating your organizational future before it happens. This chapter will seek to expand on this idea and will include an emphasis on pathfinding (direction) and decision making that lead to implementation of plans.

Principles for Planning Leaders

1. *Maintain the biblical meaning of church.* The purpose of a church is to be the people of God, a communion of saints, a called-out people in the community. The number one requirement for an administrator is to keep clear focus on the biblical meaning of church.

Unlike other organizations the church has the undeniable promise of God that His Holy Spirit will direct and empower the church for its mission. The Spirit gives power to overcome satanic forces and provides a spirit of love and self-control.

2. *Emphasize being more than doing.* Danger lies in a planning process consisting primarily of setting goals and objectives, listing and choosing from alternative strategies for reaching the goals, performing the tasks, and evaluating the results. The danger lies in the assumption that there is an ideal to be reached and that it can be accomplished by marshaling the forces to do something. Foundational to doing is *being;* therefore, emphasis should be given to *who* God's people are to be.

3. *Avoid being too data based.* Data is important, but to base your planning on data collected may send you off in the wrong direction. The difficulty often lies in the fact that the more data a congregation collects, the more confused it becomes. This approach can also enslave local churches to the supposed inevitability of demographic trends of population growth or decline. For example, a local church may tend to select a particular demographic trend and on that basis justify a decision to withdraw from active ministry effort in certain areas.

Certainly, some correlation between demographic trends and church growth exists. Some churches, however, grow in the midst of a declining population. Some churches decline in the midst of a swelling, unchurched population.

4. *Keep planning focused on the relational nature of the church.* In relation to the community, the church's task is to provide an arena where people can understand the forces affecting their lives and the lives of their neighbors and where they can get a correct perspective on time and eternity. In short, the church must focus on its relationship to God and to people.

5. *Keep planning from becoming an end in itself.* The reason churches fail

to focus on people and the ministries God has called them to is the simple fact of a focus on something else. That may be many things, including even an overreliance on administrative analysis, financial planning, and the desire to eliminate risks. Planning can become an end in itself because it may be more interesting and safer than getting on with ministry tasks.

Churches must plan, however. Planning should be used to *enhance* mental and spiritual preparedness. It should not become eternal truth which causes anything that doesn't fit the preconceived plan to be ignored.

6. *Major on strengths.* It is consequential that a church emphasize its strengths. Strengths are present in every church and precisely so because God has enabled His people to develop them. For a church to deny its strengths for all practical purposes means that it denies God. This is not to be an ego trip because the strengths are gifts from God and as such belong to the entire congregation.

Good planning begins with helping a church proclaim its strengths because good planning begins with God. To ask "What are our needs? What are our problems?" is to ask the wrong questions first.

Guidelines for Planning

The principles of planning listed above should permeate the church's attitude and total process. The following guidelines are a sequential, step-by-step process which may be expanded or rearranged to suit your own situation.

1. *Prepare for planning.* A key person in planning is the pastor. The pastor in working with key leaders and the congregation as a whole should be aware of the need and the timing for planning. The pastor is the person who knows the values of the church and expresses those values in a variety of ways. The basic philosophy and values of a church have far more to do with its achievements than do its economic resources, organizational structure, or various other aspects.

In the business world the excellent companies seem to have developed cultures that have incorporated the values and practices of their great leaders, with those shared values surviving for decades after the passing of those leaders. The enduring contribution of a chief executive comes through the formation of values that guide the organization.[1]

In preparing for planning, emphasize the values of a church's *story*. Every congregation has one; it permeates the group life of the church and is the interpreter of past, present, and future. Story is the primary medium by which the identity, goals, perceptions, and strategies are communicated. Try asking "how come?" and you will probably get a story from the church's past. The story can enhance an appreciation of the rich background of the average congregation. The local church that recounts its story gains many benefits. Narrative can identify and reinforce who and what the church is. It reveals what is important. It seems to facilitate group discussion of church life. It will reveal something of the pain in the life of the church and its needs. But most important, story can help the church to identify its mission and place in the world.

In preparing for planning, perhaps one way the church can be made aware of its story is to set up formal and informal group meetings in which people are allowed to share the parts of the church's story which have most influenced their lives. In a church with significant numbers of new people as well as many who have been members for many years, a time when both groups can share significantly their dreams and aspirations would be helpful. This would help people get to better know each other and understand how the church is perceived, and how people may be led to fulfill the mission of the church.

2. *Establish purpose in planning.* By establishing purpose, I mean first of all to have a clear statement of a church's purpose or mission. Such a statement serves as an umbrella under which the church functions in day-to-day and year-to-year ministry. Here is an example.

> The mission of a church, composed of baptized believers who share a personal commitment to Jesus Christ as Savior and Lord, is to be a redemptive body in Christ, through the power of the Holy Spirit, growing toward Christian maturity through worship, proclamation and witness, nurture and education, and ministry to the whole world that God's purpose may be achieved.[2]

Such a statement should allow the church to move forward in helping to determine its future through an appropriate planning process. If a church has no such statement at present, involve as many people as possible in the study of Scripture, history, and other church documents in writing such a statement. The pastor may find it appropriate to preach sermons on the subject.

Another step in establishing purpose and direction in planning is to develop objectives. Two approaches are currently being used in relation to church objectives. In one view objectives state the church's timeless intention to act. They are statements of ultimate ends toward which a church aims its energies. They are statements of a church's understanding of the kind of church God wants it to be.

Examples of such objectives are:

1. Our objective is to be a covenant fellowship of Christians filled with the Holy Spirit.

2. Our objective is to be a worshiping fellowship in which God encounters people.

3. Our objective is to be witnesses for Christ both in this community and throughout the world.

4. Our objective is to be a fellowship of maturing Christians whose learning results in responsible living.

5. Our objective is to be a church that unselfishly ministers to persons in the community in Jesus' name.

Another approach makes objectives more specific.[3] Here, objectives are stated in a sufficiently clear fashion that it is possible to know when they have been achieved. Thus, a local congregation that is effective in mission is seen as having a compelling passion for the achievement of very clear, intentional goals. In this approach, objectives should focus on specific groups with which the church wants to be on mission, like young adults or homebound elderly.

Whatever approach you take in the use of terminology, lifting the church's collective vision above the mundane through the eyes of mission objectives leads beyond yourselves. When a church is effectively on mission, that congregation is a group of persons living beyond selfish preoccupation. When this occurs, strengths are corporately developed, vision is lifted, and surges of energy make new levels of living possible.

As a part of establishing purpose in planning, keep in mind the individuals involved. Encourage members to remember that people are important. Hold up the truth that while a plan for the church is being developed people can also grow and develop individually as Christian persons. Be aware of ministry opportunities for encouragement to growth.

Additionally, establishing purpose in planning involves a very simple but fundamental matter. What kind of planning are you doing? Long-range, short-range, or operational?

Long-range planning sets directions for three to five years, aligns major church plans with the church's statement of mission, and sequences priorities for the expenditure of resources. The purpose is not to set the future in concrete, restricting freedom and flexibility. Rather, it is to develop an informed plan that, in the congregation's best judgment, will enable the church to live out its story responsibly and courageously. Long-range planning usually begins about halfway through the current plan so that a new plan is in place before the current one expires.

Short-range, or annual, planning usually deals with working out details for a year. This process begins several months prior to a new year and transposes long-range plans into specific, action-oriented plans related to ongoing church programs. Short-range goals, a coordinated calendar, and budget allocations should result from this type of planning.

Operational planning is regular planning done quarterly, monthly, and weekly to implement plans. This is the type of planning regularly done in meetings of the Church Council, Sunday School Council, and church staff.[4]

3. *Involve people in long-range planning.* In most churches the Church Council will be a basic unit already in place that can be used as a long-range planning committee. The Church Council is normally charged with such duties as: helping the church understand its mission and define its priorities; coordinating studies of church and community needs; recommending to the church coordinated plans for ministry; and evaluating progress in the priority use of church resources.

Whatever group you choose to use in the church should be representative of the best available human resources. These people should possess various strengths. They should be encouraged to think of the potential possessed by the church and the central fact that planning begins with God and depends on Him for its completion.

Planning should be more than collecting data and/or allocating resources. It should bring out the best in everyone for the sake of the church. Planning should be forward-looking and innovative. It should encourage the emergence of new ideas, creativity, and new solutions to problems.

Use as many people as possible in the planning process. Putting it in terms of "telling the church's story," Figure 1 provides a work sheet which can be used for people to express themselves in positive ways about the church's future.

Although warning has been given about basing one's long-range planning solely on the data collected in the community, knowing the community is important. By all means, bring into the planning process those church members who have special relationships with local government, community agencies, and businesses. Use these sources but avoid dumping too much information on the committee at the outset. Formulate a limited number of realistic questions to collect information you believe is really pertinent to your church's forward look. Ask the people to collect only the information they feel is relevant to the church.

Participation in the planning process includes the *church gathered* to consider the finalized plans. After all the input, praying, planning, and formalizing of plans, another important step follows: bringing the congregation together to hear the results. The way the committee presents its report is important. Advanced information should be given. Copies of the long-range plans should be available to any who wish to see the plans. Clarity of presentation and information should receive high priority. Questions should be anticipated and answers given during the presentation.

It should be made clear that, once adopted, long-range plans become the direction setters for the church. People, in effect, are committing themselves to participation in the fulfillment of the approved plans. If the plans are well done, they should provide a motivational atmosphere for people to join in living out the story of the church on mission.

4. *Simplify the process.* Use four simple steps for long-range planning.
- Assess the church's current situation.
- Determine primary direction for the future.
- Study strengths related to the biblical concept of church.
- Determine major objectives/goals that will assist the church in achieving its mission.

In the first step the long-range planning committee looks at certain statistics realistically. Church consultants usually say that the

Figure 1

Telling the Church's Story

List the *best* things you know that have happened in the life of our church to make its story exciting.

1. _____   4. _____
   _____   _____

2. _____   5. _____
   _____   _____

3. _____   6. _____
   _____   _____

What are one or more possibilities for ministry the church has which can help to make its future story exciting?

1. _____
   _____

2. _____
   _____

3. _____
   _____

I am interested in being a part of the church's exciting story by participation in:

1. _____
   _____

2. _____
   _____

3. _____
   _____

(Optional)
Name: _____ Phone No. _____
Address: _____

average attendance at the Sunday morning worship service is an indication of the strength of the church, not Sunday School enrollment or church membership. Most churches are larger than they think they are.

The second step has been discussed previously in this chapter; however, an additional comment should be added. In determining primary direction, the church needs to decide such things as the maximum mission potential available in the community, the total number of people to be served in the coming five to seven years, and the fundamental type of church the members want to become.

The third step has to do with a study of key strengths of the local church. This may done by comparing the church with a predetermined list or by comparison to standards derived from biblical principles and current church-life factors. The fourth part of the process, before taking the plan to the church for adoption, is to develop strategic objectives and goals to help the church to be on mission effectively.

The planning process will identify many specific human needs and hopes toward which the church can direct ministry. It is important to be selective, however, so that human and material resources are challenged but not stretched beyond capacity. To overload a church with objectives and goals could overwhelm people and diffuse the strength of the congregation so that the church ends up helping no one with anything.

5. *Maximize the results.* One temptation following long-range planning is to put the plan on the shelf or in the desk drawer for a rest; we take great pride in having finished the task and put off following through on what the church should do. Make sure that proper assignments are made and that leaders of programs, councils, and committees are clear on their duties. Have regular times to evaluate progress and check up on procedures for achieving the specified goals.

Look to see if the expected results are being achieved. Are improvements being made? Are new people being reached? Is the church making better use of its resources? If the church said it needed to reach out to the elderly, is it so doing? Is the church building on the strengths it already has?

Budgeting

Budgeting is the process of allocating resources toward goals by expressing the church's dream in dollars. Budgeting is one very important way of expressing the church's story, past, present, and most of all, what it wants to be in the future.

Set the Tone for Good Budgeting

Solid financial resources are required by today's effective churches. A biblical approach to stewardship undergirds the development of solid financial resources and helps persons to grow in their own understanding of stewardship. Saving money and the efficient use of money do not constitute an adequate stewardship theology.

A responsible biblical approach to stewardship encourages local congregations to view stewardship as an investment of money. It is an investment of money so as to (1) enlarge missional outreach in the community, (2) maximize the effectiveness of the local church, and (3) increase the number of households that contribute financially to the life and purpose of the church. Helping the church to see that its task is not to save money nor simply to spend money is extremely important. It is vitally important and biblically sound that the church view itself as investing its funds so that the church may truly be on mission.

Setting the tone for budgeting includes worship services built around the theme of Christian stewardship. Sermon suggestions are: Christian Stewardship as a Life-style (Luke 12:13-21); Acknowledging Our Source of Being (Prov. 3:5-6); Being Found Faithful (Luke 22:7-23); Growing Commitment to Cooperative Mission Giving (2 Cor. 8:1-14); and Trustworthy Stewards (1 Cor. 4:2).

Setting the tone also includes developing positive attitudes for the missionary purpose of the church. Although it is not easy to maintain a worldwide view of the church's mission, such an intentional effort pays rich dividends. To develop such positive attitudes for mission support, leaders must possess deep convictions and genuine enthusiasm themselves. Mission support is directly related to one's attitude toward the people of the world. To believe that all people are created in the image of God is to believe that all people are important and worthy of the church's mission focus. Because it is easy to lapse into self-centeredness, it is important for the church to be led to adopt a world view of mission responsibility.

Cooperation and trust lie at the heart of mission support. Such attitudes grow out of fellowship, common convictions, and mutuality. Christian faith involves Christians in a relationship with God and with other people. A cooperative attitude is endowed with a sense of belonging. For Christians it is belonging to and being involved in something bigger than and beyond themselves. An attitude of trust and cooperation is contagious and helps Christians everywhere achieve effectiveness in mission support. It validates commitment to Christ and to the concept of the priesthood of all believers.

Examine the Mission of the Church

This issue has been discussed in the first part of this chapter. It is mentioned here because of its importance to the church's stewardship of resources. If the church doesn't understand its purpose, then budgeting will become somewhat ambiguous at best.

Usually money follows mission. Occasionally the church may be the recipient of a large amount of money for which it has to determine purpose; however, the truth is usually the opposite. In many cases, the reason the congregation does not have enough money is that it has not effectively defined and put into practice a mission purpose. It may have become preoccupied with maintenance and forgotten about mission. Whenever that happens a church can usually count on diminishing giving. People want to give to mission more than they want to give to maintenance.

Many times it is rather easy to get people to give money to build buildings. This may lead to the judgment that it easier to build buildings than to give to mission causes. The reason for this may be that the buildings are specific and concrete ways for people to see how their giving is being used.

Congregations that have been specific in stating and practicing their mission objectives tend to have much less difficulty in financing those objectives and goals. Instead of saying: "Our budget is behind. We are cutting every cost possible. Would you please help us catch up?" Try saying: "Our church is seeking to reach and help many people. The money you are giving is being invested wisely in people ministries. Thanks for your giving." In summary, the church whose story includes a small mission tends to raise a small amount of money. The church whose story includes substantial mission purpose tends to raise substantially more money.

Assess Potential Financial Resources

One of the major administrative responsibilities in church finance is to anticipate the sources of income for the church. It is important to know how much money the church might reasonably expect to receive during the period covered by a new budget.

In most churches most of the money can be expected to come from the undesignated gifts of the members. These gifts are usually given through church offering envelopes through the Sunday School and the worship services. Usually smaller proportions come as designated gifts for special causes. Each church should study its own pattern as designated gifts may be more prominent in some churches than others. Other sources for some churches include rental fees from properties, memorial gifts, interest income on money invested, trusts, wills, and capital gifts.

A church may do an analysis of the occupational groups that are present in its life and ministry. Research may then be done with the local census bureau or county planning agency concerning the average income in that region for the occupational categories that are present in the congregation. With this data, the church can make a reasonable assessment of the *potential* financial resources available to it—usually 10 percent of the total estimated income of the congregation.

The church should consider its indebtedness for significant amounts of money that may be available for other purposes within a few years when debt obligations are met. One such church carefully planned well in advance how it would divide its money after a loan had been paid off. Part of it went for mission purposes and another part went for needed repairs and air conditioning of its educational building.

Develop the Ministry Budget

Two primary ways to develop a budget are described on the following pages: a line-item approach and a ministry-action approach.[5] Read the details and consider the potential for your situation; then choose the best approach.

Line-Item Budgeting

Line-item budgeting is the most common type of budget used by a church. In this kind of budget, allocation is made for each type of item where there is anticipated expenditure without regard for the particular ministry the item supports. Line-item budgeting may be done by a committee working through three important studies.

1. *What is the present situation?* This is an analysis of the church's past and present giving patterns. Look at the total undesignated gifts for each of the last five years. Determine the percentage of increase or decrease that might be expected if nothing changes.

2. *What is the potential?* Study the church's giving potential. If the potential is significantly greater than the present giving level, determine what steps would be necessary to improve financial support.

3. *Develop a proposal that will challenge the congregation.* Study the programs and budgetary needs of the church. Are there any items/areas to add or delete? What were the expenses last year? Determine the approximate amount that will provide for anticipated expenses plus some growth; compare this total with the anticipated level of support. Adjust figures for the various line items up or down to arrive at a reasonable projection of what the church will be able to do for the anticipated income.

A schedule for developing the budget is in Figure 2. You will need to determine any additional things that need to be scheduled and assign specific dates for the actions. An example of a line-item budget work sheet used by a small church is in Figure 3.

Ministry-Action Budgeting

In this approach emphasis is placed on the fullest participation of people which is possible. This process involves more people than traditional budgeting by requiring a larger budget committee and extensive use of church committees and organizations. Emphasis is also given to priorities in planning. Church entities must discover needs for ministries and project solutions. In all stages, priorities are to be determined.

Understanding and purposeful giving are emphasized. In addition to the greater involvement of people, the suggested budget format communicates more clearly the ministries to be supported. Written explanations are included with each ministry area.

Eight steps are called for in the ministry action process. The pastor, staff, and others charged with the *spending of funds* are responsible for the first two steps.

Step 1: Analyze ministries. This is an appraisal of how well the church is performing its work and will be valuable to the budget committee.

Figure 2

Budget Planning Schedule

Week 1   Finance Committee distributes lists of (1) amounts spent dur-
          ing the last twelve months and (2) the previous year's budget,
          asking committees and organizations to submit budget re-
          quests by priority and by monthly estimates.
Week 3   Committees and organizations send budget requests to the
          Finance Committee.
Week 4   Finance Committee meets to discuss requests and to propose
          a budget.
Week 6   Finance Committee and deacons meet to discuss requests
          and to recommend a budget to the church membership.
Week 7   Finance Committee mails proposed budget and a letter of
          explanation to church members.
Week 8   Church members discuss the proposed budget at a church
          business meeting.
Week 10   Finance Committee mails amended budget and letter of expla-
          nation to church members.
Week 11   Church members adopt the budget at a called church busi-
          ness meeting.
Week 12   Sunday School teachers present a lesson on stewardship.
Week 12   Finance Committee mails pledge cards and a letter of expla-
          nation to church members.
Week 13   Finance Committee sponsors Pledge Day and a commitment
          luncheon at the church. All choirs sing at the morning worship
          service.
Week 13   Finance Committee mails follow-up letters to members who
          did not turn in pledge cards.

Step 2: Propose ministry actions. This is to include written proposals of
ministries from staff members, church committees, and organizations. See Figure 4 for a sample proposal form. It calls for a description of the ministry, why it is needed, the cause, any implications
for future ministry, an alternative approach that could be used, and
when the money would be spent during the year.

Steps 3, 4, and 5 are primarily the responsibility of the budget
committee.

Step 3: Evaluate ministry actions. After all ministry-action proposals
are presented in written form, the budget committee carefully and
prayerfully evaluates them in light of the church's missional purpose. Now is a good time for this group to ask how these proposed

Figure 3

Budget Work Sheet

	Current Budget-19XX	Actual/Anticipated Totals This Year	Committee Requests	Proposed Budget-19XX
Undesignated Receipts	$_____	$_____	$_____	$_____
DISBURSEMENTS				
Missions				
Cooperative Program	_____	_____	_____	_____
Associational Missions	_____	_____	_____	_____
Local	_____	_____	_____	_____
Total Missions	$_____	$_____	$_____	$_____
Educational Ministry				
Sunday School & Church Training	_____	_____	_____	_____
Vacation Bible School	_____	_____	_____	_____
Woman's Missionary Union	_____	_____	_____	_____
Brotherhood	_____	_____	_____	_____
Youth	_____	_____	_____	_____
Total Education	$_____	$_____	$_____	$_____
Property	$_____	$_____	$_____	$_____
Debt Retirement	$_____	$_____	$_____	$_____
General Operations				
Car Allowances	_____	_____	_____	_____
Conventions	_____	_____	_____	_____
Denominational Retirement	_____	_____	_____	_____
Insurance	_____	_____	_____	_____
Kitchen	_____	_____	_____	_____
Music & Equipment	_____	_____	_____	_____
Office Equipment	_____	_____	_____	_____
Postage	_____	_____	_____	_____
Church Supplies	_____	_____	_____	_____
Payroll Taxes	_____	_____	_____	_____
Utilities	_____	_____	_____	_____
Contingencies	_____	_____	_____	_____
Total General	$_____	$_____	$_____	$_____
Personnel				
Pastor	_____	_____	_____	_____
Church Secretary (part-time)	_____	_____	_____	_____
Janitor (part-time)	_____	_____	_____	_____
Total Personnel	$_____	$_____	$_____	$_____
Total Disbursements	$_____	$_____	$_____	$_____

ministries will help the church live out the story it wishes to communicate. Priority rating must be given to each proposal. In many instances this can be done by asking such questions as "to what degree does this program make a contribution to the purpose of the church?"

Step 4: Prepare the budget. Now is the time to make decisions. List proposals in broad categories and begin determining the overall requirements for supporting the proposed ministries. Make adjustments among items and within categories according to the priorities determined in step 3.

A budget usually is organized into categories that represent the major areas of a church's ministry, such as
• World Missions Ministries
• Pastoral Ministries
• Educational Ministries
• Music Ministries
• Support Ministries
• Buildings and Grounds Ministries

In the simplest budgets, an amount would be specified for each of the major categories. For most churches, however, each category is divided into specific programs, projects, or areas of work, such as illustrated in Figure 5.

While not ignoring past giving, a total amount budgeted should usually include a challenge for growth in giving. If stewardship education is practiced and the budget clearly expresses the mission of the church in an exciting and understandable way, then members will rise to the challenge.

Step 5: Present the budget. Interpreting the proposed ministries to the church is an extremely important step. This is where the church member sees what his giving will help the church accomplish. Visual presentations through slides, posters, filmstrips, and other multimedia presentations can be extremely effective. Such presentations help broaden the members' view of what the church is doing and plans to do. Also, visual presentations can be done effectively through a budget fair or a ministry expo. These activities are festive. Informal atmosphere is created. Personal demonstrations and attractive displays depict various ministries of the church.

Every member needs an opportunity to review the proposed budget prior to any discussion. One method of communication is by direct mail. The mailing should be accompanied by a letter of expla-

Figure 4

A Ministry Action Proposal

For_____   Subject_____

1. A description of proposed plan and how it relates to the church's basic purpose.

_____

_____

_____

2. Why this ministry is needed. _____

_____

_____

_____

3. The costs to the church (in detail)._____

_____

_____

_____

4. What this will mean to the church in opportunities and cost in 2, 3, 5 years.

_____

_____

_____

5. Alternative. _____

_____

_____

_____

_____

6. Alternative. _____

_____

_____

_____

For every plan proposed there are alternatives. They are very important to the budget committee because they give variables for making judgments between one ministry and another.

Figure 5

Sample Budget Form

		Current	Proposed
I.	World Missions Ministries		
	Cooperative Program	_____	_____
	Associational Missions	_____	_____
	Direct Missions	_____	_____
	Children's Home	_____	_____
	Local Missions	_____	_____
	Total	_____	_____
II.	Pastoral Ministries		
	Pastor's Salary	_____	_____
	Housing & Utilities	_____	_____
	Associate Pastor's Salary	_____	_____
	Housing & Utilities	_____	_____
	Secretary	_____	_____
	Radio & Television	_____	_____
	Deacon Care Program	_____	_____
	Revival	_____	_____
	Total	_____	_____
III.	Education Ministries		
	Minister of Education's Salary	_____	_____
	Housing & Utilities	_____	_____
	Secretary	_____	_____
	Sunday School	_____	_____
	Church Training	_____	_____
	Brotherhood	_____	_____
	Woman's Missionary Union	_____	_____
	Leadership Training	_____	_____
	Total	_____	_____
IV.	Music and Worship Ministries		
	Minister of Music's Salary	_____	_____
	Housing & Utilities	_____	_____
	Organist's Salary	_____	_____
	Music & Supplies	_____	_____
	Special Programs	_____	_____
	Worship Supplies	_____	_____
	Total	_____	_____

V. Support Ministries
    Library   _____   _____
    Recreation   _____   _____
    Church Secretary's Salary   _____   _____
    Office Supplies/Postage
    Stewardship/Budget Development
    Auditing/Financial Records
    Travel Expense (all staff)
    Convention expense (all staff)
    Annuity Payments
    Social Security
    Special Events
    Kitchen operation/supplies
                          Total
VI. Buildings and Grounds
    Janitor's Salary
    Utilities
    Insurance
    Repairs
    Taxes
    Supplies
    Debt Retirement
    New Facilities
                          Total

Summary by Categories

  I. World Missions Ministries
 II. Pastoral Ministries
III. Education Ministries
 IV. Music and Worship Ministries
  V. Support Ministries
 VI. Buildings and Grounds
                      Grand Total

Figure 6

Flow Chart

Steps That Make Ministry-Action Budgeting a Simple Committee Procedure.

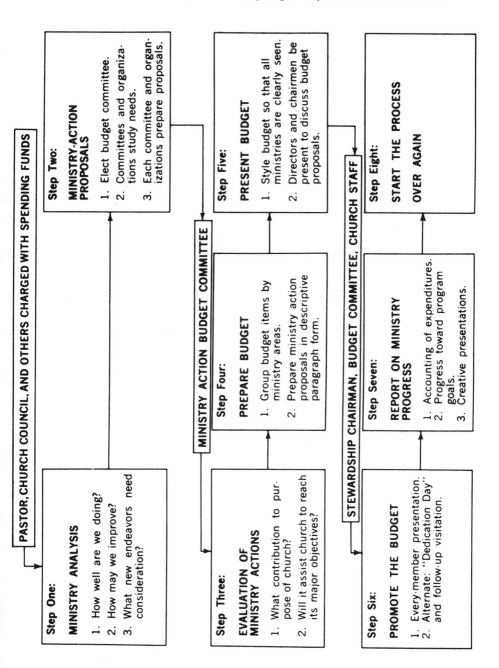

PASTOR, CHURCH COUNCIL, AND OTHERS CHARGED WITH SPENDING FUNDS

Step One:

MINISTRY ANALYSIS

1. How well are we doing?
2. How may we improve?
3. What new endeavors need consideration?

Step Two:

MINISTRY-ACTION PROPOSALS

1. Elect budget committee.
2. Committees and organizations study needs.
3. Each committee and organizations prepare proposals.

MINISTRY ACTION BUDGET COMMITTEE

Step Three:

EVALUATION OF MINISTRY ACTIONS

1. What contribution to purpose of church?
2. Will it assist church to reach its major objectives?

Step Four:

PREPARE BUDGET

1. Group budget items by ministry areas.
2. Prepare ministry action proposals in descriptive paragraph form.

Step Five:

PRESENT BUDGET

1. Style budget so that all ministries are clearly seen.
2. Directors and chairmen be present to discuss budget proposals.

STEWARDSHIP CHAIRMAN, BUDGET COMMITTEE, CHURCH STAFF

Step Six:

PROMOTE THE BUDGET

1. Every-member presentation.
2. Alternate: "Dedication Day" and follow-up visitation.

Step Seven:

REPORT ON MINISTRY PROGRESS

1. Accounting of expenditures.
2. Progress toward program goals.
3. Creative presentations.

Step Eight:

START THE PROCESS OVER AGAIN

nation and any other relevant information. A far better way to reach each home is through visitation. A church can use this means to give commitment cards to each home. Visitors can encourage members, listen to concerns, and improve understanding. In many cases, ministry opportunities will be discovered which were not previously known or responded to.

Step 6: Promote the budget. Adoption of the budget will not ensure that giving will always follow. Members must be taught, encouraged, and led to make giving commitments.

Step 7: Report on ministry progress. Regular budget reports should include all important financial data, but they should also become ministry progress reports. Such events as interviews, prayer periods, testimonies, visual aids, a review of plans, and reports on the number of people involved in specific ministry can be very helpful.

Step 8: Review and evaluate. More than just beginning again, the entire budgeting process should be analyzed and needed changes and improvements made.[6]

The flow in Figure 6[7] shows the process of ministry-action budgeting described above. This process requires a minimum of ten weeks and should be completed in the sequence described.

Additional figures are included for reference. See Figure 7 for a way of interpreting the World Missions section of the budget. A similar paragraph would be written to interpret each major category. Figures 8 and 9 are other forms that may be used in this budget development process.

Figure 7

World Mission Ministries

As we interpret our part of the Great Commission, mission ministries fall into five areas:

1. The Cooperative Program gives us a real part in everything Baptists do in more than ninety countries of the world, as well as in this nation. Through the Cooperative Program, we support nearly 6,000 missionaries, six seminaries, hospitals, colleges, homes for the aging, and children's homes around the world as well as in our state.

$27,500

2. Associational missions keep us aware of the desperate needs that are closer to home and give us a real sense of participation in ministry as these needs are met, particularly in the mission we support in our association.

$ 5,500

3. We have direct relationship with a young chaplain as he ministers at the jails and institutions in our area.

$ 1,833

4. We have a special part in the ministry of our state children's home where over 200 children are ministered to annually.

$ 917

5. Our local benevolences are growing and for this we can be thankful.

$ 917

OUR WORLD MISSION MINISTRY TOTAL *$36,667*

Figure 8

Budget Request Form

Ministry Plan and Request for Allocation of Resources
1. Name of Ministry:_____
2. Ministry Objectives: _____
_____
3. General Plan of Action (activity, date, responsible person, etc.):
_____
_____
_____
_____
_____
_____

4. Necessary Program Costs (the funds you have to have):
                    Description and Amount Needed
_____ $_____   _____ $_____
_____ $_____   _____ $_____
_____ $_____   _____ $_____
_____ $_____   _____ $_____
_____ $_____   _____ $_____
                    TOTAL $_____
5. Discretionary Program Costs (what you would like to do if you had the
   money):
            Description   Amount   Rank (1,2,3)
_____ $_____   _____
_____ $_____   _____
_____ $_____   _____
                    TOTAL $_____
TOTAL BUDGET REQUEST $_____ Date _____
Requested by: _____ Position _____

Figure 9

Worksheet for Financial Support of the Minister

(Duplicate and use a separate sheet for each staff member.)

		This Year	Proposed for Next Year
I.	Ministry-Related Expenses		
	1. Automobile Allowance		
	2. Convention Allowance		
	3. Book Allowance		
	4. Continuing Education Allowance		
	5. Hospitality Allowance		
	TOTAL EXPENSES		
II.	Protection Benefits		
	1. Insurance		
	a. Life		
	b. Long-Term Disability		
	c. Medical		
	2. Retirement		
	TOTAL BENEFITS		
III.	Basic Compensation Personal Support		
	1. Cash Salary		
	2. Housing Allowance		
	TOTAL COMPENSATION		

Notes

1. Thomas J. Peters and Robert H. Waterman, Jr., *In Search of Excellence* (New York: Warner Books, 1982), p. 26.
2. Howard P. Colson and Raymond M. Rigdon, *Understanding Your Church's Curriculum* (Nashville: Broadman Press, 1981), p. 45.
3. See, for example, Kennon L. Callahan, *Twelve Keys to an Effective Church* (San Francisco: Harper and Row, 1983).
4. For additional planning information, procedures, and sample forms, see Bob I. Johnson, "How to Plan and Evaluate" and related chapters in *Christian Education Handbook*, Bruce P. Powers, ed./comp. (Nashville: Broadman Press, 1981).
5. Information concerning the development of a budget is adapted from Lee E. Davis and Ernest Standerfer, *Christian Stewardship in Action* (Nashville: Convention Press, 1983) and Charles A. Tidwell, "Administering Educational Support Services," *Christian Education Handbook*, Bruce P. Powers, ed./comp. (Nashville: Broadman Press, 1981).
6. A simplified budgeting process based on the ministry-action concept is available for small churches or for congregations seeking to develop a budget for the first time. Contact the Stewardship Commission; 901 Commerce Street, Nashville, Tennessee 37203-3620, or write your state convention office. Information on the full ministry-action program may also be requested from these sources.
7. From *Christian Education Handbook*, p. 213.

Bibliography

Brown, Truman, Jr. *Church Council Handbook.* Nashville: Convention Press, 1981.

Callahan, Kennon L. *Twelve Keys to an Effective Church.* San Francisco: Harper and Row, 1983.

Colson, Howard P. and Raymond M. Rigdon. *Understanding Your Church's Curriculum.* Nashville: Broadman Press, 1981.

Davis, Lee E. *In Charge: Managing Money for Christian Living.* Nashville: Broadman Press, 1984.

Davis, Lee E. and Standerfer, Ernest. *Christian Stewardship in Action.* Nashville: Convention Press, 1983.

Haller, Leon. *Financial Resource Management for Nonprofit Organizations.* Englewood Cliffs: Spectrum Books, 1982.

Holck, Manfred. *Church Finances in a Complex Society.* Nashville: Abingdon Press, 1983.

Johnson, Bob I. "How to Plan and Evaluate." *Christian Education Handbook.* Bruce P. Powers, ed./comp. Nashville: Broadman Press, 1981.

McDonough, Reginald M. *Leading Your Church in Long-Range Planning, Revised.* Nashville: Convention Press, 1985.

Peters, Thomas J. and Waterman, Robert H., Jr. *In Search of Excellence.* New York: Warner Books, 1982.

Tidwell, Charles A. "Administering Educational Support Services." *Christian Education Handbook.* Bruce P. Powers, ed./comp. Nashville: Broadman Press, 1981.

8

Designing and Managing Facilities

William G. Caldwell

One of the most significant and far-reaching decisions churches ever make is the location and design of facilities in which the church will meet. A location which has low visibility or accessibility will create problems for the church in attracting people. The same problems will exist if the design of the facility does not relate to the community where it is located. For these reasons it is essential that a church give careful consideration to its facilities.

Determining Purposes of Facilities

The church must make some decisions about the basic use of church property before it can adequately determine its building and equipment needs. Most churches would feel that property and facilities should be used for worship, education, and fellowship. But each congregation needs to determine its own goals and then relate the use and maintenance of property and facilities to best meet those goals.

Some churches would emphasize worship space needs over education space needs or vice versa, while others would give priority to fellowship. Many churches with limited resources will decide to build multipurpose space which could be utilized for all three purposes. The flexibility of space should be a key factor in determining priorities in this day of high building and financing costs.

Another consideration related to the purpose of facilities would be that of weekday use and the extent to which outside community groups would be allowed to use the facilities. A church that uses its facilities six days a week will be faced with significant decisions about materials to use in construction as well as maintenance considerations. A church that is involved in sharing the use of its facilities regularly with community groups such as scouts, senior citizen groups, community interest groups, and others will need to

169

face other considerations concerning the scheduling and maintenance requirements.

The fairly recent development of large buildings for recreational
purposes has caused churches to evaluate further their purposes and
objectives for ministry. The provision of such facilities calls for
additional property (including outdoor recreation provisions), large
financial commitments (including building and equipment plus personnel for programming and maintenance), and proper policies for
the use of the facility. Even the remodeling of existing space for
recreational purposes requires the same considerations.

Whatever the decision about the basic use of property and facilities, the church must develop some system of priority use for what
it owns. Failure to do so may completely defeat the basic purpose
of what the church is about.

Designing Facilities

The design of a church facility is determined by the purposes for
which it is to be used. A number of factors must be considered
before a church can adequately provide facilities for its use.

Secure Sufficient Land

The first decision a new or an existing church will make about
facilities relates to the land needed for its purposes. A new church
will be deciding where it will locate facilities from which to conduct
its ministry. An existing church will be deciding if its present location is sufficient for its ministry or if it will need to move to another
location because of inadequate land availability at the present site.

A number of factors will be involved in decisions concerning site
selection and the amount of land needed for the work of the church.
The place where a church ministers will cause some of these factors
to be inoperable. For example, an inner-city urban church in Man-
hattan would almost ignore parking requirements because of mass
transit, but zoning requirements would be very significant.

1. *Size and shape.*—Because of the kinds of activities in which
churches engage, the suggestion of a minimum size of five acres is
frequently given. Another suggestion is to allow two acres for every
300 people in attendance. (This involves projecting the future
growth of the church.) The best shape is a large rectangle or a
square.

2. *Topography and drainage.*—The land should be fairly level with a

slight slope for drainage. Sites with problems in this area would require more space so that drainage could be designed properly. The cost of preparing a site for building and other uses must be considered.

3. *Easements and utilities.*—An investigation must be made of the kinds of easements or other access to the property which exist. Setback requirements for buildings must also be determined. If utilities are not presently available at the site, an estimate of the cost of bringing them in must be made.

4. *Zoning requirements.*—An important consideration for any site would be the zoning classification. Restrictions concerning building height, types of structures, and uses of buildings are areas that must be investigated. An attempt to change zoning classification after purchase may not be successful.

5. *Accessibility.*—The location must be readily accessible to the persons the church intends to serve. It should be at the intersection of major travel arteries within a reasonable driving time of those persons. Several entrance/exit points must be obvious. The location of buildings on the property should provide a feeling of openness and the places to enter the buildings must be prominent. Openness to people must also be considered. Provisions for handicapped persons is essential.

6. *Visibility.*—Closely related to accessibility is the need for the location to be seen easily by the people who pass by. The often repeated statement remains true: If you need a sign to point people to your location, your church should be where the sign is. Signs that can convey a changing message will add to the visibility of the church.

7. *Parking.*—Adequate parking is a must for most churches. Too many churches rely on street parking when provisions should be made on the property for people to park. Many cities have ordinances which require a certain number of off-street parking spaces. A church should do that much and more if it expects people to drive to the facility. The parking should be within a reasonable walking distance of the building, and it should be integrated with the landscaping to provide an attractive appearance. Multiple services make further demands on the parking facilities as people are coming and going at the same time. Churches with limited space may justify the expense of parking structures to provide sufficient parking. A good

site selection would be adjacent to a good-neighbor business or office space with parking facilities not used on Sundays.

Survey Program Needs

The place to begin in designing building facilities is with the program needs of the church. What needs to be done to accomplish the purpose of the church? This presupposes some basic understandings of what the work of the church is. When this is determined, then the question of programs and activities can be dealt with. All churches do not have to have every program that has ever been designed. A church will need to prioritize what it will be able to do to accomplish its purposes.

The process of surveying what the church has done in the past and what it is presently doing is necessary if the church is to plan adequately. The only way to know how to build a building is to determine what you intend to do in it.

The careful analysis of present and projected program space requirements is essential. The church will likely appoint a survey committee of competent individuals, representative of various aspects of church life, to conduct this analysis. The committee should be organized so that it will be able to study all aspects of the church life. Subcommittees should be assigned to the basic areas—education, recreation, worship, and so forth—so that they can focus on specific needs. Some types of survey instruments may need to be developed to secure information from church members concerning their ideas about church programs.

The entire committee should be involved in analyzing and evaluating the material developed by the subcommittees. The assimilation of the survey information should be provided in a condensed form for the church membership, along with recommendations for congregational action.

It is essential that a broad range of church members be involved in the survey process. Since the study looks at present activities as well as future possibilities, it is necessary to include as many people and ideas as possible. The decisions made concerning program needs should be based on accurate information and assessment of the work of the church. This will provide a proper basis for developing facility needs according to a priority arrangement.

Determine Community Needs

Another significant factor in designing facilities relates to the needs of the community in which the church is located. A part of the ministry of any church grows out of those things it intends to do to meet specific needs in the community. This may include provisions for day care for working parents, after-school care for older children, senior citizens programs, recreation programs for the community, and other types of activities in which building considerations must be made.

A number of community survey instruments are available for churches to use to determine needs which exist. Again, the approach to this kind of survey must be based on the understanding the church has concerning its purpose in ministry. Decisions concerning programs to meet community needs are just as vital as those concerning church needs. Sometimes they are even more crucial because of the additional funds, facilities, and personnel involved.

No church can do everything or provide every service which a particular community may need. The committee's thorough survey will provide the kind of information necessary for the congregation to decide what they can do and what must be left to others. Many things will not require additional facilities; decisions about them can be made apart from facility considerations.

Any community ministry decision must be made deliberately after carefully considering all of the available information. Many churches have entered specific ministries without all the facts and have not been able to sustain the work. Such activities have caused churches to lose credibility in the community. Where facility additions are required, it is even more imperative that a church gather all the needed information and weigh it carefully before deciding to provide a community ministry.

Prioritize Facility Needs

The decisions concerning what facilities are needed must be followed by decisions concerning what should be done first. The long-range projections for community development as well as the population of the ministry area of the church must be taken into consideration. What the church does first will have a definite effect on what it does later. Whether to build worship, educational, or recreational space first must be carefully analyzed by the committee and the congregation. The church that builds a large, permanent worship center first may never fill it up. A growing church may go through two, three, or more temporary worship centers before it decides about the permanent structure.

Part of the consideration concerning facilities will be related to the remodeling or refurbishing of present facilities. Unless the decision is to relocate and build everything new, present structures must be looked at from the viewpoint of the feasibility of their continued use. Sometimes the decision will be to tear down and build anew in the same place. The structural soundness of existing buildings must be evaluated by structural engineers. Local building codes must be studied to determine the extent to which existing buildings must be brought into line with current codes if extensive remodeling is undertaken. In some cases, the needs can be met by simply rearranging a few walls for more functional use of a building. In other cases, the inside of the entire building will need to be torn out and new walls put in.

A long-range plan based on the priorities which the church assigns to facility needs becomes a goal or a vision toward which the members work. Even those who may not be in complete harmony with the first stages will work at accomplishing them so that the future developments can be worked on sooner. The plan should remain flexible enough that changes can be made in the future if community or ministry changes should occur.

The basic purpose and objectives of the church must be evident in the way in which facility priorities are set. The special significance of church buildings make them different from commercial buildings. Because they are dedicated to God's work, priorities must reflect those spiritual ministries of the church and the service it provides to the community. These priority decisions will be reflected in the policies regulating the use of buildings which will be considered later.

Prepare Financial Plan

The high cost of construction and high interest rates have created significant problems for churches that need to build facilities. Through the years many different kinds of building finance programs have been used. The results have not always been good for the church. Interest payments have risen higher than missions giving. These problems point out the need for churches to plan carefully for the financing of any facility improvement.

Accumulating as much cash as possible before building is a must. The establishment of a building fund in an interest-bearing account is the first step to take. Encouraging people to give to the fund over and above their regular budget giving will help in increasing the giving. The use of such promotion ideas as "double tithing" and "fifth-Sunday building fund offerings" will help. A major fund-raising activity for many churches has been the three-year pledging campaign in which people are asked to pledge and then give weekly to the building fund. Many firms as well as denominational groups have specialized in this area of fund raising for churches.

How much cash should be raised before beginning construction? There are those who recommend that all of the funds should be in hand first. Others recommend a pay-as-you-go operation. Others would suggest from one half to two thirds of the total amount needed should be in cash. Each church will be different in terms of its needs and abilities to pay for buildings. A high interest rate, especially if the repayment is to be done over several years, could cause the total amount to be two or three times the original construction cost. A church must face the stewardship considerations of this kind of expense. There will be times when the immediacy of the building need will offset the additional cost. A significant fact for the church to remember is that it is easier to raise funds for building the facility than to raise funds for debt retirement after it is completed. The continual emphasis of the effort should not be on the building itself, but on the people who will be involved and who can be reached by this effort.

The best approach is to develop a sound financial program which can be explained to the church. It will likely incorporate a cash fund-raising approach along with a feasible, limited-payment plan for financing the remainder of the costs. Such a plan should include all of the anticipated costs related to the building project: land costs and site preparation; architectural and engineering fees; construction costs; furnishing costs; and anticipated maintenance, program, and personnel costs for the use of the facility.

Develop Design Drawings

The selection of an architect is a crucial decision for the church. The one selected should be familiar with church buildings, have experience in designing church facilities, and be willing to listen to what the church has established as the needs to be met and the priorities to be followed. The wrong decision here will further complicate an already difficult process.

The committee will need to spend time with the architect to make certain that the approach the church is taking is fully understood and that it can be implemented. Any problems should be worked out before proceeding with the project. Agreement should also be reached concerning the architect's involvement in the construction process such as the extent of supervision to be provided.

The first step will be the development of the *property utilization plans.* The best arrangement of the proposed facility along with the future buildings should be identified on the available property. It should be evident that there is enough space to provide for all that is planned on the property and that the proposal will fit the topography of the land.

The next step will be the development of the *program graphic plans* which will show the allocation of the square footage of the floor space to the various age groups and programs which have been determined by the survey. The evaluation of these plans will determine if the needs which should be met are being provided for in the proposed facility.

The final step will be the development of the *detailed drawings* which will provide the schematic design for all the areas included in the construction: foundation, plumbing, electrical, heating and cooling, roofing, ceiling, wall and floor treatment, and so forth. The specifications relating to all of these components must be stated in the way the church wants the facility finished. These become the criteria on which the bids for construction are developed. Careful evaluation of these drawings and descriptions must be made.

With all of these things accomplished, along with the appropriate review and approval, the church will be able to construct a facility that will meet the ministry needs it has envisioned.

Managing Facilities

It is not enough for a church to design and construct good facilities. The church must also be in the business of managing those facilities so that the maximum benefit can be derived from their use. It is poor stewardship indeed if the facilities are not cared for and utilized in the way in which they were intended. A number of factors are related to the process of effectively managing facilities.

Develop Facility and Equipment Use Policies

Who should determine policies for the use of church facilities and equipment? Since a policy is a stated course of action which will be consistently followed, it is essential that a responsible group be involved in determining what they should be. Since procedures vary from church to church, the group to accomplish this will also vary. However, regardless of the group—the congregation, a church committee, an official board, or church officials—the policies should be in writing and readily available when they are needed. This would include the identification of the person or persons responsible for their application. In small churches, the pastor may have this authority; in larger churches, some other staff member may be identified. In some churches, a committee or other official may be responsible.

Since policies assist in the delegation of authority, help in reaching the goals of the church, and lead to the uniform handling of all requests, it is essential that the group developing them consider the following ideas concerning good policies.

- They should be positive in nature.
- They should be simple and easily understood.
- They should be broad, allowing flexibility.
- They should be geared toward consistent application.
- They should be kept up-to-date.

The group will determine what policies are already in effect and will probably look at what other churches have in the way of policies. Resources listed in the bibliography will provide additional help.

A church may follow some system of priorities when developing policies. Preference in scheduling should be given to church activities rather than outside groups. Larger group activities may have priority over smaller group activities in certain facilities. Meetings that are conducted on a regular basis should be considered ahead of one-time or occasional meetings. All areas of the church facilities and equipment should be covered by policy statements. The group should consider worship areas, fellowship areas, educational areas, recreational areas, kitchen, parking areas, office equipment, and vehicles in the development of policies. Several sample policies and request forms are included (Figures 1-4). In order to facilitate the scheduling and use of church facilities, all rooms in the buildings

Figure 1

Sample Policy Statements

Building Use

1. The philosophy underlying policies for building use is that all church facilities shall be used to carry out the basic purpose and mission of the church. Policies should be kept in the spirit of bringing people to Christ.

2. Use of any facility shall be done in conformity with city fire and safety ordinances. These provide for the prohibiting of smoking and overcrowding in church facilities.

3. Janitors or other building personnel shall be responsible for moving all equipment and furniture when it is necessary and for replacing it for regular meetings.

4. Regularly scheduled church meetings shall have first priority in building use. Other church related meetings shall have second priority. Outside nonprofit organizations shall be eligible for building use when facilities are not being used by church groups and when their purpose is approved by the pastor and the Property Committee. Profit-making enterprises shall not use church facilities for any purpose.

Weddings

1. The philosophy underlying policies for weddings is that a Christian emphasis be encouraged and that members relate the ceremony to Christian family commitment.

2. All weddings shall be scheduled on the master church calendar with first priority being given to church members. Nonchurch members shall be allowed to schedule a wedding no earlier than ninety days prior to the event to assure the church member's priority.

3. Counseling of the couple prior to the wedding is essential. The pastor or other ministers shall conduct the counseling or be advised as to the person doing so.

4. Church members are encouraged to use the pastor and church organist for the ceremony. Guest ministers shall be approved by the pastor, and guest organists shall be approved by the minister of music.

5. In keeping with the wedding philosophy, church members shall use the facilities without charge. Nonmembers shall pay a fee for facilities a week in advance according to the following schedule:

| Sanctuary | $100.00 | Fellowship Hall | $50.00 |
| Chapel | 50.00 | Kitchen | 25.00 |

6. A minimum fee of $30.00 for the services of the janitor (including rehearsal) shall be paid by all (church members and nonmembers) since the work will be extra.

7. In keeping with safety regulations, protective materials shall be used with candles, and rice shall not be used inside nor outside the buildings.

8. The church wedding consultant shall work with the couple in the development of the wedding plans and the implementation of policies.

Figure 2

Room Scheduling Request Form

(Submit to church office at least two weeks in
advance. Form will be returned with confirmation.)

Meeting Request

Date submitted _____ Request by _____

Person responsible _____ Phone _____

Date of meeting _____ Organization _____

Type/Purpose of meeting _____

Room(s) needed _____

Time of meeting: From _____ to _____

Number expected _____ Diagram Room Arrangement on back ☐

Standing request: Every _____ until _____

Equipment needs _____

Media needs _____

Food Service needs:

    Type of service _____

    (consult with hostess after approval)

For office use:

    ☐ Approved and Scheduled

    ☐ Not approved: Reason _____

    Authorized Signature _____ Date _____

Figure 3

Wedding Request Form

(Submit as early as possible. Nonchurch members no earlier
than ninety days ahead of date requested)

Date Requested _____ Time _____

Bride's Name_____ Church Member?_____
yes/no

Address _____

Work Phone _____ Home Phone _____

Groom's Name _____Church Member?_____
yes/no

Address _____

Work Phone _____ Home Phone _____

Minister's Name _____

If Guest Minister: Address_____ Phone_____

Rehearsal Date _____ Time _____

Room(s) Required _____

Reception Time _____ to _____

Room(s) Required for Reception _____

Organist's Name _____

If guest organist: Address_____ Phone_____

Florist _____ Phone_____

Photographer_____ Phone_____

Caterer_____ Phone_____

For office use:

☐ Approved and Scheduled

☐ Not Approved: Reason _____

Authorized Signature _____ Date _____

Church Wedding Consultant Assigned _____

Phone _____

Figure 4

Record of Equipment Loaned

Item Borrowed:

Description: _____

Inventory Number: _____ Number of Items _____

Description: _____

Inventory Number: _____ Number of Items _____

Date Borrowed: _____

 I agree to be responsible for these items away from the church property. If they are lost or damaged, I will replace them or provide funds to do so.

Signature _____

_____

Office use only:

 ☐ Check out approved: Signature _____

 ☐ Items returned; date _____

 Receiver's Signature _____

should be numbered. A room assignment record can then be kept and used for scheduling as well as janitor assignments.

Plan Energy Management Measures

One of the most significant stewardship responsibilities a church has is related to the wise and proper use of energy. A lack of concern and involvement of people in energy management will result in wasteful and expensive energy use. All areas of church life relate to the use of energy from the scheduling of meetings to the selection of a temperature range, to the type of lighting fixtures used, to the turning off of lights and equipment not in use.

In planning a new church facility, careful consideration should be given to energy use. The architect and Building Committee should consider these factors.

1. *Location.*—The way in which the buildings are situated on the property will affect energy use. A balance should be maintained between the aesthetic view of the structures and the energy management view. Facing the building in such a way as to take advantage of the sun and using earth embankments for insulation are good stewardship.

2. *Landscaping.*—The use of trees and shrubs can be advantageous from an energy-use standpoint. Careful landscape planning will result in lower utility bills. Screening the sun out in the summer and allowing the sun in during the winter can be accomplished with trees.

3. *Insulation.*—Every possible part of the building should be properly insulated according to the recommended *R* value for the climate. This would include ceilings, walls, crawl spaces, concrete slabs, electrical outlets, outside pipes, duct work, caulking around wall openings, weather-stripping doors, thermal doors and windows, and attic and roof ventilation.

4. *Building materials.*—Many new building material products provide higher energy conservation. These should be considered for the building. Their use should not rule out such practical considerations as windows that open so that the building can be opened up when conditioned air is not required by outside temperature.

5. *Energy-efficient equipment.*—The selection of heating and cooling equipment with the highest possible energy efficient ratio is a must. In addition, hot water heaters and other appliances should be selected for their energy efficiency.

Many energy-management measures can be taken in existing buildings. Some are expensive but will pay for themselves in a short time. Others should not be done because of the expense and long payback period. Some can be accomplished at virtually no cost. An Energy Management Committee can be established to develop an audit of how the church is presently using energy resources and to provide suggestions for improvement in energy management.

Some no-cost suggestions would include the following ideas: set back heating temperature; lower hot water temperature; set air-conditioning temperature higher; shut off mechanical equipment when not in use; turn off lights when not in use; remove a bulb from multiple light fixtures when safety is not a factor; schedule meetings at the same time in facilities already cooled or heated. Some low-cost suggestions would include the following ideas: caulk and weather-strip around doors and windows; repair broken windows; install higher efficiency lighting where possible; use lighter colors when redecorating; use timers or photocells on outdoor lighting; lock thermostats; check efficiency of heating and cooling systems; keep filters clean and replace when necessary. Additional suggestions will be obvious when an audit is completed.

Provide Adequate Insurance Coverage

The need for proper insurance coverage by churches has long been demonstrated. The old idea of "charitable immunity" is no longer valid for a church. Too many situations are now on record to indicate that a church is subject to the same kinds of problems which face other businesses in the insurance area. A church needs insurance to meet its stewardship and moral responsibility as well as to meet practical and emotional needs. An Insurance Committee should carefully analyze the areas of need facing a church and select insurance coverage to meet those needs.

The following categories should be covered.

1. *Personnel.*—Insurance should be provided for all church employees, including staff members and other paid workers. Consideration should be given to accident and health insurance, group life insurance, disability income, workman's compensation insurance, and fidelity bonds for those who handle money. Related to these would be the provision for a retirement plan for all personnel. Leaving out any of these coverages would mean that the church might have to come up with funds to help an employee in need.

2. *Liability.*—This insurance provides protection from financial loss due to suits or claims arising from accidents on the premises or away from the premises if they relate to normal church activity. This will include the operation and maintenance of church facilities, the alteration of church properties, the sale or distribution of food, and church schools and camps. In addition, coverage should be provided for all vehicles owned by the church or used in the work of the church.

3. *Building and property.*—This insurance should cover physical damage to any property the church owns or uses. Included in the coverage would be fire insurance for buildings and contents; extended coverage for windstorm, lighting, explosions, aircraft and motor vehicles, riots, vandalism, earthquake, flood, and special coverage for glass or other valuable property; theft and burglary; and church vehicles.

The committee should follow these guidelines for providing proper coverage.

• Cover all essential areas of risk.

• Cover the largest loss exposure first.

• Have sufficient coverage (requires an inventory of property and equipment to establish replacement cost amounts on all property).

• Seek professional help (especially with appraisals).

• Select a reputable agent and company.

• Provide coverage for special events and activities which depart from regular programs.

• Use large deductibles where possible.

• Compare premium costs regularly to get reasonable rates.

• Review coverage periodically.

Effective work in this area will assure that a church is properly insured when the need arises and that property damaged or persons injured will be adequately covered.

Develop Good Housekeeping Procedures

What does good housekeeping mean for a church? It means keeping the physical facilities clean, attractive, and in good repair as a means of providing a positive witness to the community. The appearance of the facilities will speak loudly concerning the congregation's feelings about the place that is dedicated to the worship of God to say nothing of the need to protect the original investment made. Good housekeeping is good stewardship. A properly planned and executed preventive maintenance program will provide good upkeep on facilities and assure their ongoing usefulness to the church.

In order to keep buildings and equipment prepared for service, there are three types of housekeeping and maintenance programs which must be provided. The first is *operational maintenance* in which the custodial or maintenance staff performs the routine cleaning of facilities and the standard placement of furnishings. The second is *in-service maintenance* in which labor and materials are provided to place into service a damaged portion of the building or a broken piece of equipment. The third is *preventive maintenance* in which a planned program of routine service and inspection of buildings and equipment is developed to maintain service and appearance. A church should be involved in all three types for proper stewardship.

Proper organization for this type of housekeeping and maintenance program will require the use of paid personnel (full-time or part-time) as well as volunteers. The supervisory responsibility for the work should be delegated to a responsible individual to assure its accomplishment. In a smaller church, that person may be the one in charge of a committee which has the assignment of facilities. In a larger church some staff member will be given the responsibility but will likely work in conjunction with a church committee. The use of volunteers and the employment of personnel will vary according to the size of the facility. In some larger cities, contracting services are available for operational maintenance. Because of the unpredictable nature of church schedules, this outside contractor approach would have to be investigated carefully.

The person in charge would need to work in several areas to make certain that the facilities were being cared for. These would include:

- Develop inspection procedures for properties.
- Maintain an inventory of all equipment and furnishings (see last section of this chapter).
- Develop maintenance policies and procedures.
- Prepare budget recommendations for maintenance.
- Maintain records for maintenance.
- Contract for outside maintenance firms when needed.
- Develop preventive maintenance program including forms and reports needed.
- Oversee budget expenditures and development of contingency funds for large items.

• Supervise personnel in maintenance program.

The development of forms and records is an essential part of a good housekeeping program. The ability to keep up with what has been done and what needs to be done is necessary for good facility upkeep. The proper maintenance of equipment requires a record of its use so that it can be serviced at regular intervals. The sample custodian's checklist will serve as an example of the kinds of forms which will be helpful in building maintenance (Figure 5). Other forms could be used for weekly, monthly, and periodic assignments. The frequency of use in a specific part of the facility will determine the housekeeping requirements.

Develop Adequate Lighting and Sound Systems

Due to the nature of the activities conducted in church facilities adequate lighting and sound systems are essential. Improper lighting can be a safety hazard as well as present problems for persons trying to read or study printed material. An inadequate sound system will prevent persons from hearing and understanding much of what is being said in worship services or other large group gatherings.

Figure 5
Custodial Daily Work Checklist

Name of Custodian_____

Area/Rooms Assigned_____Week of_____

(Initial tasks when completed)

Duties	M	T	W	T	F
Dust all furniture, equipment, window sills, etc.					
Clean all glass doors					
Pick up and empty trash					
Vacuum carpets					
Clean water fountains					
Damp mop tile floors					
Clean stairwells					
Clean rest room urinals, basins, toilets					
Damp mop rest room floors					
Fill towel and toilet tissue holders					
Special assignment (see below)					

Special Assignment:

In most cases, adequate lighting provisions will be made at the time of building construction. When this does not happen, it becomes necessary to correct the problems with additional lighting where needed. A study should be made of the various classrooms, office areas, hallways, entrances, and rest rooms as well as the worship area to determine if the lighting is sufficient. Each area will have its own needs in terms of the amount of light. A light meter can be used to determine if the required amount of foot candles of light is present in the more crucial areas. The ability to control lighting with spots and dimmers is especially helpful in worship areas. In classrooms and hallways, changing from incandescent to florescent fixtures will provide better lighting as well as save energy.

The acoustics of a building are also determined at the time of construction. The type of floor, wall, and ceiling materials used will affect the sound in a room. A noisy room can be deadened by placing carpet on the floor or acoustical treatment on the walls and ceiling. Other types of acoustical treatment can be used to make a "dead" room more alive. Expensive sound systems can be installed to enable persons to hear what is being said. Unfortunately, sometimes after spending large sums of money the hearing problem still exists. The advice of experts must be sought to provide answers to acoustical problems.

Perhaps the major problem with sound treatment relates to the worship area. The problem is complicated by the need to amplify music and the speaker by using the same system. The approach with music is to make it sound like it comes from all over the room whereas the desire with a speaker is to make the voice sound like it comes from the person speaking. These two different approaches create problems for the sound system. Proper installations will take into account the size and acoustical treatment of the building and its equipment. A number of microphone outlets will be needed for the multipurpose use of musicians and speakers. Good quality speakers can be focused to direct sound to all parts of the room. The amplifier, mixer, tape recorder, and other equipment must be of sufficient quality to provide the kind of sound reinforcement needed.

Maintain Sufficient Heating and Cooling Systems

The days of the hand fan have long since passed as an adequate means of keeping people comfortable at church. The key word is *comfort.* Whatever people have become accustomed to in their homes and in other public places regarding heating and cooling should be seen as the norm for the church facility. The installation of adequate systems for this purpose should be done in the construction of the building. Proper maintenance of the equipment will provide for its long-term use. The type of system will determine the type of maintenance which must be done. Because of construction design, some systems will need to operate year round to provide conditioned air in the facility. In buildings where windows can be opened, there likely will be several months during the year (depending on the climate) when the equipment will not need to be used.

The maintenance of this equipment requires good record keeping to enable service to be done at the proper intervals. In some instances the church maintenance personnel will be able to provide the proper service requirements. In most situations, the maintenance will need to be done by outside contractors who will provide the proper service within the appropriate time frame. (See Figure 6.)

Develop Proper Security Measures

The need for security in church facilities has been highlighted in recent years by increasing reports of vandalism, burglary, attacks on persons, arson, and other unfortunate events. No one likes to think of the church as a fortress where everything is locked up, but proper steps should be taken to protect the church property and the lives of members.

Several factors should be considered in the internal security of the buildings. A key control policy should be established to provide for the issuing of keys to proper persons and to keep a record of keys issued. Certain areas and rooms should be locked when not in use. These areas include offices, library and media rooms, equipment rooms, kitchen, supply rooms, and the like. All equipment should be identified with the church name and control number and should be put away when not in use.

Special precautions should be taken relating to security of confidential records, computer access, and money-receiving and counting activities. Churches with weekday child care and school programs should provide training for workers relating to security precautions for children. A plan for evacuating the buildings should be developed and publicized.

Figure 6

Equipment Inventory Record

Type of Equipment _____

Located at _____ Inventory number _____

Description _____

Model No. _____   Cost   _____

Serial No. _____   Shipping   _____

Date Purchased _____   Installation   _____

From _____   Taxes   _____

Trade-in allowed _____   Total   _____

Service contract agreement date to be renewed _____

Warranty _____

Repairs and Maintenance

Date	Description	By	Amount

Additional consideration should be given to the external security of the buildings and grounds. Doors and windows should be provided with adequate locking devices. Landscaping around the building should not block the view of windows and doors so as to provide cover for a burglar. Outside areas including the parking lots should be equipped with sufficient lighting for nighttime use. It is wise in some areas to develop parking lot patrols when people are in the building to protect vehicles from theft. A committee or special group in the church could take responsibility for providing the patrol.

Many churches have felt a need to install alarm systems for better protection of the property, especially when no one is on the premises. There are several types of systems available for the church to use. Some simply make a noise while others are tied directly to an alarm service company or to the local police or fire station. A church should carefully investigate the types of systems available before it selects the one to install.

Maintain Grounds and Parking Areas

The appearance of the church grounds and parking areas should serve as an inspiration to others in the community to improve the appearance of their own property. Similar to proper building maintenance, they serve as a testimony to the attitude of the church members concerning the place where they worship. Grounds that are not cared for may be communicating a lack of concern which is not characteristic of the church. One indication of concern is an attractive sign identifying the church and providing information about the services which can be read easily from the street.

Grassy areas around the facilities can do much to enhance their appearance amid all the brick and concrete. These areas must be fertilized, watered, and mowed regularly if they are to remain attractive. It is also helpful for them to be edged to keep a neat appearance. In some churches this responsibility is assigned to the custodial staff. Others will secure outside help for this purpose. Although professional persons may be hired, this is an excellent place to utilize youth in the community who can provide this service. If volunteers are used, there must be a clear understanding of the responsibilities involved or the appearance will likely suffer.

Landscaping with trees and shrubs can provide a helpful addition to the attractiveness of the facilities. Professional help will be an advantage here in the selection and care of the proper plants. The choices should be made in the interest of energy considerations as well as appearance. The plants and trees chosen should enhance the beauty of the facilities without hiding them or blocking the view of drivers entering or leaving the parking area.

Walkways and parking areas must be designed in a way that will facilitate the easy access of people to the buildings. Ramps and close-in parking should be provided for older persons and the handicapped. Covered loading and unloading areas should be considered for parents with small children and for use in inclement weather. In areas of extreme winter weather, surfaces should be treated to prevent falls.

The design of the parking areas should be planned to accommodate the maximum number of cars and still provide sufficient driveway areas. The parking angle used should be easily negotiated by all drivers. Entrances and exits should be provided in two or more locations far enough apart to prevent backup during busy traffic times. The city-zoning codes must be examined and followed in determining the amount of parking to be provided.

The parking area should be surfaced to provide all-weather use. Even though more expensive to install, concrete provides a longer-lasting and more easily maintained surface. The parking spaces should be clearly marked and kept painted, so drivers will know where to park. The feasibility of parking structures should be investigated when limited land is available or when the cost of ample land for surface parking is prohibited.

As discussed earlier, sufficient lighting should be provided for all grounds and parking areas. The security factor is significant as well as the safety factor for people using the facilities. In addition, the lighting of the building or one special feature of the building such as the steeple will serve as an advertising focal point at night. All outside lights should be on a timer or a dusk-to-dawn automatic switch so that the areas are illuminated when needed. Additional lighting may be needed where outside grounds or parking areas are to be used for recreational purposes. Special lighting (as well as additional parking area) may be needed for church vehicles when stored on the parking lot.

Develop Property and Equipment Inventory Procedure

Perhaps one of the most neglected areas in church facility management is a workable system for keeping up with property and equipment owned by the church. From the standpoint of insurance requirements (in case of fire or theft) as well as good stewardship, such a system needs to be developed and utilized. A church that must continually replace hymnals, kitchen equipment, tables, and chairs because they "disappear" is not providing a good model for its members nor acting as a good steward of its resources. Taking an inventory of present equipment as well as developing a procedure for keeping up with additional purchases is required.

The Building and Grounds or Properties Committee should initiate the inventory procedure. It may be as simple as counting and listing all tables, chairs, educational furniture, kitchen equipment, and so forth or as involved as securing tags or stickers with control numbers and affixing them to every item. Whatever approach is taken, a listing of all items is necessary and a record kept as to where they are located. Policies relating to the borrowing of equipment would include a form to use in recording that information. All existing equipment should be identified as to approximate date of purchase, cost of the item, and the amount of time used in the case of motors or other items which require service.

An inventory record of all new items should be started at the time of purchase and maintained for the life of the item. Any warranty information or instructions for use should be filed in a related folder. The record form should include all information necessary for providing maintenance for the item. (See Figures 6-9.)

Facilities which are properly designed and managed will go a long way in helping the church fulfill its mission. A lack of attention to facilities will not only handicap the church in its work; it may provide a negative witness to the community.

Figure 7

Report of Vehicle Use

This form should be completed by the driver of each vehicle at the time the vehicle is returned.

Date(s) of use_____

Group or person responsible _____

Destination _____

Reason for use_____ Acct. No. Charged_____

Driver _____ Phone _____

Vehicle Used:

_____ (Vehicle description)

    Odometer reading:

        End of trip _____

        Beginning of trip _____

        Total miles _____

_____ (Vehicle description)

    Odometer reading:

        End of trip _____

        Beginning of trip _____

        Total miles _____

Maintenance Needs: Please list any repair needs or conditions to be corrected which you observed on the trip.

_____

_____

Driver's Signature_____ Date _____

Figure 8

Inspection/Maintenance Report
Property and Building Exterior

Item/Area	Inspected Date	By	Location	Condition	Action Needed	Action Performed Date	By
Church Sign							
Doors/Windows							
Drains							
Exterior Walls							
Lawn, Shrubs							
Metal Flashing, Gutters, Down Spouts							
Walkways							
Parking areas							
Outside Equipment							

Figure 9

Inventory/Inspection Report

Room No. _____ Made by _____ Date _____

Item	Condition			Repair Needed	Recommendations	Number
	Good	Average	Poor			
Ceiling						
Walls						
Floor						
Lights						
Curtains						
Drapes						
Blinds						
Carpet						
Tables						
Chairs						
Piano						
Chalkboard						

Bibliography

Anderton, T. Lee. *Church Property/Building Guidebook*. Nashville: Convention Press, 1980.

Belknap, Ralph L. *Effective Use of Church Space*. Valley Forge: Judson Press, 1978.

Chambers, Fred R. *Creative Sight and Sound for the Church Musician*. Nashville: Convention Press, 1978.

Egan, M. David. *Concepts in Building Firesafety*. New York: John Wiley & Sons, Inc., 1978.

Gray, Robert N. *Managing the Church*. New York: NCC Publication Service, 1977.

Hoffman, Douglas R. *The Energy-efficient Church*. New York: Pilgrim Press, 1979.

Keogh, James E. *The Small Business Security Handbook*. Englewood Cliffs: Prentice-Hall, Inc., 1981.

Myers, Marvin, author/comp. *Managing the Business Affairs of the Church*. Nashville: Convention Press, 1981.

Owensby, Idus V. *Church Custodian's Manual*. Nashville: Convention Press, 1974.

Privette, Jerry A. and McAdams, Howard D. *Church Energy Handbook*. Nashville: Convention Press, 1980.

Sack, Thomas F. *A Complete Guide to Building and Plant Maintenance*. Englewood Cliffs: Prentice-Hall, Inc., 1976.

9

Planning Special Congregational Events

Robert D. Dale

Special congregational events put the minister's management skills—especially planning skills—on public display. These special events are common, high-profile happenings. Three of the most demanding are weddings, funerals, and revivals.

Each of these is spotlighted in this chapter as an example of and model for the administrative care that must support all types of special activities.

Planning Weddings

Weddings are occasions when the minister wants especially to be sure everything goes according to plan. Weddings are so public and so sentimental that the wedding party, the minister, and the plan are all on display. Because churches want to avoid misunderstandings about weddings, many have developed statements of wedding policies. (For an example of church policies for another special event, funerals, see Figure 1.) Several aspects of planning for weddings deserve careful attention.

Guiding Premarital Counseling

Ministers often find premarital counseling unfulfilling. They feel frustrated because engaged couples usually want a ceremony, not counsel. One professional counselor friend complains that these couples are "in a state of madness." Consequently, engaged couples usually aren't at a stage of life where they are interested in making decisions; for them, the decision is already made.[1] They want a wedding now, and they'll worry about the issues of building a married relationship later. Rather than trying to guide a decision-making process for the already decided, you may want to open a discussion forum for two people who will establish one new family. A forum provides a setting in which a minister can raise basic questions about marriage and husband-wife relationships, and a couple can take advantage of that setting to make sure they have thoughtfully discussed the full range of concerns they will face in marriage. The minister provides the setting, the questions, an objective listening ear, and some coaching in communication and conflict management processes. The couple responds with frank answers and direct conversation.

Whether you prefer more traditional counseling approaches or the forum style of premarital preparation, you may want to use some reading material to introduce issues and to prime the conversational pump. For example, the book by Jerry and Karen Hayner, *Marriage Can Be Meaningful*,[2] is a helpful resource. If the engaged couple reads this or some other mature book a section at a time, even the inexperienced counselor can work with young couples with more confidence. Many ministers request a minimum number of conversations with the engaged couples whose weddings they have been asked to perform as an integral part of the overall wedding planning process. Discussing the wedding ceremony itself is only one part of premarital counseling.

Rehearsing for the Wedding Ceremony

The wedding rehearsal is a time to clarify what everyone is to do and when he or she is to do it. Rehearsals also are times to calm everyone's anxieties and to reassure them that the plan will work. Therefore, all of the wedding party and all of the officiants need to attend the rehearsal. The exact time and place should be clearly communicated to every person who is expected to take part in the rehearsal.

Some couples enlist the assistance of a bridal consultant. If so, the consultant will also attend the rehearsal and will provide an additional resource to the minister in planning for the wedding. Consultants are generally expert in the etiquette of weddings but have no input into the content of the ceremony.

A variety of customs surround weddings and rehearsals. For example, some brides subscribe to the old superstition that it's bad luck for a bride to take any active part in the rehearsal of her wedding and prefer to use a stand-in during the rehearsal. Additionally, different denominations have varying traditions relating to weddings. The rehearsal provides the occasion for everyone to understand the traditions that apply to this particular wedding.

Before the Wedding Ceremony

The timing of several preceremony events can be crucial. Consider this countdown.

• One hour before the ceremony—the ushers arrive, put on their boutonnieres, and seat lady guests by offering their right arms. If designated seating areas are preferred, the bride's section is on the left side (from the rear of the sanctuary), and the groom's section on the right.

• Thirty minutes before the ceremony—the organist begins playing music. If candles are used, they are lighted at this time unless the minister instructs otherwise. The groom and best man should arrive and go to the minister's study or another meeting place designated by the officiating minister.

• During the final twenty minutes prior to the ceremony—some churches have facilities for all of the wedding party to use in dressing for the ceremony. If the wedding party dresses away from the church, the timing of several arrivals needs to be considered. The groom's parents arrive at the church about twenty minutes prior to the ceremony. The bride's mother arrives at the church about ten minutes before the scheduled beginning of the ceremony. The bride and her father arrive at the church just minutes before the ceremony and join the bridesmaid(s).

Immediately prior to the ceremony's beginning, an usher seats the groom's parents on the right front pew. Then, the bride's mother is seated on the left front pew where she will later be joined by the bride's father. No one is escorted to a pew after the bride's mother has been seated. Guests who arrive late must either stand or quietly seat themselves in the rear of the sanctuary. If an aisle runner is used, it should be unrolled at this time. If wedding songs are planned, the soloist should sing them just prior to the processional.

Guiding the Ceremony Itself

The ceremony proper commences with the processional. The minister, groom, and best man take their places at the front of the center aisle. When the organist begins the wedding march, guests should follow the lead of the bride's mother. If she rises, all guests should also stand. The order of the processing group is ushers, bridesmaid(s), maid or matron of honor, ring bearer, flower girl, and (after the organist increases the volume of the march music) the bride and her father.

Most ministers use some version of the traditional Episcopal wedding ceremony.[3] When customized vows are preferred, the minister should guide the writing of the vows closely, be sure the vows are carefully memorized, and make a copy of the vows and carry them with him during the ceremony itself in case of an embarrassing lapse of memory on someone's part.

What If Someone "Speaks Now"?

Occasionally, a wedding ceremony develops an unexpected glitch. For instance, what are the minister's options if after asking, "If there is anybody present who has any objections to this marriage, let him or her speak up now or forever hold his peace," someone speaks up with an objection? What if an old flame of the bride or the groom chooses the wedding as an occasion for making a public complaint? Or what if future in-laws don't like the prospective mate their child is about to marry? Are these concerns reason enough to stop a wedding? What should you do?

According to justices of the peace, the only valid reason for halting a wedding is when the marriage wouldn't be legal. While the law related to marriages may vary somewhat from state to state, several issues commonly constitute illegal marriages.

• If either the bride or groom has a prior undissolved marriage.

• If the parties are related to each other in a manner prohibiting marriage in that state.

• If either of the parties is under age.

• If either of the parties is judged to be incompetent or insane.

• If either of the parties is involuntarily intoxicated or drugged.

Consult a justice of the peace or an attorney in your state to see if the instances mentioned above are the law in your state or if additional causes apply also. Review the law and save yourself uncertainty and a wedding party embarrassment.

After the Ceremony

The recessional begins the final element of the ceremony. The order of the recessional is the reverse of the order of the processional with the bride and groom exiting first and the best man escorting the bride's honor attendant. If the guests stand during the recessional, they should be seated following it until after the ushers have returned and escorted the bride's parents and then the groom's parents out of the sanctuary. The aisle runner isn't removed. If the wedding party wishes, the minister may invite the guests to the reception at the close of the ceremony.

Planning Funerals

The Bible notes that there's "a time to die" (Eccl. 3:1-2). About one percent of the American population dies each year. On the average, residents of the United States experience a bereavement because of a death every six years. Funerals have always been emotionally difficult and structurally challenging services for the minister to lead. No longer, however, is death considered a dirty word in our culture. Americans are more informed about the event of death and the process of grieving.

Why Have a Funeral?

Funerals are changing. Wakes aren't very common any more. Increasingly, families are closing caskets at funerals and even having memorial services after the burial. Do funerals have a purpose any longer?

A funeral is both a family ceremony and a community event.[4] In the first place, funerals demonstrate the strength of our "credit networks." Our families and friends rally around us. Our sense of solidarity with them supports us. Second, funerals provide official farewells. This painful passage in our lives is clearly marked by the ceremony, the body, and the gathering of mourners. And, of course, funerals allow us to share our spiritual values.

The Minister's Role in Funeral Planning

Your role when a death occurs is multifaceted. The family of the deceased, the polity and policies of his or her church, the funeral customs of the local area, the funeral director, and any special military or fraternal groups that may request participation must all be dealt with considerately.

In relationship to the family of the deceased, you extend your most crucial ministry. In most cases, you will have known and cared for the deceased previously. When the deceased has suffered some extended terminal illness, you will already have established a pattern of care and may have made some plans concerning the funeral with the deceased. When a death occurs, make a prompt, generally brief, comforting home visit and offer any assistance needed.

The funeral director generally contacts the minister who will officiate at the funeral, and together they structure the arrangements for the service and burial. In most cases, the family of the deceased will leave the details of the funeral service to the minister. If the family requests a favorite Scripture, hymn, or item in the service, consider such appeals carefully and grant them as often as is appropriate.

Your composure at the funeral service is crucial to all of the mourners, especially the family. A brief home visit and prayer before the service, calm demeanor in the conduct of the service, firm handshakes, and sincere efforts to comfort and help will provide emotional structure and practical assistance to the deceased's family. The proof of your care of bereaved families is shown through your ongoing counsel with family members during the difficult and extended period of repairing their social network after the funeral.

No difference in your care of others should be apparent. Prominent church members, marginally participating members, and non-members should be treated alike. In fact, nonmembers may be reached for Christ and for church membership because of your, and the church's, thoughtfulness and thorough care during bereavement.

In relationship to local customs and congregational policies regarding funeral services, you should be knowledgeable and sensitive. Even if you disagree with some of these customs, don't choose a public funeral to create a test case for your views. Use other congregational settings to discuss issues and clarify church practices. Work to develop policies such as in Figure 1 that can be used to inform and guide members of your church.

Additionally, you should know and practice consistently the local customs regarding any fees paid to persons who assit with funerals. Be prepared to advise about appropriate fees to pay an organist, soloist, janitor, and so forth. Often this information will be requested by the funeral director. In any event, ministers should never ask for a fee for conducting funerals although they may choose to accept travel expenses incurred in fulfillment of their professional responsibilities.

In relationship to previous ministers who are asked by grieving families to return to the field and to conduct funerals, the current

Figure 1

Funeral Policies for Our Church

The Christian gospel of peace, hope, and triumph is nowhere brought into sharper focus than at the death of Christians. Although we who believe in Christ sorrow at the death of persons we love, we don't grieve "as others do who have no hope. For since we believe that Jesus died and rose again, even so, through Jesus, God will bring with him those who have fallen asleep" (1 Thess. 4:13-14, *RSV*). The plans Christians make to face death are a testimony of faith.

Christians ought to assemble, not to mourn the dead, but to confess our faith in a living Lord. Generally, since the funeral is a service of worship, it should be held in the church building and should itself be a witness to hope and fellowship.

On the basis of this affirmation, the statements below are offered for the guidance of our own members in the matter of funerals.

1. When a death occurs in the church family, the pastor should be called immediately. This call will give you the benefit of the pastor's solace and experience in making funeral arrangements.

2. Since a Christian funeral is a worship service, it is recommended that the funeral service be held in the church, that the congregation join in the singing of hymns of victory, thanksgiving, and fellowship, and that the pastor lead the service, drawing heavily on the comfort of God's Word.

3. The pastor will help the family select the hymns, Scriptures, and other elements of the funeral service to ensure the centrality of the theme of our victory over death through faith in our Savior.

4. When the funeral service is held in the church, with the physical remains present, it is recommended that public viewing of the deceased in the service be discouraged. Private or public viewing of the body may be arranged prior to the funeral service.

5. In order that worshipers may center their thoughts on the comfort and strength God provides, a memorial service may be held without the physical remains of the deceased, which may be committed to the earth prior to the service.

6. A simple casket is as appropriate as an elaborate one since the deceased's worth isn't determined by the cost of the funeral arrangements. Therefore, the church will provide a suitable cloth with which to drape the coffin for services which prefer this courtesy.

7. Families are encouraged to recommend to concerned friends the opportunity of making memorial gifts to the church or designated charities. Members of the church are reminded of the importance of acts of thoughtfulness and practical concern to the living during the grief process.

8. Because the funeral service is regarded as one appropriate function of the body of Christ, no fees of any kind are charged for the use of the church's facilities or its personnel.

minister should abide by the family's wishes. Anyone who returns to a previous field of service should be certain the current minister is informed. Invite the current minister to join in conducting the funeral service unless the family prefers otherwise. In any funeral in which more than one minister is officiating, all of the ministers should be fully aware of the responsibilities of each of the other officiants.

In relationship to funeral directors, you should major on spiritual and emotional assistance and leave the physical arrangements to the funeral director. While you may occasionally encounter a difficult person in the funeral home business, you will discover that most funeral directors are sensitive public servants. You may accompany grieving church members to the funeral home to make the final arrangements if members request your assistance in making decisions during difficult times.

In relationship to military or fraternal groups, you should acquaint yourself with these groups' prescribed rituals. When conducting funeral services that include these groups, carefully coordinate funeral services and graveside committals with their representatives. The Defense Department will, upon request, provide ministers with copies of their pamphlet on conducting military funerals.

Planning for Revivals

Some churchmen suggest that revivals are no longer an effective evangelism approach. That isn't the opinion of the more evangelical groups. For example, over 40,000 local church revival meetings were reported by Southern Baptist congregations during one recent year.

While revivalistic methods can become gimmicks and lose their credibility with Christians and non-Christians alike, good planning undergirds wholesome evangelism. A thorough, refreshing treatment on evangelism suggests a framework for prerevival planning.[5] Several planning questions need to be raised by any congregation projecting a revival as an element of its evangelistic witness.

What is the purpose of our revival? The pastor and other church leaders in evangelism and ministry should guide the congregation in determining the specific purpose of their revival. Will the meeting concentrate on outreach? On building up the existing Christian fellowship? On both?

When is the revival scheduled? As far in advance as possible, the date of the revival needs to be calendared. The date may need to remain tentative until the preferred preacher and singer can be enlisted. Care should be taken to avoid dates that compete with major community events or holidays.

Who will lead the revival? The pastor and others who may be charged with selecting the revival preacher and singer should carefully enlist leaders who can best help the congregation reach its goal for the meeting. The pastor himself, pastors of neighboring churches, and vocational evangelists provide an array of possibilities for personnel.

How will we organize to reach our goal? The church's evangelism committee (and special groups as needed) can arrange for prayer support, publicity, music, visitation, testimonies, hospitality, finance, ushers, and special emphases. In small churches, one person may be able to coordinate each of these activities.

How will we finance our revival? Misunderstandings over finances can tarnish your revival's impact quickly. Several options are used by congregations to underwrite the necessary expenses of revivals. Some churches include an item in their budgets for the total cost of their revival personnel and other expenses. Other churches use only freewill offerings. A few churches cover expenses out of their budgets, then use a love offering to show their appreciation for the preacher and singer. Whatever custom a church finds most comfortable, it should pursue its approach openly but without detracting from the revival's primary goal. If revival leaders are required to travel long distances, an advance on their expenses or a prepaid ticket is a thoughtful courtesy.

Are we involving most of our resident members in revival preparation? Prospect visitation, prayer support, and a plan for discipling every person who registers a public decision allows every member to contribute more than attendance to a revival's success. Overall involvement and careful preparation can plant the seeds for the Holy Spirit's cultivation and ripening.

Plan, Plan, Plan

Special events deserve the minister's thorough efforts in planning. Special congregational events should be remembered for positive results, not for what went wrong. Planning helps special events unfold in predictable stages.

Figure 2

Special Event Planning Form

1. Event _____ Date _____ Time _____
2. Purpose/For _____ Approx. attendance _____
3. Person in charge _____ Phone _____
4. Facilities needed
   _____ Auditorium (seats XXX)   _____ Nursery Ages? _____
   _____ Chapel (seats XX)   _____ Playground
   _____ Parlor/Bride's Room   _____ Room(s) # _____
   _____ Fellowship Hall   _____ Kitchen (space only)
   _____ Office Reception Area   _____ Parking Lot (East side)
5. Equipment needed
   _____ Sound System   _____ 16 mm Projector
   _____ Piano   _____ Slide Projector
   _____ Chalkboard   _____ Tape Recorder/Player
   _____ Easel   _____ Record Player
   _____ Table(s) Number? _____   _____ Kitchen Equipment
   _____ Chairs Number? _____   _____ Other: _____
   _____ Equipment/supplies will be provided by the following:
         Company/Person _____ Phone _____
6. Preparation and cleanup of facilities
   Janitor needed? _____ (Required for nonchurch function.)
   Payment due, if nonchurch function $_____ Date due _____
   If church function, person in charge _____
7. Arrangement of facilities
   Sketch on the back of this form the room arrangement(s) desired. Show locations
   of tables, chairs, flower arrangements, and other items that will need to be set up.
8. Schedule and Participants
   List below or attach to this sheet the schedule/agenda for this event and a list of
   program participants.

Person requesting _____ Date _____
Approved by _____ Date _____

Notes

1. For a useful classic book and a more recent resource on ministering to premarried, see Russell L. Dicks, *Premarital Guidance* (Philadelphia: Fortress Press, 1963) and Bobbye and Britton Wood, *Marriage Readiness* (Nashville: Broadman Press, 1983).

2. Jerry and Karen Hayner, *Marriage Can Be Meaningful* (Nashville: Broadman Press, 1983).

3. For an extremely helpful resource for planning wedding ceremonies, see Marion D. Aldridge, *The Pastor's Guidebook: A Manual for Worship* (Nashville: Broadman Press, 1984), pp. 72-97.

4. Bill G. Bruster and Robert D. Dale, *How to Encourage Others: A Resource for Preaching and Caring* (Nashville: Broadman Press, 1983), pp. 69.

5. Delos Miles, *Introduction to Evangelism* (Nashville: Broadman Press, 1983), pp. 287-99.

Bibliography

Aldridge, Marion D. *The Pastor's Guidebook: A Manual for Worship.* Nashville: Broadman Press, 1984.

Bruster, Bill G. and Dale, Robert D. *How to Encourage Others: A Resource for Preaching and Caring.* Nashville: Broadman Press, 1983.

Dicks, Russell L. *Premarital Guidance.* Philadelphia: Fortress Press, 1963.

Hayner, Jerry and Karen. *Marriage Can Be Meaningful.* Nashville: Broadman Press, 1983.

Miles, Delos. *Introduction to Evangelism.* Nashville: Broadman Press, 1983.

Wood, Bobbye and Britton. *Marriage Readiness.* Nashville: Broadman Press, 1983.

10

Church Publications

Bruce P. Powers

To a great extent, the personality of a church is conveyed through church publications. How a congregation thinks and feels about its life usually is reflected in its publications. Not consciously, perhaps, but nevertheless there is a direct relationship.

For example, look at your church bulletin. What story does it tell about the personality and character of your congregation? And look at the newsletters and other printed materials. Which ones make the church look best? How do they compare with the materials you see from businesses and community organizations in your town?

In this chapter you will find some ideas to spruce up your printed communications. Pick out the ones that appeal to you and that have possibilities for your situation. Then take a notepad and decide how to make the needed changes.

Following the administrative procedures, there is an idea section containing information on a variety of topics related to the preparation of printed materials.

General Considerations

1. Be clear about your message. Exactly what is it you are trying to communicate? The best messages are:
• Concise—the writing is tight, direct, and clear;
• Energetic—they are compelling, full of action verbs, and devoid of trite phrases and useless words;
• Respectful—they allow the reader to interpret and make decisions without overselling or dictating conclusions.

2. Be clear about your target audience. Are you speaking to insiders or to outsiders? Are you trying to communicate with an age group or with all ages? Is a message specifically for all persons in a worship service, or is it for those who are members of a Sunday School class?

3. Is there a planned design to the material, or is it sort of pieced together? Look at a newsletter or bulletin. What stands out? Is this what you want to emphasize? Look at your church's material through the eyes of a stranger. What are the most important items or activities? Where would you look first, and how would you be guided through the printed messages? What would you remember? Why?

4. Look at the title of your newsletter or bulletin, and the contact information. Would a stranger be able to

- Tell the full name of the church?
- Address a letter to the church?
- Call the church office?
- Ask for the pastor or other minister by name?
- Tell what the various sections or columns are about?

If a stranger would have trouble with any of these, so would many church members.

5. What type of paper is used, and what does it look like? Is it light colored, clean, and crisp looking? Is it heavy enough so that printing on one side doesn't interfere when you read the other side? Is there a good contrast between the printed material and the paper, so reading even in dim light is easy?

6. Who edits—decides what goes into and prepares—your church publications? Has this person developed skills in church communications and does she/he feel good about the job being done? Consider providing some helpful resources for this person such as those listed in the bibliography. And, when possible, encourage participation in a church publications workshop provided by your denomination or other church-related organization.

Administrative Guidelines

The following guidelines will assist you in developing an administrative plan for your church.

1. One person on the staff should be in charge of church publications. Although work might be delegated, this person would plan, organize, direct, and approve all editorial matters.

2. Develop a policy statement that describes the purpose, content, distribution, and costs for each regular publication. Have this approved by the appropriate person or group. New publications would be approved in the same way.

3. Develop a production schedule for each regular publication.

Indicate the dates by which various actions must be completed and the person responsible if other than the editor. See Figure 1 for a sample production schedule.[1]

4. Use a planning form, as illustrated in Figure 2, for each issue of a church publication. These forms could be prepared ahead of time for each week. Staff members then could easily plan ahead for major emphases and arrange to treat themes over a series of issues. More time could be allowed for important writing assignments, and the editor could give more thought to layout and design. Such planning would enhance publications and help them serve as educational aids as well as promotional tools for church ministry.

5. Follow the same planning scheme for special brochures, promotional materials, and other related items. Plan thoroughly and far in advance of the date needed.

6. Develop a layout form for all regular publications. This will enable you to visualize materials while still in the planning stage and will cut down the time spent in editorial and typing work. This form is a sketch or copy of the actual publication with all material that *changes* missing. In designing an issue, you place new material in the blank areas. For example, a Sunday bulletin form might include a square on the front indicating the number of characters across and the number of lines available for typed copy. See the illustration in Figure 3.

7. Keep a file copy of every publication. Place regular items such as bulletins and newsletters together in a binder for easy reference. Occasional items such as brochures can be filed together in a publications folder.

8. Review annually the effectiveness of church publications. This can be done by the church staff, the Church Council, or other authorized group of leaders. Guidelines for evaluation and suggested ways of developing an annual plan for publications are included in books listed in the bibliography.

Ideas to Enhance Your Work

1. Design content of materials based on the target audience. In publications designed for the total congregation like a weekly newsletter, focus on general items such as the pastor's message, church family news, program promotion, and people features. Avoid a number of personal columns that *have* to be filled each week.

2. Space is precious; use it wisely. Information that applies to a

Figure 1

Weekly Newsletter

Sample Production Schedule

Thursday	Meet with staff to plan next week
Friday	Compile materials Write or secure commitments to prepare articles
Monday	Secure all materials and complete writing/editing using information gained from weekend activities
Tuesday	Prepare camera-ready copy, or submit copy according to agreements with printer
Wednesday	Newsletter printed and folded
Thursday	Label, sort, and package newsletter Deliver to post office according to local requirements
Friday	Newsletter delivered to homes

Figure 2

Publication Planning Form

Title: _____ Editor: _____

Date to be listed on publication: _____

Date needed:_____ Give to whom: _____

PRODUCTION SCHEDULE:

Date _____ *Action*

_____ Planning meeting with _____

_____ Complete assignments for items to be written

_____ Deadline for receipt of all items

_____ Prepare copy

_____ Print or deliver to printer

_____ Finish processing

GENERAL PLANS FOR THIS ISSUE:

ARTICLES OR INFORMATION TO SECURE:

What   *Person Responsible   Due Date*

1. _____   _____   _____

2. _____   _____   _____

3. _____   _____   _____

4. _____   _____   _____

5. _____   _____   _____

6. _____   _____   _____

7. _____   _____   _____

8. _____   _____   _____

Figure 3

Sunday Bulletin Layout Form

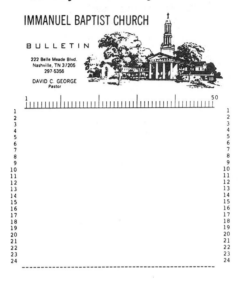

few, such as a report to a committee, might better be sent via photocopies in an envelope.

3. Establish a news-gathering system. Determine what information is needed and how often. Enlist representatives who can gather and perhaps write the needed articles. Determine an appropriate publication schedule, as described earlier in the chapter, and advise assistants of due dates.

4. Keep freshness in your publications. Materials that are overly predictable lose their communicating power. Try some of these ideas.

• Study books on the layout and design of church publications.

• Exchange materials with other churches by placing each others' names on your respective mailing lists.

• Collect publications that appeal to you and keep them in an idea file.

• Clip line drawings and related artwork from reading materials that will be discarded; you can use them in promotional materials. Such items also are available commercially as are rub-on letters, borders, arrows, and other useful art. Some denominations publish

proofs and stencil cutouts; check with your book store or denominational office.

• Attend a church publications workshop.

5. Become acquainted with proofreading marks. These are used
by printers and professional editors/writers to save time and to
indicate specifically what is to be done when preparing a publication. Marks often used in preparing church publications are illustrated in Figure 4.

6. Learn the vocabulary used in dealing with church publications. Many of the words you will use are listed and defined in
Figure 5.

7. Select a regular printer to handle all of your publications.
Before doing this, determine the types and amounts of items normally used by the church over a year. Then visit several printers.
Discuss your needs, look at their products, and secure a list of prices
and/or quotes. Select a printing firm that not only has good prices
but that can produce what you need within the time framework that
you must operate. Often you can negotiate with the printer concerning the amount of layout and design that must be done in your
office and the amount that will be done by the printer.

8. Develop a form sheet to use, and learn how to write press
releases. Give facts: what, who, when, where, and why. Tell the
most important information in the first few sentences, then give
details. Type double-spaced on one side of 8½-by-11-inch white
paper. A sample form is in Figure 6.

9. Make an appointment to meet with each of the local editors,
newscasters, and other persons responsible for deciding what news
is distributed to the public. Discuss the requirements for submitting
information, time schedules, and specific persons to whom you
should relate. Discuss the types of information that would be
printed or broadcast.

10. Be dependable. Get information together on time, in the right
form, and to the right person.

11. Secure a style manual or a secretarial handbook for your office.
Use this for reference whenever you are in doubt about how to
communicate in print. Check with your book store or denominational office to determine if a specific manual is recommended for
your situation. Several manuals in general use are listed in the
bibliography.

12. Proofread, proofread, proofread! Don't let careless mistakes
make a joke of the church's image.

Figure 4

Proofreading Marks

Mark	Meaning
¶ The news is good.	Begin new paragraph
No ¶ The news is good.	No new paragraph
The¶news is good. It	Delete (may be drawn through a letter or may be attached to a circle that encloses material to be deleted)
Stet The news is good. It	Leave as it was; let stand
Th news is good. It	Insert item shown
The is news good.	Transpose material indicated
The news is good.	Insert a space
The news i s good.	Take out the space; close up
The news is good.	Print in boldface
The news is good.	Use italic style printing
The News is good.	Make the letter lower case
the news is good.	Make the letter a capital
The news is good.	Move copy to end of box (may be left, right, up, or down)

Figure 5

Church Publications Vocabulary

Bruce P. Powers

Listed below are words often used in dealing with church publications. I have collected them through the years from workshops, courses, and working relationships with printers and publishers. Get acquainted with these terms, and your ability to communicate in this field will improve measurably.

Artwork - any material prepared by hand as camera copy
Bleed - an illustration that runs off the edge of the paper after trim
Blowup - an enlargement of a photograph
Box - typed copy enclosed by a printed border
Bullet - a solid circle of print, generally used for emphasis; make one with a typewriter by filling in an o

By-line - the author's name at the beginning of a story

Camera-ready copy - finished copy and artwork pasted on a page for duplication just as it appears

Caps - capital letters

Center spread - two facing center pages of a publication

Clip art - artwork that can be cut out and pasted onto a master for reproduction

Coated paper - type of paper with hard, smooth finish that makes pictures look better

Copy - material to be photographed or composed

Copy desk - where all written material is edited and given headlines before being published in a newspaper

Cover stock - thick paper suitable for booklet covers

Credit line - information about the source of copy or illustration

Cropping - changing the size or proportions of a picture

Deadline - the last time to get copy in for publication

Dummy - a made-up model of what the finished version will look like

End - Typed at the end of a news release (—end—, also —30—)

Filler - short item inserted to fill space in a publication

Flush - even with the margin

Flyer - an inexpensive piece of printed promotional material

Font - a complete assortment of type characters of one face and size

Glossy - a shiny-surface photograph

Layout - Arrangement of text and artwork on a page

Lead (pronounced like seed) - opening paragraph in a news story that gives the essential facts

Line drawing - artwork; a sketch or illustration

More - when written at the bottom of a page, information is continued on the next sheet

Pasteup - see Camera-ready copy

Point - the printer's basic unit of type measurement (approximately 1/72 of an inch)

Proof - printed examples of type and/or illustrations on which corrections can be made

Rub-ons - sheets of letters and artwork; put a letter where you want it, rub gently, and the letter transfers to the master you are preparing; also called transfer type

See-through ruler - a large, transparent ruler marked with a grid; used to arrange materials on a master

Transfer type - see Rub-ons

Trim size - the final size of pages or other printed matter after trimming

Widow - paragraph endings of less than full measure occurring as the first line of a page

Figure 6

Information Release

Name of Writer   Release Date/Time _____
Position   For Immediate Release _____
Church or Organization   Release at Will _____
Mailing Address   (Indicate *one* of the above.)
Telephone Number

                              SUBJECT: (state major focus)

Begin typing here. (Follow these guidelines.)

- Use short paragraphs.

- Do not hyphenate words.

- Use wide margins on sides, top, and bottom.

- Do separate lines of a paragraph.

- If a second sheet is needed, type —more— at the bottom of the sheet before going on.

- After the first sheet, type your name, first three words from the subject, and the page number in the upper left corner.

- At the end of your release, type —end— .

- It is not necessary to write a headline for a news release.

—end—

Note

1. Information for this item is adapted from George W. Knight, *How to Publish a Church Newsletter* (Nashville: Broadman Press, 1983), p. 6.

Bibliography

Craig, Floyd A. *Christian Communicator's Handbook,* rev. Nashville: Broadman Press, 1977.
Chicago Manual of Style, The, 13th ed. Chicago: The University of Chicago Press, 1982.
Eckersley-Johnson, Anna L., ed. *Webster's Secretarial Handbook.* Springfield, Mass.: G. & C. Merriam Co., 1976.
Knight, George W. *How to Publish a Church Newsletter.* Nashville: Broadman Press, 1983.

11

Food Services

William G. Caldwell

The extent to which a church is involved in food services will vary greatly from church to church. In some churches, there will be little or no activity relating to food whereas other churches will have several full-time personnel and an extensive operation in food services. Regardless of the extent of the activity, a number of considerations must be made for the food service operation to be effective in a church.

Determining Food Service Purposes

A church must decide what it hopes to accomplish with food service activities. This decision will affect the approach taken to serving and funding meals. When it is seen as a ministry of the church, it will be used to enhance what the church is trying to do. The following purposes should be considered for a food service ministry.

Encourage Fellowship

There is something about sitting down to a meal together that encourages the fellowship and friendship of those who are involved. The informality that exists along with the amount of time it takes to eat a meal contributes to the opportunity for people to get better acquainted with one another. New members can be encouraged to participate in food service activities as a way to meet church members and to develop friendships.

Support Programs

Providing a meal is often the best way to get people to participate in some activity at the church. A regular Wednesday evening meal will encourage members to attend the prayer service and other program activities which may be scheduled at the same time. A special missions emphasis or some other ministry of the church will more likely be better attended if a meal is included.

Foster Involvement

Many churches utilize volunteers in the food service operation. This provides the opportunity to involve people in the ministry of the church who might not be willing to serve in leadership roles. Adequate planning and scheduling will be necessary to make the most of volunteer involvement.

Provide Convenience

The opportunity to eat at church will offer a convenient way for many individuals and families to participate in church activities. This will be especially true on weeknights when there would not be time for people to get home from work, prepare and eat a meal, and then get to the church for a meeting.

Develop Spiritually

The emphasis on physical food should not overshadow the need for spiritual food. Every meal service activity should be seen as a means to help people grow spiritually. When the food service operation is seen in this light, the ministry opportunities are unlimited.

Designing an Efficient Church Kitchen

The design of a kitchen will have a great deal to do with how it is used and how well it contributes to the effectiveness of the operation. Whether a church intends to serve meals from a potluck supper approach, a completely prepared and served approach, or a caterer approach, the design of the kitchen will help or hinder the process.

Location

The kitchen is best located on the ground floor of the building with easy access to the outside for receiving deliveries, servicing equipment, and disposing of garbage. It must be accessible to water, sewer, electric and gas connections, and have an outside wall or ceiling access for exhaust fans. It should be near an interior corridor and directly adjacent to the dining area.

Space

The amount of space needed will be directly related to the type and frequency of meals served and to the number of people involved. A completely volunteer operation will require more kitchen space than a completely paid operation. The space should be adequate for storage and refrigeration of food, preparation and serving of meals, cooking equipment, washing and storage of dishes and utensils, and the movement of people. A room size equal to 20 to 25 percent of the dining area should be considered. It should also be large enough to allow for growth.

Arrangement

The way in which the kitchen is arranged will have a definite impact on its efficiency. If people continually get in the way of each other while trying to work, problems will exist. If the arrangement does not allow for an orderly flow of the activities relating to meal service, it will be difficult to operate effectively.

The usual arrangement is to have the preparation area in the center, with storage and dishwashing facilities to either side of the back and the service area facing the dining room.

Ventilation

Adequate ventilation is essential for a good kitchen operation. The hot, odor-filled air should be exhausted and replaced by fresh air once every two or three minutes. The exhausted air should be moved directly outside. A separate heating and cooling system for the kitchen works best when tied in to the exhaust system. Filters relating to the system should be cleaned and changed regularly.

Sanitation

A church must be extremely cautious about the sanitation and health aspects of its kitchen. Even though the local health inspectors may not visit the church, everything that is required of restaurants should be done by the church. The health of the people being served requires the church to be diligent in its own inspections and thorough cleaning of the facility. Those who work in the kitchen should have a health certificate or a food handler's certificate and should follow all the standard rules of hygiene around food. The kitchen and storage areas should be treated regularly to prevent insects and rodents from thriving. Leftover food and garbage should be removed promptly. Any outside doors or windows should be provided with screens and maintained regularly.

Equipment

A church must recognize that the church kitchen is not a home kitchen. This will have significant bearing on the selection of equipment as well as policies for use. The amount and type of equipment needed will be determined by the frequency of use, number of people served, and type of service utilized. For most churches, commercial or institutional equipment should be installed. If a church never plans to cook a meal, however, it would not require extensive equipment. Used equipment can frequently be obtained from local suppliers or from restaurants going out of business.

The cost of stainless steel equipment will be greater but offers real advantages in upkeep and cleaning capabilities. The equipment should be purchased with a long-term outlook rather than the immediate cost factor. The amount of equipment secured should relate to the regular, normal activities of the kitchen. On those once-a-year occasions when more is needed because of an extremely large gathering, consideration could be given to renting equipment, moving the gathering to a larger facility, or using a caterer.

Walls and Floor Treatment

The construction of the kitchen should take into account the heat, moisture, and sound which will be generated as well as the need to be easily cleaned and maintained. The surfaces should be covered with material that provides for these considerations. The sanitation of the facility will relate directly to this consideration. If proper acoustical treatment is not done, the proceedings in the dining area or other areas of the church will be limited because of the kitchen noise. As with equipment, proper construction will be more expensive but much more effective in the long run.

Operating Food Services

Designing a good church kitchen is the beginning of a good foodservice ministry. Using the kitchen in the best possible way requires careful thought and planning concerning its operation. Even the best arranged and best equipped kitchen will not operate itself. Proper selection of personnel, menus, and the process of serving will determine the effectiveness of the operation.

Develop Policies

Policies for the operation and use of the church kitchen are needed for the same reasons as any other church facility. Guidelines are needed to avoid problems and to define responsibilities. They should be protective but not restrictive and should be followed by all who use the food services. Most churches will find it helpful to have a committee to develop the policies. This group will consider carefully the needs of the church and the needs of the kitchen staff. The committee can also serve as a liaison between the church and the food service personnel in the implementation of policies and procedures. All aspects of the work of the kitchen and food services areas should be covered. See Figures 1 and 2 for a sample policy statement and a schedule request form.

Figure 1

Kitchen Policies

1. The kitchen and food services operation of the church are to be used primarily by the church and its organizations. Outside, nonprofit groups desiring to use the facilities should make a written request 30 days in advance to be considered by the Food Services Committee and director providing there is no conflict with a scheduled church function.

2. The schedule request form shall be completed by all groups wishing to use the facilities. Written approval must be received before the facility can be used.

3. The Food Services Committee and director shall have supervision of the kitchen at all times. The director or a trained volunteer shall be present whenever the kitchen is used. Food service personnel shall have health certificates.

4. Agreements for purchasing food and supplies must be made with the director at least one week in advance of the activity to assure adequate financial arrangements are made. For church groups, the costs will cover the food and supplies. For outside groups, the costs will include food, supplies, labor, and an estimated amount to cover utilities and janitorial expense.

5. Keys to the kitchen and storage areas will be issued only to employed food service personnel. These areas will be kept locked when not in use.

6. Kitchen and dining room equipment to be loaned for use outside the church building will follow the equipment policy procedure in consultation with the food services director.

7. The organization sponsoring a meal shall arrange for volunteers to assist with serving and shall be responsible for arranging and decorating the dining area.

8. The Food Services Committee and director shall be responsible for maintaining an inventory of equipment and supplies and preparing a budget for additional equipment and supplies as needed.

Figure 2

Food Service Request Form

Date received _____ Date of meeting _____
Organization _____
Type of meeting _____ Number expected _____
Time of meeting: From _____ to _____
Person in charge _____ Phone _____
Area needed _____
Type of meal service: cafeteria _____ buffet _____ plates served _____
Menu suggestions: Meat(s) _____
    vegetables _____
    salads _____
    desserts _____
    drinks _____
Cost desired: _____
Do not write below this line
_____
Charges: Dept. _____ Account _____ Amount _____
Cleared on church calendar _____
Menu approved _____
Personnel assigned _____
                 Approved _____

Recap.
Food cost $ _____
Supplies   _____
Labor   _____
Total $ _____
Per plate cost $ _____

The church should also make a decision about the procedure to follow in the matter of reservations or the number of people to prepare for when a meal is served. Most churches that serve a weekly meal will be able to forecast the expected attendance on the basis of the time of year, special programs, and the like and will not use a formal reservation system. Those who use a reservation system will have to determine the procedure for making reservations, the deadline for canceling reservations, and the procedure for collecting from those who do not attend. In the case of banquets or other special meals, tickets should be sold or a number of plates should be guaranteed by the organization responsible. The cost of all meals should be determined in advance and paid for by those who attend.

Enlist Personnel

The selection of personnel for the food service operation is critical to its success. Most churches will use a combination of paid and volunteer help. One person (whether paid or volunteer) should be selected as the food service director. Some of the characteristics needed by this person are:

1. An outgoing personality
2. Ability to work in harmony with others
3. Emotional maturity
4. Ability to communicate
5. Interest and experience in kitchen management
6. Understanding of food service purposes
7. Dependable and energetic

These same qualities should be looked for in other persons who will be enlisted to work.

The number of persons needed will be determined by the type of food service activity in which the church is involved. A regular, weekly meal will likely involve some paid personnel who will work every week. The food service director will plan the meals, purchase the food and supplies, and direct the persons who will be involved in cooking and serving. Volunteers can be enlisted to assist with the serving and initial cleanup. It is usually wise to use paid personnel in the dishwashing operation.

Helpers will usually be available from within the church membership. Utilization of youth and senior adults is a wise procedure. Enlisting volunteers from Sunday School classes, mission organizations, or other church organizations should be done for the weekly meals or the occasional banquets. Some of the tasks will require a limited amount of training but most of the jobs to be done can be accomplished by any willing person.

Determine Serving Methods

The arrangement of the kitchen and dining facilities will affect the ways in which food is served. This should be considered in planning a facility, but it will have to be lived with once the facility is constructed. If there is not enough room or equipment to cook a meal, then it would be unwise for a church to plan anything more than a potluck dinner. If the facility has been planned for multiple serving capability, then the decision can be made on the basis of the number of persons and the type of group to be served. The economics of the meal should not be the only consideration. The ages of the persons will be a factor as well as the type of group: families, children, senior adults, or others. The amount of space available and the amount of time allowed for the meal will also need to be considered since some serving methods require more space and take more time than others. The following methods should be considered:

1. *Family style.*—The food is placed in bowls on the tables; persons serve themselves; requires enough servers to get the food to the tables while it is still hot; cost factor usually greater.

2. *Cafeteria.*—This requires counter-serving space where food can be kept hot or cold; offers selection; not good for persons who have trouble making decisions; cost is controlled since price is determined by selection made; requires servers behind counter.

3. *Buffet.*—This requires serving space where food can be kept hot or cold; allows persons to serve themselves amount they want; cost factor usually greater.

4. *Plate service.*—Plates are picked up at one location already served; requires enough servers to put food on the plates as people come in; offers portion and cost control; taking plates to the table would require more servers.

Plan Menus

The food service director should be responsible for planning menus in keeping with the type of meal to be served and the type of group involved. The sponsoring organization should provide input based on the cost factor as well as the occasion. Basic suggestions relating to menu selection include the following: simplify the choices; balance the menu from a nutrition standpoint; contrast textures, flavors, and colors; consider the age group involved; consider the workload and personnel available for cooking; stay within budget limitations.

A regular Wednesday-evening-meal program must also be planned from the standpoint of variety since the same people will be eating every week. Some basic items can be selected and rotated over a period of time. Seasonal items can be included when they are available. The attractiveness of the items as they appear on the plate will have a great deal to do with the taste of the food.

Purchase Food and Supplies

Because of the high cost of food it is necessary for the food service director to shop carefully and wisely in purchasing food and supplies. If the amount purchased is large enough, institutional distributors will deliver to the church, and wholesale prices can usually be obtained. However, for most churches one distributor will not be able to supply everything that is needed, and the best approach is usually a combination-buying procedure utilizing both retail and wholesale outlets.

It is best to plan in such a way that major purchasing is done only once a week, so the best prices are secured, and time is not wasted. Quantity purchases can be made when price considerations and storage capabilities are favorable. Quality should not be sacrificed for price. Poor-quality food service will affect participation and probably cost more in the long run.

A food service director will discover over a period of time who the best distributors are and where the best deals can be made. Taking advantage of special sales is good when there will be a need for what is on sale in the immediate future. Any deliveries made to the church should be checked for quality and quantity of items ordered.

Determine Costs

All of the factors relating to the food service operation must be calculated when figuring the cost of meals and services. Many churches will provide for equipment, supplies, and labor through budget allocations and therefore only charge for the cost of food when determining a per plate charge.

A church must decide how it will provide the cost of the food service ministry. If different charges are to be made on the basis of the organization or activity involved, the policies should identify the differences. In most cases where an outside group is involved, the church should plan to recover all of the costs incurred.

Prepare and Cook Foods

All of the activity relating to food services can be a complete waste of time if the food is not prepared and cooked so that it looks and tastes good. The menu selection must be done on the basis of the amount of time and number of personnel available for cooking. The choice of using prepared foods or cooking from ingredients will also be made on the time and personnel considerations.

When more than one meal is involved, consideration must be given to oven space, refrigerator/freezer space, and utensils available for multiple use. Planning ahead will enable the food service director to be aware of upcoming situations and do some preparing and cooking ahead of time when storage facilities are available.

Cleanup Procedures

Proper and thorough cleanup is a vital part of any food service program. A food service director must be just as concerned for cleaning up and putting items in their proper place as any other part of the operation. Volunteers may be effective in the initial cleanup of the dining area and in bringing the dishes to the dishwashing area, but it will probably be best to pay someone to do the actual washing of dishes, pots, and pans and putting them in the storage areas. Some churches have had good success in employing teenagers for this work. Adequate provisions will need to be made for getting all garbage to the outside storage area until it can be disposed of properly. Nothing should be left out in the dining or kitchen area which might be attractive to rodents and insects.

Special Food Services Programs

In addition to the regular, weekly meals in which the church may be involved, there are a number of special activities the food services ministry may consider. Each of them will have specific concerns which will have to be dealt with if they are to be successful.

Weddings

Most church weddings will have food service needs. The rehearsal dinner may be held at the church, and most likely the wedding reception will be held at the church. The food service director will need to be consulted in these situations unless the church has a separate person who acts as a wedding consultant. Even when this is done, there must be communication about the use of the kitchen and serving equipment.

Receptions

There will be other receptions at the church given to honor staff members or others in the church membership. The church may have a committee which helps to plan such occasions. Careful planning with the food services director is necessary for these events.

Banquets

All kinds of banquets may be conducted at the church. Examples would include leadership banquets, Valentine banquets for youth or adults, deacons banquets, Christmas banquets, Thanksgiving banquets, youth banquets, Sunday School class or department banquets, and the like. Decisions will have to be made about the time, the cost (reservations or tickets), the decorations, the need for extra equipment or supplies, and the type of serving to be done. The food services director should always be willing to work with any group that wants to plan a banquet.

Picnics

Many churches utilize picnics as an informal means of fellowship. Since most of these would be held away from church facilities, careful planning would have to be done by the food services director to accomplish these activities. Decisions would have to be made about securing the site, facilities available at the site, the food to be furnished by the church or the members, the supplies to be provided (including tables and chairs), and the cleanup process.

Conclusion

The food service ministry can be a valuable asset to the work of the church when it is conducted properly. The wise church will secure competent leadership which will plan and conduct the ministry, so it will make a contribution to helping the church achieve its purposes.

Bibliography

Anderton, T. Lee. *Church Property/Building Guidebook.* Nashville: Convention Press, 1980.

Box, Doris. *The Church Kitchen.* Nashville: Broadman Press, 1976.

Brown, Richard and Cook, Melva. *Special Occasion Cookbook.* Nashville: Broadman Press, 1983.

Hatfield, Antoinette. *Food for Fellowship.* Waco: Word Books, 1972.

Hitchcock, Mary J. *Foodservice Systems Administration.* New York: Macmillan Publishing Co., 1980.

Knoll, Anne Powell. *Food Service Management.* New York: McGraw-Hill Book Co., 1976.

Morgan, Sarah. *The Church Supper.* St. Louis: The Bethany Press, 1976.

Myers, Marvin. author/comp. *Managing the Business Affairs of the Church.* Nashville: Convention Press, 1981.

12
Legal Matters
William G. Caldwell

One of the most difficult areas with which the church must relate is that of the law and the legal ramifications of the church and its feelings of immunity or separation from the state. Many churches act out of ignorance or a stance based on the separation idea which says that the church has no dealings with the state. Every minister and every church should become knowledgeable of those basic legal matters which apply to the work of the church. The problem with general statements relating to those matters is the variance of state and local regulations concerning them. A related problem is the continual change in laws and their relationship to churches. This chapter seeks to point out areas of concern without giving legal advice. A qualified, local attorney is the best source of detailed information.

Determining Needs for Legal Advice

Every church will have need for legal advice at some point in its ministry. The need will vary according to the kinds of activities, building programs, and ministries in which the church is involved. A major consideration in this area will involve the ability to know when to seek legal help and the best approach to take when the situation calls for it.

Select an Attorney

A church should seek a reputable, competent attorney who will be sympathetic and understanding of the special legal needs of a church. An attorney who is a member of the congregation may not be the best choice. The need for objectivity in legal matters could be a problem for one who is too closely related to the situation. A church should be willing to pay for the services rendered and not expect discounted or free advice. For a small fee some attorneys will serve on a retainer basis, always ready to provide the service needed.

In selecting an attorney it is wise to check with other churches to discover if they have found one who has helped them. State and local bar associations and legal aid societies may be other sources of information. The specialty of the attorney is important. Most churches will not need a person who specializes in criminal law. The more common areas of need would relate to real estate, contracts, employment, liability, and general family law. The selection process should include an interview to allow the attorney to become familiar with the church, its leadership, and the specific areas of concern relating to legal services. The status of the church as a nonprofit entity would need to be understood by any attorney who would work with a congregation.

The church should feel free to discuss with the attorney the schedule of charges which is used for services rendered. If a retainer fee is to be used, some negotiation of the amount would be in order based on the expected time involvement and the frequency of advice needed. Once a selection has been made, there should be freedom by the church or the attorney to change or terminate the relationship if the need arises.

Situations Requiring Legal Advice

Numerous and rapid changes are taking place in legal matters that may have impact on the local church. At the national level the Internal Revenue Service continues to issue rulings which will affect the church. In addition, tax code changes and tax court decisions make it necessary for the church to keep up with those areas which will affect its work. At the state level, decisions are being made concerning day-care centers and school operations which will affect those churches that offer such services. At the local level the taxation of properties owned by a church continues to be explored. There are also many local ordinances which affect a church in its building program and the operation of church activities. Many of these situations will require the church to secure competent legal advice. Ignorance of the law will not be a valid excuse if the church is guilty of failing to abide by its legal responsibilities.

There are times when the church may be required to go to court to resolve the problem which exists. There are several considerations the church must make when this happens.

1. *Stewardship.*—What is the responsibility of the church from a stewardship standpoint? If a person has attempted to swindle the church, the court may be the only place to deal with the problem. The church must analyze the situation from the perspective of the wise and proper use of its resources.

2. *Safety.*—The responsibility of the church to provide adequate safety precautions is sometimes overlooked and may result in a court case. The church must not hide behind any spiritual excuse when its negligence concerning the safety of its members and guests is involved.

3. *Fraud.*—In the case of a company which has demonstrated outright fraud, the case may have to be settled in court. The church may have a responsibility to keep it from happening to others who might be treated in a similar matter.

4. *Public relations.*—Going to court should always be the last resort. It will be embarrassing and difficult and may have a negative effect on the image of the church in the community.

A change has come from the time when the doctrine of charitable immunity protected the church from lawsuits. More and more, the trend is toward close inspection of all nonprofit institutions—including churches—as to the ways in which they abide by the rules and regulations of society. Churches must set a good example in all those situations where they are required to do certain things—even going beyond the minimum expectations to do more than is required.

Role of Trustees

The work of trustees in a church will vary according to the structure within which the church operates. In most instances they will be the official group to sign papers and otherwise represent the church in legal matters. They thus will act as the agent of the church in transacting business. In some cases the pastor acts as the agent of the church. It is important that the pastor or the trustees know and have evidence of the authority possessed in acting for the church. Entering into a contract outside that authority could result in personal liability for any loss or damage to the church or any outside party. When acting for the church, there must be clear indication of the role of agent on behalf of the church. This will eliminate any personal liability in the case of a dispute. Advice from an attorney can be helpful in this area. The section on incorporation provides additional information regarding this responsibility.

In some organizational structures trustees may perform additional responsibilities for the church. They may act as the Building and Grounds or Maintenance Committee, the Personnel Committee, or serve in functional areas relating to insurance and like matters. In most cases, these structures have been arrived at over a period of time and work well for the church using them.

Resolving Grievances

A church would do well to establish a procedure for dealing with disputes, disagreements, or grievances which are bound to develop in spite of the best of Christian intentions. It is tragic when such disputes make it to the court system to be resolved. Every effort should be made to settle such matters within the framework of the church structure.

A written procedure for this process should include the following ideas.

The immediate supervisor should be the first person involved when an employee has a problem. A written record should be made of the grievance and the attempt to deal with it. Several efforts may have to be made to resolve the issue. If the difficulty cannot be dealt with at this level, then the next level of supervision should be involved. All of the records of the attempts to solve the problem should be reviewed, and additional solutions explored.

If the supervisors cannot develop a satisfactory solution, it is helpful to have some type of a committee (personnel, pastor/parish relations) made up of qualified church members who relate to personnel matters. These persons would be brought into the discussion to give greater insight into possible solutions. In some organizations they would have the final word. In others, the congregation would have to be involved or a denominational group would be called in as arbitrator if the grievance could not be resolved. Every effort should be made to deal with such matters in the church rather than securing an attorney and going to court.

Utilizing Legal Help in Specific Areas

There are a number of specific areas where the church will be wise to secure legal help. The extent of the help needed will be determined by the nature of the situations and the degree to which the state or county has gotten involved in the affairs of the church. Each church will have to determine for itself the extent of the need and the legal advice which may be necessary. A word of caution: this is not the place to hide your head in the sand and pretend that something will go away, especially if you pray hard enough! Issues must be dealt with, and legal help will be necessary in many areas.

Incorporation

A church is not required to become incorporated as a nonprofit religious corporation. Each state has its own regulations concerning the status of a church as a nonprofit organization. The office of the secretary of state is the appropriate place to get information about the incorporation procedure. The procedure will vary if the church is an independent body—a congregational-type church governed solely within itself; or a dependent body—a church governed by a hierarchical form of government, so that the church itself is a member of a larger organization.

The process usually involves the assembling of members for the specific purpose of approving the documents relating to incorporation. These will include the charter stating the name and purpose of the organization; the bylaws which include the powers and responsibilities of the officers, the members' rights and privileges, the meetings of the body and provisions for dissolving the body; and the minutes which will detail the conduct of the meeting which approved the incorporation. All of this information will be filed with the appropriate fee for recording the action. It may be advisable to have an attorney look over the documents to be sure they are in order.

The effect of incorporation is to create a legal entity which the law recognizes for purposes of holding title to real estate, executing contracts, and performing all functions necessary in conducting the civil affairs of the church. It does not take away the spiritual nature or purpose of the church. While the main advantage relates to the insulation from liability for individual members, there are several other advantages to incorporation.

- The church can hold property in its own name.
- It restricts the duplication of the church's name.
- The church has continued life.
- It protects creditors.
- Certain states offer tax benefits.

- It helps the church obtain multirisk insurance.
- The church has a greater opportunity for obtaining loans.
- The church is a separate legal entity.
- It protects church members and trustees.

The advantages of incorporation seem to far outweigh the potential problems of remaining a society in the eyes of the state. The advice of an attorney will be helpful in determining the proper procedure to follow for a local church.

Liability

The church and the minister are not immune from responsibility for their actions because they are in the religion business. There is a responsibility which extends to anyone who is related to the activities of the church in terms of their care and protection. A church may be called upon to provide compensation for anyone—members, visitors, employees, or others outside the church—when its negligence results in any loss or damage. The act of negligence may result from the doing or not doing of something that a reasonable person would do or not do in a similar situation. The interpretation of what is reasonable has varied from state to state and usually is decided by a judge or jury when the question of negligence reaches the courtroom. The church should make every effort to keep from being negligent as well as to provide adequate insurance coverage for protection from unforeseen situations. The provision of *workers compensation* insurance coverage for employees and *public liability* insurance coverage for property and vehicles in significant amounts should be made.

The minister as a professional also has concerns about the proper performance of responsibilities. This is evident in those acts as an agent of the church but also in those acts as a professional person, particularly in the area of counseling. The subject of "malpractice" by a minister is becoming one of legal significance. This is due to vague interpretations of a minister's liability when advice given a counselee leads to harmful results. Again, the negligence question is open to interpretation but has become the object of suits which have been filed.

Related to this concern is that of privileged communications between a minister and a counselee. The state statues vary as to the extent to which a minister could be required to testify concerning such communications. The main difference in some states is the conducting of formal counseling sessions as opposed to informal conversations. The minister should consider the type of counseling which is done and be extremely cautious in directing a person to do something. If the concerns in this area continue, it would be wise to secure minister's malpractice insurance to protect against damages which may result from court decisions.

Taxation

The subject of taxation of churches is extremely complicated and open to various interpretations. The idea that a church is tax exempt does not remove the responsibility the church has for filing certain forms and for paying some taxes. It is further complicated by the differing requirements of federal, state, and local laws relating to churches.

1. *Federal taxes.*—A church is usually automatically exempt from federal taxes because it is a church. Other religious organizations must request exemption from taxes and the right to receive tax deductible contributions as a religious organization defined in Section 501(c)(3) of the Internal Revenue Code. (A church should have a copy of this section and the related publication on applying for exempt status.) The Internal Revenue Service uses several characteristics to determine if a church qualifies for exemption. Among these are the following.

- A legal existence
- A formal code of doctrine
- A membership not associated with another church
- An established place of worship
- Regular religious services
- An ordained ministry
- Schools for training ministers

A church may have activities which are not separately incorporated and are therefore recognized as units of the church. It may also have separately incorporated activities which are controlled by the church and are therefore recognized as an integrated auxiliary of the church. A federal identification number is issued for the church to use in filing forms or other documents with the government.

2. *State taxes.*—In most states, churches are exempt from paying the state sales tax on items purchased for use by the church. A tax exempt number is required in some states while others simply recognize the name of the church for exemption. The property tax

code will also vary from state to state in terms of what is or is not exempt as church property. A church should investigate what its tax responsibilities are in the state where it is located.

3. *Local taxes.*—The same variance in taxation exists at the local level. Local sales taxes and local property taxes are levied against churches in some communities. A church should not assume that all of its properties and purchases are tax exempt but should investigate what is required and what process must be followed to obtain exemptions when they are allowed. In recent years many local authorities have attempted to levy taxes on parking lots, parsonages, excessive land, and other church property in an effort to broaden the tax base in a local community.

4. *Employment taxes.*—A church is responsible like any other employer to withhold taxes from an employee's wages and to pay those taxes along with some the church must pay to the proper authority.

Income taxes (including state and local where applicable) must be withheld from all employees according to the tax guides provided. The exception to all employees applies to the ordained minister (and to the licensed or commissioned minister who performs substantially the same functions as the ordained minister) who is considered self-employed and files quarterly returns along with the payment of the self-employed rate of Social Security taxes.

A newly ordained minister within the second year of ordination may file a request for an exemption (which is irrevocable) from Social Security coverage on religious grounds. The opposition must be by reason of conscience or religious principles to acceptance of Social Security benefits (or other public insurance) for services as a minister. Economic considerations for opposition are not valid. (The church may withhold amounts from salary for these taxes at the request of the minister.) All other employees, whether paid by the hour, day, week, piecework, or percentage are included. In addition, the church must file a form on independent contractors who are paid more than $600 during a calendar year for services rendered.

The church must keep appropriate records and file the proper forms with the employee and the taxing agencies as instructed. The most recent ruling on Social Security taxes requires the church to withhold the stated amount from all employee's wages and to match that amount from church funds when making the quarterly payments. Failure to do so can result in tax liens and penalties for failure to comply with the regulations. A church should consult with the state to determine if other wage and hour laws apply to the church.

5. *Unrelated-business income taxes.*—A church may be subject to taxes based on business income which is not directly related to the work of the church or which the church receives from debt-financed property. A church should carefully examine its receipts in these areas and determine if it should file the proper forms for reporting such income and pay the appropriate taxes required.

6. *Federal excise tax.*—In certain cases a church may be exempt from paying the federal excise tax which is levied on certain items purchased. This is especially true for church-related schools. The proper form should be secured and filed for the exemption.

7. *Unemployment tax.*—A church is usually exempt from federal and state unemployment taxes. An investigation should be made with state authorities to discover the requirement in each state. A church may be permitted to participate voluntarily in these programs in some states.

Employment Practices

A church should establish policies relating to the employment of personnel, so it will not be guilty of inconsistency in hiring practices. Even though churches are not required to follow the government mandated policies regarding equal opportunity employment, every effort should be made to assure a nondiscriminatory approach in employment. A church may want to employ only church members, but that should be a consistent policy and not an excuse used only when it is convenient to keep from hiring someone. A lack of consistency in hiring practices could result in a discrimination suit being filed against the church.

It is also wise to be cautious in case it becomes necessary to terminate an employee. A supervisor should carefully record any action taken to reprimand an employee and document the effort made to improve performance. This documented record should be placed in the employee's personnel file. It is helpful if the record also includes a signed statement by the employee acknowledging the agreement to improve performance. If repeated attempts to rectify the inadequate performance are not successful and termination becomes necessary, the records will provide sufficient information to indicate that the church was justified in its action. If a church does not follow such a process, there is a good possibility that an employee would have legal grounds for a lawsuit.

Wills and Estates

The whole matter of wills and estates represents a significant area of legal concern for the church and the Christian interested in the total concept of stewardship. The advice of those trained in the field is essential for good planning because of the complex nature of government rules and state laws regulating the disposition of an estate. Many churches have a special committee to promote the concept of making a will or establishing a trust as an act of Christian stewardship. Some churches are fortunate enough to have attorneys, bankers, or accountants who can assist church members in this area.

The advantages of estate planning must be shared with the congregation. The need to put things in order should be evident to the Christian. The desire to protect one's assets in the way an estate is settled should be of major concern. Good planning will minimize the effect of taxes and other administrative costs relating to settling the estate as well as provide for the efficient and timely distribution of property.

The making of a will is essential to the completion of estate planning. Without a will, state laws specify who benefits from the estate. By making a will, the *individual* specifies who is to benefit. The assistance of an attorney is not required, but it is highly recommended. The complexity of legal terminology is such that a person may not say what needs to be said unless an attorney assists with the preparation of the will. A church can and should encourage the inclusion of Christian causes in making a will so that a person who has supported the church while living can reflect that support in the disposition of the assets of the estate. Since a will can be changed anytime prior to the death of the person, it should be reviewed and updated as changes in circumstances should dictate.

General Family Law

There are several areas of legal responsibility which the church will not face directly but may be called upon to deal with because of the involvement of church members in these matters. The church that has a day school or child-care program will more than likely have to make some decisions concerning policies it will follow in its responsibility to children enrolled.

Perhaps the most common area of concern is that of family violence. This includes spouse abuse as well as child abuse. Many churches and ministers are being faced with counseling decisions as well as legal decisions relating to the reporting of such activities. Many states and communities now have laws concerning the responsibility of school officials to notify the proper authorities when there is obvious evidence of child abuse. The very nature of the work of the church which involves visits into the homes of members and prospective members may result in the discovery of situations where abuse is apparent and must be dealt with. Some of the legal implications of these situations may call for the advice of an attorney.

The increasing occurrence of divorce has created many cases of spousal and child support which may cause difficulties for the church. Since religion is such a vital part of life, some have charged that church involvement has been the cause of alienation and separation. Wise counseling is necessary in such situations. Several well-publicized cases have presented the need for schools and child-care programs to be extremely cautious in their policies concerning the release of children to relatives or others who may not have the legal right to take the child. Temporary or permanent restraining orders may have been issued by the court which the church will be involved in enforcing. A church cannot ignore its responsibilities in this area if it desires to be effective in its ministry to the community.

There may be other areas of family responsibility that will affect a church in its work. There have been situations in which court-ordered counseling has been related to the church. The activity of child adoption may involve a minister with families in the church. The problem of court-directed grandparent access may affect the church. It is not necessary that a church or its ministers become experts in these family matters as they relate to legal requirements. It is necessary that a church and its ministers realize that all of these situations can and do affect the work of the church and that legal advice be sought when it is needed.

Contracts

One of the most obvious areas in which legal advice is helpful and necessary is that of making and keeping contracts. A church will have many situations when the services of an attorney will be needed to draw up, interpret, or evaluate a contract. Since a contract represents a legally binding agreement between two or more parties, it is essential that the document be accurate, clearly understood, and prepared according to legal requirements. This is necessary for the protection of the church as well as for the other parties involved.

As discussed earlier, the church acts through its authorized agent to enter into a contract. In most cases this agent would be the trustees who have been given the authority to act on behalf of the church. The trustees can only act within the authority given and cannot bind the church to contracts which have not been approved. A pastor or other minister of the church should not assume the role of agent for the church in matters of contract. If this is done outside the minister's authority, personal liability may result.

Legal advice is necessary when any real estate purchase is anticipated. In many cases it is helpful to have an attorney who specializes in real estate law. It is never wise to "do it yourself" no matter how well meaning church members may be. The need for a title search to assure a clear title to the property, the need to examine the contract to be sure it says what it should, the need to draw up a deed that provides protection for the church, and the need to properly identify any restrictions which may apply—all point to the necessity for legal advice in real estate transactions.

Other contracts which involve major purchases or agreements lasting for more than one year should also be evaluated by an attorney. Any transaction involving an executor or agreements requiring the church to guarantee something should likewise be evaluated. Any expense the church may have to bear for these services may well be savings in the long run if it protects the church from faulty contracts or agreements.

Copyrights

There is no excuse for a church or its ministers to be ignorant of the copyright law and its application to the work of the church. A copy of the current law and forms for application for copyright registration may be obtained free of charge by writing to the Copyright Office, Library of Congress, Washington, DC 20559. The new statute which became effective on January 1, 1978, made some significant changes in the copyright system. A church is required to follow the law in its use of material belonging to other persons.

One of the first things any church should do is to go through files of educational and music materials and dispose of all copied materials which were made without permission. This would provide a good example for church members as well as remove the church from any illegal activity in this area. As the church becomes familiar with the law, it will know what practices it should follow in using copyrighted material.

Generally speaking, the church should not make copies of any material when doing so would affect the sales of those materials. Exceptions are allowed for the purposes of criticism, comment, news reporting, teaching (including copies for classroom use), or for research purposes. Copyrighted musical works are also covered, but exemptions are allowed for certain types of nonprofit use. When in doubt, it is usually wise and very simple to request permission for use from the copyright holder. One area where churches should be very careful is in the reprinting of material from the church paper or bulletin of some other church. Even if the other church had received permission to use the material, it would not be right for another church to use it.

Conclusion

There are many circumstances in the life and work of the church in which legal advice is necessary. The wise church will secure an attorney and seek help when it is needed. The cost involved may be well worth the damages and court costs avoided or the public image preserved if proper legal procedures are not followed.

Bibliography

Buzzard, Lynn R. and Ericcson, Samuel. *The Battle for Religious Liberty.* Elgin, Ill.: David C. Cook, 1982.

Foshee, Howard B. *Broadman Church Manual.* Nashville: Broadman Press, 1973.

Hammar, Richard R. *Pastor, Church and Law.* Springfield, Mo.: Gospel Publishing House, 1983.

Hopkins, Bruce R. *The Law of Tax-Exempt Organizations.* New York: Ronald Press, 1979.

Myers, Marvin. author/comp. *Managing the Business Affairs of the Church.* Nashville: Convention Press, 1981.

Schmidt, Richard F. *Legal Aspects of Church Management.* Los Angeles: Financial Executives of Christian Organizations, 1980.

13

Establishing a Mission/ Starting New Work

Bob I. Johnson

The idea of new work produces many images in the minds of concerned Christians. The image of a new congregation rising out of the dreams and aspirations of concerned church members is the first example that may appear. New work images may also take the shape of satellite programs, special target groups of persons, and new units of work similar to or exactly like what the church has already been doing. In one sense, new work can be anything from beginning a Sunday School class for a group not currently being served to the establishment of a new mission-type congregation.

The emphasis in this chapter will fall more on new congregation-type ministries; however, one should remember that beginning any new or additional ministry places new demands on a church. Both involve giving up something and gaining something since a new situation is created.

What a New Work Allows

New work allows a church to align itself with a stream of others who have through vision and purpose established new work in their communities and around the world. It helps a church to carry out the command of Christ as found in Matthew 28:18-20, commonly called the Great Commission.

New work allows a church to have a part in formation of new communities or new groupings of persons within communities. New work allows the church to experiment with alternative models of congregational style and to recognize the diversity in the new institutions which may distinguish them from the sponsoring church or churches. Participating in the development of new work can also help to eliminate racism and traditionalism among the mother congregation. It also allows, and forces in some cases, the

243

sponsoring group to relate to other churches within its denomination and even to churches in other denominations.

The creation of new work offers the church a fresh and challenging opportunity to express its own Christian faith. It forces the church to rethink its theology and its purpose and to provide models for Christian service and ministry. It forces the church to reach out in evangelistic efforts toward persons hitherto unreached by this particular congregation. In short, it allows the church to make faith a verb.

The Prebirth of New Work

The hopes for good results from many worthwhile projects often turn to frustration due to hasty preparation and decision making by the church. While some ideas can germinate quickly and find ready acceptance within a congregation, the case generally is that a congregation needs time to mull over significant decisions. People must raise all possible objections and then move together through a studied decision. New work falls into this kind of category. Following are several suggestions for prebirth activities for a church considering new work.

1. *Determine the mind-set and readiness for new work of the congregation.* What things are important to the congregation? What things are given emphasis in the worship services and in the printed materials published by the church? Does the church have a status quo mentality, does the church have fellowship problems within, or is the fellowship basically strong and healthy? Sometimes, if negative factors are present to a fairly mild degree, challenging the group to undertake new work can serve as an antidote in the situation. This is where leadership needs to possess and exercise good diagnostic skills. To push a church to sponsor new work while it has serious, unresolved internal problems may serve only to exaggerate those problems, causing them to fester and worsen.

2. *Determine the true mission interest of the church.* The church may be a heavy contributor to mission offerings and to the denominational plan of cooperative giving; still, the people may not have the real interest to pay the price in time and money to establish a new work on sound footing. Use formal and informal ways to survey the interest and willingness of church members in becoming new spiritual parents.

3. *Get the congregation to verbalize its story and see the reason for establishing*

new work. Often church members are not aware of the verbal and nonverbal cues they are communicating. Perhaps persons who have been members for a longer time and those who have been members a shorter time are not quite sure how to relate to each other in sharing their dreams and aspirations for the congregation.

One example of overcoming this problem is to sponsor one or more informal dialogues among various groups in the church. Perhaps at a Sunday night fellowship the longer-termed members can talk about what it was like in the past, the sacrifices the founders and supporters through the years had to make, and what they need from the church and are willing to contribute to and through the church. Newer members could be encouraged to express those things which have benefitted them in the past in other churches where they have been members, what they bring in their gifts and attitudes, and what they are willing to commit of themselves to this present congregation. Summarize some of the history of the church and point out the story the church has been telling the community by both its verbal and nonverbal expressions.

Point out how the church was begun and suggest that the church may have come to a time when it needs to consider expressing itself in new and different ways.

At an appropriate point explain to the congregation that new work is being considered informally. If possible, point out the specific needs which have given rise to the possibility of new work. Allow questions and seek to have as much information as possible to give people. Do not make commitments before the church is ready to move deliberately.

Providing a Healthy Birth

After working through informal discussions and study with the congregation, review all the factors with the Church Council or, if the church has one, the Missions Committee. When there is a strong conviction of God's leadership among the congregation and within the council/committee, draft a formal recommendation that the church proceed to establish new work. Promote this recommendation and advise that it will be considered at a specified church business meeting. At this meeting the church should formally adopt a proposal to sponsor new work and approve procedures to guide the development.

The following steps might be presented as guidelines.[1]

1. *Elect a Mission Committee specifically for the new work.* This may be a new committee, or it could be an ongoing Church Missions Committee. Regardless, this group requires a mandate from the congregation to give positive and enthusiastic leadership to the implementation of the mission project.

Elect five to seven people who are spiritually mature, positive toward mission outreach, concerned about people, able to relate well with people who may be different, and who are able to analyze situations and make good decisions. Above all, they must be warm-hearted, loving people who by faith can see possibilities and act when others may be immobilized.

If possible, have representatives who can give special assistance related to church educational organizations, worship services, and outreach activities. The most competent, mission-minded layperson should chair the committee. The pastor should, of course, be an ex officio member.

Upon election, the committee should schedule a work session with the director of associational missions or of regional/state missions. During this session, the committee will be briefed on their duties and receive information concerning possibilities for new work.

2. *Select the geographic area of mission need.* Determine the general area in consultation with the director of missions and/or the associational/regional/state missions committee. Gather data to pinpoint specific possibilities for location and/or types of work. From the research, select one or more specific target groups of persons to be reached by the new work.

3. *Prepare the church for the new work.* Develop a strong motivational climate for the new work by sharing information, discussing possibilities, and describing needs that the church will be able to meet. Inform the congregation about the location and type(s) of work that will be developed. Study ways to use gifts of the sponsoring group to energize people in the target area. Begin recruiting volunteers who can assist with surveys, Bible studies, home visitation, worship, and fellowship activities.

4. *Cultivate the mission field.* Take a community survey to locate the unchurched and the unaffiliated persons of your denomination. Using resources from your denominational missions director, determine who the primary prospects are, where they are located, and

possible strategies for establishing a trusting relationship with them.

Be alert to every opportunity for exposure and ministry. Choir concerts, fellowship Bible classes, home visitation, recreational projects, and tutoring classes are some possibilities.

5. *Begin a fellowship group.* This is the first step toward establishing an ongoing mission point. After relationships have been developed and some local support is apparent, the Mission Committee will determine the best location and target persons with whom to begin a home/office/storefront fellowship mission and/or a fellowship Bible class.

One of the laypersons should be in charge and facilitate a cooperative plan of inreach and outreach for volunteers from the sponsoring church and local participants. They would come together for fellowship, worship, Bible study, prayer, support, and planning. They would reach out into the community to identify and enlist prospects who are unchurched.

When the group is too large for one home/location, divide into two groups that can meet in different parts of the target area. When at least four such fellowship groups are functioning, a good nucleus for a congregation is underway.

Periodic rallies of the fellowship groups should start when there are three or four groups. At first, about once a month would be adequate. Work on building fellowship, enthusiasm, and motivation for taking the message of Christ to others.

6. *Start a mission chapel.* If and when the new work is large enough and the expressed need for a central location is strong enough, begin plans for a mission chapel. You might begin with a Bible study and worship service each week at a central location, as well as continue the fellowship groups as a means of growth and community ministry.

Consider using public facilities such as a school building or community meeting hall. Other possibilities are motel conference rooms, a recreation room in someone's home, a vacant store, or even a mobile home.

Before the chapel is established, relationships with the sponsoring church must be carefully defined. Clarify finances, membership, ordinances, calling of a mission pastor, and other pertinent issues. For sample guidelines, see Figure 1, "The Church's Relation to Its Mission," at the end of the chapter.

Other items to be completed before beginning include the following.

- Enlist and train leaders for the mission chapel.
- Secure location and gain approval from the church and any other agencies that may be required.
- Publicize the chapel and encourage participation at the first service.
- Mobilize fellowship groups to prepare the location and promote participation.
- Secure needed equipment and supplies. Put out a sign if permissible.

7. *Determine the financial plan for the chapel.* If not determined earlier, specific procedures should be established to handle aid from the mother church, contributions from chapel participants, and the expenditure of funds by the chapel leaders. Financial aid should be limited, with a phaseout planned from the beginning. Stewardship education should become a part of chapel activities as persons are prepared to assume the right and responsibility to determine their own future.

As the mission chapel develops toward maturity, the election of a chapel treasurer and the transfer of funds to the chapel treasury may be a good training step toward constituting the new church.

Another step toward self-direction comes as the chapel considers calling a full-time pastor to replace the interim provided by the sponsoring church. The usual guideline is that a mission congregation should delay calling someone until at least 50 percent of the pastor's support can be provided from chapel offerings.

8. *Develop building plans.* When the mission has sufficient strength and stability to take on this task—and when their growth and ministry require it—the selection of a permanent location begins. Once again, the director of missions is a key helper as well as those persons in the mother congregation who are providing ongoing support.

Much time should be devoted to a study of options, raising of funds, and motivation of mission participants. A modest, attractive, and complete first unit is the goal rather than a large facility designed to hold several times the present number.[2]

9. *Constitute the church.* The Mission Committee of the mother church should be convinced that the mission group is fully commit-

ted to the mission of Christ's church and the responsibilities of a local church for carrying out that mission in the world.

When all concerned are sure that the mission congregation is spiritually mature and sufficiently stable to become a self-governing church, a date can be set to incorporate the new church.

The preparation of a church constitution and bylaws is most important and should be done two or three months before constituting.[3]

The constituting service is held in cooperation with the sponsoring church, sister churches in the area, and the director of associational/state missions. An organizing council is formed of representatives invited from sister churches. This group meets prior to the service, examines the group's request, and recommends at the appropriate time in the service that the mission be constituted into a church. A sample outline of such a service, a format for a church constitution and bylaws, and an example of a church covenant appear at the end of this chapter (Figures 2-5).

Working for Effectiveness

The emphasis on church growth has naturally reminded many people of numerical growth. Numerical growth is important; however, effectiveness is more important. Many people are writing on what makes an effective church. The new work should especially pay attention to the research and to the findings to aid the overall health of its existence. New churches can instill principles of effectiveness perhaps more easily than can older congregations. Kennon Callahan has distilled from his research twelve keys to effectiveness.[4] They are: (1) specific, concrete missional objectives; (2) pastoral and lay visitation; (3) corporate, dynamic worship; (4) significant relational groups; (5) strong leadership resources; (6) streamlined structure and solid, participatory decision making; (7) several competent programs and activities; (8) open accessibility; (9) high visibility; (10) adequate parking, land, and landscaping; (11) adequate space in facilities; and (12) solid financial resources. To be effective, a church does not have to have all twelve of these characteristics; it should have almost all of them, however.

The new congregation and certainly the pastor would do well to study Robert Dale's book *To Dream Again* during the first year's existence of the new work. There the church could learn before it ever experiences the life cycle of a church.

An effective new church will certainly be marked by an intentional ministry. The new congregation will understand what it is supposed to do and how it will go about fulfilling its purpose. As a Christian community of persons, the group will be careful that all its activities contribute to the primary task of the church. The effective congregation will operate through a planning process that includes goals and strategies that can be evaluated in terms of its purpose reflected in the New Testament. The effective congregation will institute a plan of evaluating its ministry and its opportunities.

Winning and discipling new members will be important to the effective church in its early years. Time should also be given to the effective assimilation of new members into the congregation so that the church can be one in which all members have a part and a stake in its success.

The church should be helped to have a clear image of itself which manifests itself in a specific way in its community. The church will know what it is about and each member will be able to express and defend that purpose. The effective church should work to have the strength to face the future in which surprise, excitement, and expectation can be incorporated into its life.

Figure 1

The Church's Relation to Its Mission

It is important that a good relationship be maintained between the church and its mission, and this does not just happen. It must be worked for: the lines of communication must always be open.

Communications between the church and the mission will be easier and more effective if they are carried on through the Church Missions Committee representing the whole church and a group, preferably the mission's steering committee. Thus, better understandings will be developed before matters are communicated to the congregations of the church and the mission. Each will receive its communications through its own representatives who can present them in the light of the viewpoints of its people.

In reality, the mission *is* the church. It is simply the church meeting in a different place or satisfying a special need: it is the church, extended.

1. Relationship

An understanding of the relationship between the church and its mission can be stated in an agreement or bylaws.

(1) The mission and the church should agree on the pastor of the mission.

(2) The mission pastor should be a member of the sponsoring church.

(3) Evangelists for mission revivals should be agreed on by the mission pastor and the pastor of the church.

2. Church Membership

All persons who qualify for church membership should be urged to join the sponsoring church. Mission members can be received:

(1) By baptism

After profession of faith and request for baptism at a mission service, the person's name will be submitted to the sponsoring church for vote. Baptism is administered by someone authorized by the church.

(2) By letter

After a request for membership at a mission service, the person's name will be given to the church for vote and for obtaining the church letter.

(3) By statement

After a request to be accepted by statement at a mission service, the person's name and statement will be presented to the church.

3. Business

The mission meets for business only to recommend items of business to the sponsoring church for its consideration. All items shall be offered at least one week before the church's monthly meeting. (Items which are considered emergencies may be presented anytime.)

(1) A written report of the mission should be made to the sponsoring church at the monthly business meeting. The report is to be presented by the church Missions Committee.

(2) The church Missions Committee and the mission nominate officers and teachers and present their names to the church for approval.

(3) The observance of the church ordinances—baptism and the Lord's Supper—should be held according to plans approved by the sponsoring church.

(4) The mission should give complaints and correspondence to the church Missions Committee.

4. Tithes and Offerings

(1) All tithes and offerings from the mission should be kept in a separate fund and handled according to the plan designated by the sponsoring church. The use of the mission fund shall be subject to the approval of the church. The mission fund shall be used for the mission. When the mission is constituted into a church, all funds become the property of the new church.

(2) The mission is urged both to give a definite percent of its tithes and offerings through the Cooperative Program and to plan to increase this percent in future years.

(3) The mission should consider giving a proper percentage of its receipts to the associational mission program.

(4) Checks shall be signed and bills paid by the one authorized and in the way designated by the church. All checks written and all bills paid shall be reported and approved each month in the regular business meeting of the church.

(5) The mission should use the Bible and denominational curriculum materials.

(6) When both the sponsoring church and the mission feel that the mission is strong enough to organize into a New Testament church, they should express this desire to the church Missions Committee. The Missions Committee should present this to the church for action. Plans should be made for the service.

(7) The sponsoring church should do all it can for the mission to enable it to do all it should for God. Prayer for the mission is essential. The mission should pray for, love, respect, and cooperate with the church for the mutual blessings of both.

5. Property

Property owned by the sponsoring church may be sold or transferred at the discretion of the church. It is suggested that when a mission is ready to constitute as a church, that deeds be in order so that property may be transferred without delay.

Figure 2

Constituting a New Church

1. How to Constitute

(1) A church Missions Committee, after counsel with the pastor of the sponsoring church and with the mission, recommends to the sponsoring church that the mission should be constituted into a church.

(2) The mission and sponsoring church can receive much aid from other Baptist churches when the mission is ready to be constituted. These steps have been used.

   a. Set date to constitute.
   b. Inform and seek assistance from associational missions committee and director of associational missions.
   c. Invite neighboring Baptist churches to send representatives to form a council. Invite state director of missions.
   d. Form a council at the meeting to constitute the mission into a church by choosing a moderator and clerk. This meeting can be held before the mass meeting.
   e. Council hears reasons for the church's being constituted.

2. Service of Constitution

(1) Devotional

   Hymn: "The Church's One Foundation"

   Scripture: Matthew 16:18-19; Acts 2:41-42; 1 Corinthians 12:27; Ephesians 4:11-13; Colossians 1:18

   Prayer

(2) The report of the council. The council recommends to proceed with the constituting of the mission into a Baptist church.

(3) Recommendation from the sponsoring church is read and approved by the mission congregation. The adoption of this recommendation formally constitutes the new church (see Figure 3).
(4) Election of the officers and committees of the new church.
   a. The moderator of the council may serve as temporary moderator for the further proceedings.
   b. He should at this time hear the report of the previously appointed nominating committee. The names of church officers and committees may be presented for election.
   c. A pastor should be called according to the plan previously adopted.
(5) If it is advisable to give the new church title to the church property, the transfer should be presented.
(6) Incorporation is desirable and should be acted on at this time.
(7) If the new church desires a constitution and bylaws (see Figure 4 for a work sheet), a committee should be appointed to draft them.
(8) Worship service
   Hymn: "To God Be the Glory"
   Offering
   Sermon: The message should include a charge to the pastor and the people. The universal scope and cooperative privileges should be emphasized.
   Invitation for charter members
   Reception of charter members
   Benediction
   Charter members are greeted and commended on their new beginning by members of the council and visitors.

A new Baptist church should petition the association at its next annual meeting for fellowship. Some associations provide petitionary letters to be received by the association's executive board at any time in the year subject to the approval of the association. The proper preparation and service for the constituting of a new church can mean much to the new fellowship in its getting a good start and in its future ministry.

Figure 3

Recommendation for Constitution

(The sponsoring church submits for adoption by the new church a recommendation prepared in advance. The following format will serve as a guide.)

Whereas we believe that there is a need for a _____church in this community, and *whereas* we believe we have found God's divine guidance after prayer;

Whereas we have consulted with fellow Christians and neighboring churches, and *whereas* we have called a council to consider this matter and the council has recommended we proceed with the constituting of the new church;

Be it therefore resolved that we do now enter upon the organization of a new _____ church under the direction of the council composed of the members:

_____   _____
_____   _____
_____   _____

representing these churches:

_____   _____
_____   _____
_____   _____

Be it further resolved that we adopt this as our church covenant:
(The covenant should be included in the resolution.)
Be it further resolved that we adopt the following articles of faith:
(to be inserted)
Be it resolved that our name shall be the:
(to be inserted)
Be it further resolved that these resolutions be signed by all charter members and that this document be preserved with the official church records.
Be it further resolved that this church cooperate with these denominational bodies:
(to be inserted)
Be it further resolved that our gratitude is hereby expressed to the sponsoring church and to God for His divine guidance.
Witnesses on this date:
(Space for signatures of charter members may be provided here.)

Figure 4

Sample Format for Constitution and Bylaws

Constitution

A constitution reflects the basic truths and accepted patterns of interaction among members of an organization. Statements regarding the following items are usually included:

1. Preamble

    "We declare and establish this constitution to preserve and secure the principles of our faith, and to govern the body in an orderly manner. This constitution will . . ."

2. Name

    "This body shall be known as the

    _____, located at

    _____.

3. Purpose (Objectives)

    (a listing of timeless statements of intention)

4. Statement of Faith

5. Polity and Relationships

Bylaws

These are written guidelines agreed upon by members to direct the activity of the organization. Such statements focus on procedures to be followed and, as such, are more susceptible to modification as needs change than are statements in the constitution.

Bylaws are designed to assist the organization in fulfilling its purpose. Items often included are statements regarding:

1. Membership
2. Organizational Structures/Programs of Work
3. Officers
4. Committees
5. Meetings/Special Observances
6. Finances/Organization Operations Manual
7. Amendments (how to make changes in the constitution and bylaws)

Figure 5

Church Covenant

Since we have committed ourselves to Jesus Christ and have experienced the acceptance, forgiveness, and redemption of God our Father, we covenant together as members of this church that with God's help through the guiding presence of His Spirit:

We will walk together in brotherly love.

We will show loving care for one another and encourage, counsel, and admonish one another.

We will assemble faithfully for worship and fellowship, and will pray earnestly for others as well as for ourselves.

We will endeavor to bring up those under our care "in the nurture and admonition of the Lord."

We will seek, by Christian example and personal effort, to win others to Christ and to encourage their growth toward Christian maturity.

We will share one another's joys and endeavor to bear one another's burdens and sorrows.

We will oppose all conduct which compromises our Christian faith and will uphold high standards of Christian morality.

We will prove the reality of our conversion by living godly, fruitful lives.

We will maintain a faithful ministry of worship, witness, education, fellowship, and service.

We will be faithful stewards of our resources and abilities in sharing the gospel with people of all nations.

As a result of this covenant relationship, we will seek earnestly to live to the glory of God who brought us out of darkness into His marvelous light.*

Church covenant of the Immanuel Baptist Church, Nashville, Tennessee

Notes

1. Information in this section is adapted from an uncopyrighted "Guide for Establishing New Churches" published by the Home Mission Board, 1350 Spring Street, NW, Atlanta, Ga. 30309.

2. Information on small church facilities and architectural services is available from the Church Architecture Department, 127 Ninth Avenue, North, Nashville, Tenn. 37234.

3. A helpful booklet that describes the process and gives a sample constitution and bylaws is "The Church Constitution and Bylaws Committee" available from Materials Services Department, 127 Ninth Avenue, North; Nashville, Tenn. 37234. You can also request assistance from your associational director of missions or your denominational office.

4. Kennon L. Callahan, *Twelve Keys to an Effective Church* (New York: Harper and Row), 1983.

Bibliography

Callahan, Kennon L. *Twelve Keys to an Effective Church.* New York: Harper and Row, 1983.

Dale, Robert D. *To Dream Again.* Nashville: Broadman Press, 1981.

McDonough, Reginald. M., comp. *A Church on Mission.* Nashville: Convention Press, 1980.

Redford, F. J. "Guide for Establishing New Churches," an uncopyrighted booklet. Atlanta: Home Mission Board of the Southern Baptist Convention.

Smith, Ebbie C. *Balanced Church Growth.* Nashville: Broadman Press, 1984.

14

Administration in a Small Church

Mark Short

Lyle E. Schaller has written an interesting book entitled *The Small Church Is Different.*[1] In his premise he draws some conclusions as to the differences noted in large and small churches. These differences center around people, fellowship, and mission. Our culture seems to worship bigness and success, often to the detriment of the fellowship. When the small church senses its mission and uniqueness, it will not try to force the program of the large church onto its smaller membership.

A pastor of a small church recently told of the blessings that came from the smaller fellowship. His testimony reflected how God had led him to a rare treasure—the intimacy of the little flock. This pastor made this cogent statement: "It is fulfilling and enriching to minister to the few, while at the same time refusing to be content with remaining small."[2]

In addition to the thousands of pastors serving full-time in smaller churches, there are many others who carry the title of "Bivocational Pastor." Dual-role ministry has been around since the apostle Paul. These pastors generally preach, lead, and minister in their churches during the hours they are away from their full-time secular jobs. In some states as many as one fourth of the churches are staffed by bivocational pastors. Their ministry is especially taxing due to the fragmentation of their responsibilities. There will continue to be a growing need for bivocational pastors as new churches are begun. John Y. Elliott wrote, "The recent surge of interest in dual role ministry is evident in almost every Christian denomination in the United States."[3]

Regardless of the status of the small-church pastor—bivocational or full-time—there can be great satisfaction in giving leadership to a New Testament church. Joining with thousands of others in similar circumstances, each pastor of a small church is involved in the same overarching objective as every other pastor and church, regardless of size. Leaders can effectively guide their churches in fulfilling their appropriate portion of God's work where they are with the resources God has provided.

Organize to Meet the Objective of the Church

An organization is a social system of relating people to each other to accomplish the goals of that organization. The small church will organize itself in such a way as to reach the objective of winning people to Jesus and nurturing the believers. Two suggested plans of organization are listed to meet the needs of churches with fewer than 300 members (see Figure 1).

Committee Structure for the Small Church

The small church should exercise care to keep the organization from becoming cumbersome with too many committees. A small church in Louisiana with only thirty-eight members recently reported that it had eighteen regular church committees! The organization had become so overpowered with committees that it could no longer function effectively.

Personnel should be carefully chosen to staff the committees. People who are willing to work, have aptitudes in the areas of need, and understand the task should be selected to serve. The smallest church can have a committee training time in preparation for the new year of work. Committee task descriptions should be interpreted to committee members.

You will need at least three key committees to care for the crucial functions of recruiting volunteer teachers and leaders, managing church property, and handling church finances.[4]

Nominating Committee

The basic responsibility of the church Nominating Committee is to locate, screen, and recommend to the church qualified persons to fill all church-elected positions requiring volunteer leaders.

The duties of the Nominating Committee are:

1. Locate, interview, screen, and recommend qualified persons for all church positions requiring volunteers (church program organization leaders, church service program leaders, church committee members, and general church officers).

Figure 1

Organizational Possibilities

Suggested Unit	Churches with fewer than 100*	Churches from 100-300
STAFF	Pastor: Full-time or Bivocational Music Director: Part-time or Volunteer	Pastor Music Director Part-time Secretary Part-time Custodian Part-time
DEACONS	1 Deacon per 15 family units	1 Deacon per 15 family units
CHURCH OFFICERS	Trustees, Clerk, Treasurer	Trustees, Clerk, Treasurer
CHURCH COMMITTEES	Nominating, Stewardship, Property	Nominating, Stewardship, Property
SUPPORT SERVICES	Media Services Director	Media Services Director
PLANNING IMPLEMENTING, EVALUATING	Church Council	Church Council
SUNDAY SCHOOL	Classes for each age group	Departments for each age group
CHURCH TRAINING	Member training for each age group	Member training for each age group
BROTHERHOOD	Brotherhood Director	Brotherhood Director Baptist Men, Royal Ambassadors
WOMAN'S MISSIONARY UNION	WMU Director	WMU Director Age level Organizations
MUSIC MINISTRY	Music Director, Pianist, Choir	Music Director, Pianist, Choirs

*Resident Members

2. Counsel with church leaders regarding need for volunteer workers and the performance of present volunteer workers.

3. Develop and operate by a plan that distributes leadership according to priority needs.

4. Nominate qualified members for special church committees approved by the church during the year.

5. Present names of recommended workers to the church for approval.

Property Committee

The Property Committee is responsible for the care of all church property and buildings. It also makes studies and recommendations regarding need for additional space and furnishings for church program organizations.

The duties of the Property Committee are:

1. Make regular inspection of all church property and keep current inventory of all furnishings and equipment. Recommend policies regarding use of church property and furnishings.

2. Make annual study of space needs and allocation to determine if adjustment is needed. Recommend additional space if needed for growth.

3. Develop and make recommendations regarding maintenance policies and procedures.

4. Develop and make recommendations regarding adequate insurance on all buildings, equipment, and furnishings.

5. Develop recommendations regarding annual budget needs and administer maintenance budget.

Stewardship Committee

The Stewardship Committee is responsible to the church for stewardship planning, stewardship promotion, and administration of church finances according to church financial policies.

The duties of the Stewardship Committee are:

1. Develop and recommend to the Church Council an overall stewardship information plan.

2. Develop and recommend a church budget to the church.

3. Plan and direct the church's budget subscription plan.

4. Conduct studies and make recommendations to the church concerning proposed expenditures not included in the budget.

5. Review expenditures periodically in terms of budget allocations and recommend adjustments to the church as necessary.

6. Develop and recommend to the church financial policies and procedures.

In addition, ad hoc or temporary committees may be appointed by the pastor and Church Council to meet one-time, short-term needs of the church. A temporary committee will cease to function at the conclusion of its mission.

It seems feasible and desirable to structure regular church committees on a rotating basis over a period of three years with two thirds of the membership being retained each year. One third of the committee will be new, three-year term members.

Church Council in the Small Church

The task of the Church Council is to plan, implement, and evaluate the work of the church. Its membership consists of pastor, music director, secretary, Sunday School director, Church Training director, Woman's Missionary Union director, church treasurer, church clerk, and chairman of the deacons.

The Church Council meets monthly with tasks as wide ranging as calendar planning, use of facilities, future church programming, and allocation of limited resources. It meets to act instead of react. Truman Brown, Jr., suggested that a "church council can be the means for motivating program organization leaders to put their full enthusiasm and resources behind the priority need of the church."[5]

The evaluation process is overlooked in many churches. One of the strengths of a good Church Council is its willingness to set some standards for any activity in the church and carefully weigh the results of that activity by the predetermined standard. The congregation should then be apprised of this evaluation.

Record Keeping in the Small Church

One of the essential tools of good administration in any endeavor is the provision for adequate records. For educational organizations, the addition of a good record system provides the means by which the organization can measure growth and effectiveness. The general church membership role not only gives data on resident as well as nonresident members but, in some cases, provides legal proof of church membership.

Records may be easily established if someone is willing to do the initial work in starting the record system and in maintaining that system. The system should be simple and accessible.

The church, regardless of size, also has a legal responsibility to carefully maintain a giving record of each member. Amounts given are posted to the individual members account each week. Offering envelopes are stored for up to five years to fulfill requirements of the Internal Revenue Service.

Financial Planning and the Small Church

Large churches with diverse memberships can often accommodate seasonal shortfalls in church receipts. The smaller church can experience painful problems in paying salaries, being faithful in mission giving, and repaying loans during difficult times. With adequate financial planning, many of these problems can be avoided. Care should be exercised when adding new staff or borrowing money for capital improvements.

Implications for the Small Church

Administration is simply a tool to accomplish the goals of the church. If there is no vision, planning, staffing, coordinating and evaluating, the work grinds to a halt, and people become frustrated in their Christian walk.

Cyril Barber[6] told of the personal inspiration he received from reading Nehemiah. Barber's administrative skills in planning, organizing time and resources, and motivation of others have come to him from this Old Testament leader.

Each congregation, whether large or small, can reap the benefits of good administration if leaders and members rely on the biblical principles of Nehemiah and if they exercise good common sense.

Notes

1. See Lyle E. Schaller, *The Small Church Is Different* (Nashville: Abingdon, 1982).

2. See J. Grant Swank, Jr., "The Big Deal of the Small Church," *The Christian Ministry*, July 1984, p. 19.

3. See John Y. Elliott, *Our Pastor Has an Outside Job* (Valley Forge: Judson Press, 1980).

4. An overview of the work of these committees and other information helpful to a small church are included in Howard B. Foshee, *Broadman Church Manual* (Nashville: Broadman Press, 1973). The committee descriptions are adapted from this source.

5. See Truman Brown, Jr., *Church Council Handbook* (Nashville: Convention Press, 1981), p. 4.

6. See Cyril J. Barber, *Nehemiah and the Dynamics of Effective Leadership* (Neptune, N.J.: Loizeaux Brothers, 1976).

Bibliography

Allred, Thurman, ed. *Basic Small Church Administration.* Nashville: Convention Press, 1981.

Engstrom, Ted W. *Your Gift of Administration.* Nashville: Thomas Nelson, 1983.

Mintzberg, Henry. *The Nature of Managerial Work.* Englewood Cliffs: Prentice-Hall, 1980.

Myers, Marvin, author/comp. *Managing the Business Affairs of a Church.* Nashville: Convention Press, 1981.

Schaller, Lyle E. *The Small Church Is Different.* Nashville: Abingdon Press, 1982.

15

Cooperative Relationships

Bruce P. Powers

Churches are not independent bodies. They always function in an environment of mutual support and shared ministry with primary emphasis on faithfulness to Christ's mission. A church may be related formally to other Christian bodies, as in an association or denomination, or it may choose to function as an independent unit among Christian churches. Regardless, the commission of Christ requires that all congregations develop the best means possible to function effectively as His representatives.

Church Polity and Organization

Your church and denomination have a way of working together. The organization you have and the procedures you follow are called *denominational polity.* Polity is a statement of principles and guidelines that determine a Christian institution's form of government and procedures for working together. The same New Testament principles that guide local church government apply as far as possible to the practice of denominational government.[1]

Whether rigid or flexible, clearly defined or vague, there is an expected way of working together for the common good. To the degree that you understand and support these expectations you can guide your congregation in contributing to and drawing from the larger resources God has entrusted to His people in support of the church's worldwide mission.

Most major denominations have a basic source book that explains the how and why of church and denominational polity. These are used as resources for church leaders and as educational aids for church members. The purpose is to make Christians full participants in church and denominational activities, thereby contributing to order, effectiveness, and harmony.[2]

It is imperative that church leaders grasp the principles by which their denomination functions. In the absence of clarity about purpose, relationships, and procedures, a church inevitably finds itself divided—either within its own house or in opposition to sister churches.

Stewardship of Resources

Effective Christian service depends on a sharing of resources. By combining spiritual and material gifts from God, churches can extend and enrich their witness in ways not possible for a single congregation. For example, most churches cannot publish their own Sunday School materials, provide homes for children or the elderly, establish a college or seminary, provide salary assistance for hundreds of ministers in pioneer missions areas, or send missionaries around the world in an orderly and systematic way.

But by combining resources, churches can band together in enterprises which would be impossible alone. The people of God and the body of Christ become a reality as we bring ourselves together in an overall purpose and plan.

At the same time, all bodies do not possess the same resources. Consequently, congregations that are richer must contribute a greater share while those less able will give less. And church missions and new congregations that are needy will be assisted by others—for *giving* and *receiving* are both part of the stewardship of resources.

How This Works

Most evangelical churches follow a plan whereby local resources are shared among the home congregation and the various needs supported by the denominational group(s) with which a church is affiliated. For example, a large portion of church contributions will go toward costs incurred by the local congregation in its activities of worship, education, ministry, and proclamation.

A smaller portion will then be designated to denominational and other church-approved causes beyond the local church. The usual practice is to determine an appropriate percentage of contributions that will go to each denominational group. Then, this amount will be deducted periodically from contributions and sent to the designated body. Thus a church supports its own life as well as contributes to the larger mission of the church throughout the world.

How decisions are made about the channeling of contributions to various causes varies widely from denomination to denomination, and even among churches.

A denomination in which each church decides for itself what shall be contributed is greatly dependent on an accurate understanding of and commitment to denominational causes. Churches in such situations may give or not give, or adjust the amount of their contributions, depending on local sentiment regarding denominational activities.

Nevertheless, among denominations that depend on voluntary cooperation, there is a general expectation that at least 10 percent of local contributions will be sent to state/regional and national bodies. An additional 2 to 4 percent will be given to local causes through an association or other organization representing local churches. These contributions are intended for the use of the larger bodies, according to the *polity* of the denomination.

Other denominations assign a share of the cost of cooperative activities to individual congregations. Church leaders then work out a budget that will enable the local group to meet their own needs as well as contribute their proportionate share to the common work.

Benefits of Cooperation

When churches work together, they combine their resources and channel their individual efforts into a united, systematic plan to propagate the gospel regionally, nationally, and throughout the world. Such organized efforts provide practical and efficient ways to conduct a worldwide Christian enterprise on behalf of individual churches.

At the associational level, cooperation enables churches to be involved in these and other activities.
- Starting new churches and mission points
- Sharing Christian fellowship
- Supporting each other in times of need
- Approving persons for ordination to the gospel ministry
- Determining criteria related to denominational recognition
- Assisting each other with leadership training for volunteer workers in church programs

At the state convention level, churches have opportunity to extend the functions of education, proclamation, and Christian service through a state or region. Such activities provide services to participating churches as well as an outreach ministry to unchurched persons. Depending on the availability of resources, conventions might be involved in these activities.

- Developing and promoting methods and resources to assist local churches
- Developing and leading churches in statewide ministry and outreach projects
- Providing leadership training for volunteer church leaders
- Promoting home and foreign missions
- Receiving and distributing cooperative offerings from participating churches
- Assisting associations in their work
- Publishing a newspaper to inform church members and to promote denominational causes
- Operating Christian colleges and schools
- Operating benevolent enterprises such as hospitals and homes for children and the aged
- Operating camps, assemblies, and conference centers

At the national level, major emphasis is placed on achieving an overall structure and design for the services and ministries required by churches in the denomination. Such activities may be developed and coordinated in one location or may be administered from a variety of locations. Regardless of the arrangement, the polity of the body determines policy and organization, and tells exactly how decisions are made concerning denominational causes. This information is detailed in the constitution and bylaws of the body.

Activities of a national body might include these items.

- Developing and publishing curriculum materials
- Developing and promoting financial plans to assist churches
- Operating national conference centers
- Providing theological education for ministers
- Administering home mission activities
- Administering foreign mission activities
- Developing and promoting leadership training programs
- Publishing and distributing through public means information related to the emphases and work of the denomination

Looking to the Future

The future for Christian work is bright as long as cooperation is acknowledged as a basic New Testament principle. Together, churches can more nearly be the body of Christ on mission to the

world. James L. Sullivan, an astute observer of denominational relationships, suggested that there is no option for a local church. For
it is the lordship of Christ over the church and its mission to the
world that is of utmost importance. "Even as churches defend their
autonomy—their right to self-government—they ought also to defend theonomy, God's authority over them.

"A local church cannot remain fully Christian if it stays local in
concept and action," says Sullivan. A church must have a burden
for the whole world. There must be a delicate balance in which there
can be freedom of action and at the same time cooperation in the
fulfillment of the Christian mission.[3]

Notes

1. The author is indebted to Allen W. Graves for insights concerning church polity that
he has shared through personal conversations and his writings.
2. Several books on polity are listed in the bibliography. Consult your denominational
office or book store to determine the exact title currently recommended for your church.
3. James L. Sullivan, *Rope of Sand with Strength of Steel* (Nashville: Convention Press, 1974), p.
119. See also, James L. Sullivan, "Nature and Importance of a Local Church," *Baptist Polity*
(Nashville: Broadman Press, 1983), pp. 17-27.

Bibliography

Graves, Allen W. *A Church at Work: A Handbook of Church Polity.* Nashville: Convention
   Press, 1972.
McDonough, Reginald M. ed. *A Church on Mission.* Nashville: Convention Press,
   1980.
Mead, Frank S. *Handbook of Denominations,* seventh ed. Nashville: Abingdon Press,
   1980.
Sullivan, James L. *Baptist Polity.* Nashville: Broadman Press, 1983.
_____. *Rope of Sand with Strength of Steel.* Nashville: Convention Press, 1974.

Examples of Denominational Polity Resources

Airhart, Arnold, et al, eds. *Church of the Nazarene Manual.* Kansas City: Nazarene
   Publishing House, 1980.
Book of Discipline of the United Methodist Church. Nashville: United Methodist Publishing
   House, 1984
Constitution and Bylaws of the United Church of Christ. n.p.: Executive Council of the
   United Church of Christ, 1984.
Constitution, Presbyterian Church (USA), Part II: The Book of Order. New York: Offices of
   the General Assembly, 1981.
Gause, R. H. *Church of God Polity.* Cleveland, Tenn.: Pathway Press, 1958.

Graves, Allen W. *A Church at Work: A Handbook of Church Polity.* Nashville: Convention Press, 1972.
Maring, Norman H. *American Baptists: Whence and Whither.* Valley Forge: Judson Press, 1968.
Sullivan, James L. *Baptist Polity.* Nashville: Broadman Press, 1984.

16

Staff Relationships

J. Ralph Hardee

At any given moment, for any given staff member, staff relationships at a *feeling* level are, in varying degrees, either "good" or bad." To illustrate, if a staff member is asked, "What are your feelings about staff relationships?" words that are either basically *positive* or basically *negative* will be used to describe one's feelings. And almost every response—whether with reference to *overall* staff relationships, to relationships with another *specific* staff member, to *overall* relationships with the church, or to relationships with a *specific* church member or group—will fall into one of the following four categories.

1. Good, and getting better
2. Good, but not getting better
3. Bad, but getting better
4. Bad, and getting worse

Apparently, there is no such thing as "neutral" feelings about staff relationships! It is my assumption (and conviction!) that the feeling norm for staff relationships should be that they are good and getting better. This chapter offers some suggestions to staff members committed to that norm which can facilitate movement toward its achievement.

Covenanting: A Key to Improving Staff Relationships

A church staff is defined by Jerry Brown in *Church Staff Teams that Win* as "A group of Christian persons who in response to a divine and ecclesiastical calling willingly covenant with God, a local congregation, and one another to live out their vocational mission sharing responsibility and authority for enabling the church in its mission."[1] Included in this definition is a critical factor affecting one's feelings about staff relationships: *covenanting.* It is a key to improving staff relationships.

271

Covenanting: Concept

Four highly significant inferences about covenanting can be drawn from Brown's definition. First, covenanting is a mandatory activity for staff members. Second, covenanting is a continuing activity for staff members. Third, covenanting is to be done with God, with a church, and with other staff members. Fourth, covenanting involves shared responsibility and shared authority among all staff members. Each of these inferences also has a significant corollary. First, covenanting should be both encouraged and engaged in by all staff members. Second, covenanting should begin during one's prestaff experiences and continue throughout one's tenure as a staff member. Third, covenanting should encompass all three parties—God, church, other staffers—for every staff member. Fourth, covenanting should include both dimensions—responsibility and authority—for all staff members. The suggestions in this chapter all derive from my attempt to take these implications seriously.

"All churches have covenants with their staff members," Brown wrote. "They are well defined or ill defined, written or unwritten, official or unofficial, openly agreed upon or unmentioned or assumed. It is not a choice of whether there will be a covenant between a church or staff member; rather it is a choice as to the kind of covenant they will have."[2]

Covenanting: Commitment

All that Brown says about covenants between a church and its staff members applies to covenants between and among staff members! There will not be well-defined, written, official, openly agreed upon covenants by either a church or its staff members unless there is a commitment—a genuine commitment—to covenanting by all the parties involved. I think Wayne E. Oates was right when he concluded that "the most common cause of bad staff relations is the failure of both the church and the staff member to get their covenantal and contractual relationships clear at the outset of their work together."[3] In another book I expressed an opinion which I want to reaffirm here: "It is imperative for church staff ministers to be certain that their covenantal and contractual relationships with each other—and with the church—are clear. When staff ministers do not work at the task of making explicit the commitment and expectations that are implicit, misunderstandings arise, conflict ensues, and malcontention results."[4]

The Contents of Covenants

Staff ministers do not serve very long on a church staff before becoming aware that the expectations which are held by church members, other staff members, and they themselves about their role and function are numerous, varied, and often conflicting. While some expectations are apparent to everyone—perhaps even specified in writing—and others may be evident enough to be "sensed" by a perceptive staff minister, many may be unknown (or "hidden") to a particular staff minister. When expectations clash or are not met, problems arise in staff relationships.

For the optimal potential in staff relationships to be realized, there must be a high degree of correspondence between a staff member's personal expectations, the expectations of church members, and the expectations of other staff members. The testimony of scores of staff ministers I know is that where there is not a clear understanding by *all* parties of the expectations of *each* party, there is apt to be misunderstanding. And misunderstanding appears to be especially prevalent when inadequate effort is made by a staff member to clarify these expectations both during the process of coming on staff as well as during his or her tenure.

Because clarity of expectations among all parties is prerequisite to healthy staff relationships, it is appropriate for each party to ask the question: What are the common understandings that we must have in order to work together most redemptively? The content of a covenant helps to answer this question.

The "Standard" Covenant

Although a church staff is likely to have access to many documents which provide information on how the staff is to work together, it seems to me that every church should provide for its staff at least one document in which the "givens" of staff work are clearly stated. It should be perceived as the standard covenant common to all staff members. It should be the *primary* reference document which guides the church staff in their work together. An example standard covenant is included here for reference.

Basic Principles to Guide a Staff in Their Planning and Working Together

Spiritual

1. All staff members love the Lord, love the church, love each other, and behave like Christians.

2. All staff members are predisposed to joy.

3. There is among all staff members a spirit of humility and submission.

4. All staff members maintain a daily devotional time, and during this time they intercede in prayer for all other staff members.

The Scripture on which these spiritual principles are based is Galatians 5 which speaks of the "fruit" of the Spirit rather than the "fruits" of the Spirit: "The fruit of the Spirit is love," and it is manifested in "joy, peace, longsuffering, gentleness, goodness, faith, meekness, temperance" (vv. 22-23). For the church staff, joy is love's strength; peace is love's security; long-suffering is love's patience; gentleness is love's conduct; goodness is love's character; faith is love's confidence; meekness is love's humility; and temperance is love's victory. Every staff member—without exception—should be committed without reservation to the faithful practice of these spiritual guidelines.

Administrative

1. The staff is a shared ministry leadership team, and there can be only one chief of staff.

2. There is ongoing attention given to covenanting in order to ensure clarity in policies and guidelines.

3. There are regular staff meetings with adequate time devoted to both short-range and long-range planning.

These guidelines affirm the validity and necessity of the ministry of each staff member. Ministry which is to be united in effort and objective but divided in responsibility is to be expected. The pastor is acknowledged as having the church-assigned responsibility of being first among equals. While diversity of function among staff members is recognized and accepted, wholeness and unity in the ministries of all staff members is affirmed. There is a commitment to expending whatever time and energy it takes to ensure that all staff members have clear understandings of expectations and ample opportunity to participate in all planning processes affecting their work and ministries.

Practical

1. Each staff member is encouraged to think and function as a "full" minister and a team member.

2. There is good communication—especially when there is a problem.

3. Each is loyal to each other, and all are loyal to the church and to the Lord that we serve.

These guidelines provide for great latitude in the responsible use of freedom in exercising one's ministry to the fullest extent possible. A high level of trust, openness, relationship, interdependence, and maturity among staff members is assumed.

The "Special" Covenant

In contrast to a standard covenant which clarifies the expectations that all staff members and the congregation hold in common, a "special" covenant clarifies the agreements, understandings, and expectations that are unique for each staff member. Special covenants can be classified into three types.

• Maintenance Covenant with a Church (how you will be supported)

• Mission Covenant with a Church (what your job will be)

• Mission Covenant with a Staff (how you will work with others)

Although these will vary from situation to situation, each of them will be developed in some form. In the simplest form they will be informal working agreements, determined primarily by tradition and the ways in which various people mesh in their personality and work styles.

In more developed forms, there will be church-approved statements concerning how the congregation expects staff members to work together, and specific job descriptions for each position. (These were presented earlier in chapter 4.) And staff members will intentionally work on the issues that will bring them together into an effective ministry team.

On the following pages, you will find the essential information to work on these issues. I have described each of the types of special covenant and suggested ways to build solid agreements prior to and during your tenure with a local congregation.

Maintenance Covenant with a Church

What is it? A maintenance covenant specifies the resources provided by a church for maintaining a minister's ministry. The purpose of a maintenance covenant is to (1) clarify the personnel policies of a church as they relate to a specific staff minister and (2) clarify the financial resources provided by a church for a specific staff minister.

Where is it negotiated? A maintenance covenant is usually negotiated with the Personnel Committee, the Finance Committee, and/or a Pastor Selection Committee, and approved by the church. For a staff member, negotiation of a maintenance covenant may start with the Pastor Search Committee, or Personnel Committee. For a pastor, it starts with the search committee. Depending on the situation, it then moves to the Personnel Committee and/or the Finance Committee before approval by the church.

When is it negotiated? Thorough negotiation of a maintenance covenant should take place at the outset of one's ministry in a church. There will never be another time as opportune as this for negotiation of this covenant. A staff minister should use this opportunity wisely to ensure that an equitable salary, benefits, and housing allowance are provided for adequate maintenance of his or her ministry. There should be an annual opportunity for renegotiation of selected contents in the maintenance covenant with the Personnel Committee and/or the Finance Committee.

What is its content? Information about any or all of the following may be included in a maintenance covenant: employment policies and procedures (interviewing, calling, moving expenses); salary (arrangements, administration, review); office and equipment; housing allowance; automobile allowance; travel expense; basic work schedule; vacations; holidays; sick leave; time off for personal reasons; personal/professional development; sabbatical/study leave; advancement; tenure; grievances; insurance; retirement plan/pension; dismissal policy and procedures; release/resignation.

A maintenance covenant may be in the form of a checklist (such as in Figure 1[5]) or in the form of a contract (such as in Figure 2[6]). It should be noted that these examples in the figures are oriented solely to the resources often provided for a pastor. With minor modifications, however, these forms could be used for any staff member.

The maintenance covenant between a church and a staff ministe written form. It is too important to trust to memory or promise.

Mission Covenant with a Church

What is it? A mission covenant specifies the functional responsibilities assigned by a church to a specific staff minister. The purpose of a mission covenant with a church is to clarify what the church expects a specific staff minister to do. It answers the question: What is my work responsibility? Its focus is almost exclusively on the relationship which a staff minister has with the church. This type of covenant is typically called a job description. It should be in written form.

Where is it negotiated? The channels for negotiating a mission covenant are usually the same as the ones available to negotiate the maintenance covenant. However, for certain staff members, such as a minister of music, additional opportunities for negotiation may be available (like through a Music Committee).

When is it negotiated? Like the maintenance covenant, primarily at the outset of one's acceptance of a position. *Schedule adequate time to negotiate this covenant!* Many sessions with various persons/groups may be necessary. An opportunity for review and/or renegotiation of a staff member's mission covenant with a church should be provided annually by the Personnel Committee and/or the Finance Committee.

What is its content? A staff member's mission covenant with a church should be much more than just an organized listing of duties and responsibilities—as important as that is. It should also contain the vision which a staff minister and the church have for that person's overall ministry. Sample descriptions of the duties usually expected of staff ministers are included in chapter 4.

Mission Covenant with the Staff

What is it? This covenant focuses on the role of a minister as he or she is involved with other staff members. The focus of this covenant is more on knowing how one functions in a team relationship rather than what one does; more on knowing how one does his or her work than on what is achieved. Its purpose is to: clarify the quality of relationship which now exists; clarify the perceptions each minister has about how he or she is to work with every other person on the staff; and clarify how in their working together the

Figure 1

Check List for Clarity in a Call

	YES	NO

1. Church moves/provides moving expenses?

2. Church provides housing for pastor, family?
   If yes, in what form?
   Pastorium _____
   Allowance _____
   If allowance, how much monthly? _____

3. Church provides utilities or allowance? If yes, amount:
   Electricity $ _____
   Phone $ _____
   Water $ _____
   Other $ _____

4. Church assists pastor in purchasing home?
   If yes, indicate the following: Provides down payment as gift or loan in the amount of $ _____
   at an interest rate of _____ % to be repaid at $ _____ monthy. Amount to be paid in full within
   _____ days of termination as pastor.

5. Monthly salary to begin $ _____ with review for increase at the end of:
   Months _____ (How often? _____) Year _____
   Recommendation for increase to be made by _____ committee.

6. Monthly car allowance provided?
   If yes, in the amount of $ _____ per month and _____ ¢ per mile for distant travel on
   church business.

7. Church provides insurance coverage? If yes, how much?
   Health $ _____
   Life $ _____
   Retirement $ _____

8. Church provides annual book allowance?
   If yes, annual amount $ _____

9. Church provides weekly days off? _____
   If yes, number of days _____
10. Church provides annual, paid vacation? _____
    If yes, number of weeks _____ first year; second year _____ and thereafter _____
11. Is pulpit supply paid by church for vacation absences? _____
12. Church provides time off for:
    Revivals? _____
    State Convention? _____
    Southern Baptist Convention? _____
    How much time for revivals? _____
13. Is pulpit supply paid by church for these absences? _____
14. Are expenses paid to conventions? _____
    Wife included? _____
15. Church provides time off for bereavement? _____
    If yes, how much time? _____
16. Church provides time off for illness? _____
    If yes, amount of time annually _____
17. Are salary and benefits paid during time of illness? _____
    For how long? _____
18. Supply minister paid by church? _____
    For how long? _____
19. Church provides annual physical examination for pastor? _____
20. Pastor is designated as supervisor of other staff? _____
    If no, who is designated and for which staff members? _____
21. Time off is provided for study leave and training conferences? _____
    If yes, how much time annually? _____
22. Does church pay cost of job-related training? _____
    If yes, how much of total cost? _____
23. _____
24. _____
25. _____

Figure 2

Specific Agreements (These Will Vary from Church to Church)

Annual Financial Arrangements

1. VOCATIONAL COMPENSATION
   Base Salary: to be paid .... $

   _____ Housing Allowance _____ Parsonage Rental Value

   _____ Utilities Allowance _____ Utilities Estimate

   TOTAL $ _____

2. FRINGE BENEFITS

   Retirement Plans: _____ % of

   Vocational Compensation $ _____
   Family Health Insurance:
   _____ Pastor's Part _____ All

   Life Insurance on Pastor _____

   Disability Insurance on Pastor _____

   Tax Deferred Annuity _____

   TOTAL $ _____

Annual Time Arrangements

The church acknowledges that the pastor's work cannot be rigidly regulated because of the nature of ministry. Crisis situations and emergencies along with meetings and a heavy schedule may alter the pastor's schedule and sometimes necessitate his arranging his work and leisure at his own convenience. Despite week-end work and evening obligations, the pastor must find some time to spend with his family and for his own personal needs.

1. Day(s) a week off _____

2. Weeks for vacation _____

3. List holidays _____

4. Study leave time _____

5. Revivals or Sunday engagements _____

6. Total number of Sundays for church-paid pulpit supplies _____

   Vacation time _____

   Conventions or conferences _____

3. PROFESSIONAL EXPENSES
   Car Allowance: to be paid _____ $_____

   *Conventions and Meetings _____

   Book Allowance _____

   TOTAL $_____

4. NECESSARY EXPENDITURES
   Social Security Tax Allowance:
   _____ Half _____ All $_____

   Workman's Compensation _____

   TOTAL $_____

5. ANY OTHER CONSIDERATIONS
   Christmas Bonus or Cash Gift $_____
   Homeowners Insurance on
   Parsonage _____

   TOTAL $_____

_____ Study leave _____

_____ Revivals and engagements _____

7. Sick leave arrangements:

8. Any other arrangements:

*Professional Expenses, Conventions and Meetings

_____ For expenses at meeting attended as pastor

_____ Includes pastor's spouse when she accompanies

_____ For study leave and continuing education

_____ For civic club membership expenses

_____ To be used at pastor's discretion

_____ Pastor to give account for reimbursement

_____ Surplus belongs to _____ pastor _____ church

quality of relationship between and among staff members can be significantly strengthened.

Where is it negotiated? Anywhere two or more staff ministers get together, this covenant will be—consciously or unconsciously—in the process of negotiation.

When is it negotiated? As with the other types of covenants, much attention should be given at the outset of one's ministry to negotiation of a mission covenant with colleagues. Unlike the other types of covenants, however, this covenant requires continuing renegotiation on a regular basis. Rule of thumb: touch base with other staff ministers as often as possible—not because you have to, but because you want to! When staff members both solemnly and joyfully enter into a mission covenant with one another, the outcome is a better relationship and a clearer understanding of how they can most effectively work together and enjoy the Lord's work.

What is its content? Brown suggested a number of key issues for dialogue by a church staff team when it comes together.[7] These can serve as guidelines in determining the content of this covenant. The issues relate to each person's understanding of self and others in the areas of: value system; self-image; the goal, nature, and work of staff ministry; church expectations of a staff; leadership style; and church personnel policies and procedures.

These and other issues considered significant by staff ministers could be a part of the content of a staff mission covenant. It is unlikely that all of these issues will ever be discussed fully, and they need not be discussed in any particular sequence. However, none of them should be avoided or ignored in mission covenanting within a staff.

Covenanting: Negotiating One's Ministry

In a book which he edited, John Biersdorf described negotiation as the way that a church staff and a church work together to make the possible become a reality.[8] From this perspective, ministry is viewed as a continuing process of negotiation with a variety of persons and/or groups. The negotiation of covenants becomes the means through which the realities of one's ministry emerge: its shape and focus, its impact and effectiveness, its victories and defeats, its style and flavor, and its public and private significance. Biersdorf stated: "We negotiate our identity, our professional space, our work, our specializations, our relationships, the expectations people have of us, our study leaves, our salary and other rewards, our organizational and geographical location, and our pattern of development and growth."[9] The covenanting approach to ministry advocated in this chapter is consistent with Biersdorf's perspective on negotiation.

The negotiation of covenants enables a minister to accept personal responsibility for ministry by taking the initiative in purposefully directing one's life as much as possible rather than simply allowing it to be determined by past and present pressures. It is a *proactive*—in contrast to a *reactive*—ministry stance.

How does a minister develop a proactive posture in ministry? According to Biersdorf,

> It involves having both vision that gives our career intentionality, and effectiveness in realizing that intention. It requires a style that is open and that trusts the partners in the negotiations to make their unique contributions to the realities that will emerge out of the negotiations. It means identifying the issues that are important and meaningful for the church and developing a consensus about the most effective strategies for addressing those issues. Negotiation as an organizing principle for ministry is an explicitly dynamic image.[10]

And so it is!

In sum, convenanting through negotiation, that is, becoming proactive in determining the direction of one's ministry, rests upon the preconditions of mutual respect, mutual trust, mutual support, and open communications. The more attention given by a minister to creating these preconditions, the higher the probability that covenanting through negotiation not only *can* but *will* become the guiding principle for a church staff and a congregation in their work together.

Notes

1. Jerry W. Brown, *Church Staff Teams that Win* (Nashville: Convention Press, 1979), p. 23.

2. Ibid., p. 63. Brown provides information about "Contracting the Covenant" on pp. 63-64.

3. Wayne E. Oates, "Factors Hindering Effective Staff Relationships," *Search* (Summer 1971), p. 24.

4. J. Ralph Hardee, *Formation for Christian Ministry*, eds., Anne Davis and Wade Rowatt, Jr. (Brentwood, Tenn.: J M Productions, 1981), p. 187.

5. From Bruce Grubbs, *The First Two Years: A Pastor's Guide to Getting Started in a Church* (Nashville: Convention Press, 1979), pp. 9-10.

6. From Brightie E. White, Jr., "For the Pastor-Church Relationship: A Covenant," *Baptist Program,* Dec. 1982, p. 7.

7. Ibid., p. 60.

8. See John Biersdorf, ed., *Creating an Intentional Ministry* (Nashville: Abingdon, 1976).

9. Ibid., p. 18.

10. Ibid., p. 19.

Bibliography

Biersdorf, John, ed. *Creating an Intentional Ministry.* Nashville: Abingdon, 1976.

Brown, Jerry W. *Church Staff Teams that Win.* Nashville: Convention Press, 1979.

Davis, Ann and Rowatt, Wade, Jr., eds. *Formation for Christian Ministry.* Brentwood, Tenn.: J M Productions, 1981.

Grubbs, Bruce. *The First Two Years: A Pastor's Guide to Getting Started in a Church.* Nashville: Convention Press, 1979.

Review and Expositor (Winter 1981, LXXVIII, No. 1) Southern Baptist Theological Seminary (Issue on "Church Staff Relations").

Schaller, Lyle E. *The Multiple Staff and the Larger Church.* Nashville: Abingdon, 1980.

17

Managing the Minister's Personal Life

Robert D. Dale

What does it take to live happily and healthily in our hectic world? One formula for effective functioning includes a spouse who loves you, a job that challenges you, and five friends whose faces light up when they meet you. Add your personal faith in Christ to these three factors—a mate, a calling, and a tribe of encouragers— and you have the raw materials for managing the personal dimensions of your ministry.

Effective ministry requires effective support-system management. Why? Because ministry is a stressful, wear-and-tear calling and because ministry is a vocation of attrition for ministers and their families. The give, give, give of caring for others causes some ministers to give out and others to give up.

We who minister must receive in order to give to others. Thankfully, the Christian faith has rich resources for ministerial support: prayer, the Holy Spirit, and the fellowship of other believers.

Three major aspects of managing personal dimensions of ministry will be spotlighted in this chapter: marriage and family relationships, career development, and the general elements of a well-constructed ministry support system. Overall, managing your personal life as a minister involves a variety of concerns.

- Enriching your marriage and family living
- Handling family stress
- Charting your career span
- Planning for career growth
- Discovering the stages in a minister's career cycle
- Balancing your support network
- Managing personal and professional stress
- Avoiding burnout

Enriching Your Marriage and Family Living

Ministers are reminded by biblical instruction to be responsible managers of their marriage and family relationships. When discussing the ministers' qualifiers and disqualifiers, the apostle Paul links home management with church management (1 Tim. 3:5). To fail in family relationships is to be disqualified as a church leader.

When family living is viewed as a lifelong process, managing household relationships becomes an ongoing practice of updating our promises and vows to our family members. Consider the stages of a family and the recommitments that are basic for each phase.[1]

1. *The happily-ever-after family.* Newlyweds view family life simply: we love each other. Life is a romantic fantasy of rainbows, roses, and rendezvous.

Then the "I never knews" begin to be discovered. New and disappointed revelations come to light: the early morning grouch, the inability to balance a checkbook, the irritating habits. The "I never knews" reveal the essential double-edged nature of relational growth and raise up several occasions for the renewing of promises.

- Building a new family unit separate from the two families of origin
- Developing a mutual partnership
- Learning to disagree agreeably
- Accepting personality differences as growth opportunities, not as threats, flaws, or faults

2. *The "making-ends-meet" family.* Two paycheck families make up the majority of American households currently. In fact, for many families, two incomes are a necessity rather than a career option. Ministers increasingly are finding making ends meet is a state of family living instead of a passing stage. Several important promises need to be considered for these families.

• Keeping work from becoming a wedge between family relationships

• Avoiding letting jobs becoming the primary at-home topic of conversation

• Developing a joint plan for managing both incomes

3. *The "bundle-of-joy" family.* Parenthood creates family in its fullest sense. Especially when the child has been planned and prayed for, births of babies are really blessed events. Conversely, the introduction of new babies into the family circle creates strains—loss of

schedule flexibility, added expenses, care responsibilities, and potential neglect of the primary husband-wife relationship. These challenges suggest some additional updating of vows.

• Seeing children as unique persons, not rivals or substitutes

• Developing a parenting style appropriate to your current family situation

• Keeping the husband-wife relationship strong as a base for family health and effective parenting

4. *The "expanding-world" family.* This stage is a blossoming phase for both parents and children. Adults are putting down roots and investing in their careers. Many husbands are feeling more independent; some wives are returning to school or entering the work world again. Children are entering school and developing a circle of friends beyond the family. New commitments also confront this family.

• Facing power struggles as the family's interests diversify

• Resisting the child-centered family which neglects the fundamental husband-wife relationship

• Coping with deadening routines

5. *The "breaking-away" family.* Teenagers have a habit of storming the family fortress in their attempts to grow up and develop their own personalities. At this stage of family life, a double bind often develops between children's adolescent search for identity and direction and parents' "middlescent" search for identity and direction. Both generations face similar struggles simultaneously. A range of renewed promises present themselves to this family.

• Admitting that some tension is natural in families

• Adjusting discipline approaches as teens become more responsible decision makers

• Resisting the temptation to become pals with children and go through a second childhood

• Creating family boundaries which are flexible enough to provide children with both protection and freedom

• Preparing the husband-wife relationship for the empty-nest stage

6. *The "untying-the-apron-strings" family.* Launching children into their own independent lives is both exciting and frightening. Excitement arises from watching our parental influences and emotional investment in our children being tested in others' lives. Fright frequently emerges in the discomfort of letting children go and seeing

the family circle shrink. Mothers who have focused exclusively in childrearing feel the trauma of losing their identity when they launch their children. Becoming obsolete looms large on these families' horizons. Crucial new promises face these families too.

• Passing the torch to younger generations gracefully

• Coping with the loss of children's dependency and facing the evidences of aging

• Seeing children as only one aspect of our legacy to the world

7. *The "empty-nest" family.* This is a husband-and-wife family again. The real test of this family stage is the health of the spouses' relationship. Grandparenthood opens a new, and generally more relaxed, dimension of parenting. Painfully, the empty nest can refill as children lose jobs or divorce and as aged parents become dependent on their adult children. Three generations are learning to relate to each other in new ways during this stage. A number of recommitment opportunities emerge at this stage.

• Concentrating on spouse rather than children

• Becoming in-laws

• Nurturing another generation as grandparents

• Assisting aging parents

8. *The "three generations" family.* Most families experience intergenerational relationships involving at least three generations. In reality, Grandma is the third generation in many families. Grandmothers who have lived traditional life-styles are confronted with an unfamiliar role—putting themselves first. Another rare role some members of the third generation face is great-grandparenthood. Several decisions call for updating promises for three generation families.

• Affirming the present when you have so much past

• Freeing and encouraging children and grandchildren to live their own lives

• Identifying with grandchildren without isolating the generation in between

Each stage of family living takes on its own texture and challenges. The test of healthy families is how well they recognize the stage they're in and how completely they update their faith and actions to their stage.

Handling Family Stress

The minister's family is both a great resource and a heavy responsibility. Parenting is an increasingly demanding role. Some family counselors refer to parent burnout, the condition of trying to be superdad or supermom with only ordinary resources. Burned-out parents feel tired, depleted, numb, angry, and blue. Stressed families are not fun for either parents or children. Mothers are a bit more apt to burn out than fathers, especially if teens are in the home.

Parents are waking up to the magnitude of stress modern teens face. Suicide, for example, is the second highest cause of death among teenagers (following accidents). The incidence of teen suicide has nearly doubled during the past decade. What are the primary teen stresses?

- Peer pressure
- Personal appearance
- Parental expectations
- College and career decisions

Being Adolescent: Conflict and Growth in the Teenage Years, a new study of teenagers' activities, private thoughts, and emotional ups and downs, yields some interesting findings. Teens use forty-two hours weekly in leisure activities and thirty-eight hours in schooling. Teens spend 19 percent of their time with other family members; less than 5 percent of their time is spent alone with one or both parents. Dramatic mood swings of only fifteen minutes in duration are normal. Contemporary parents apparently need to devote more time and patience in their parenting efforts.[2]

Preteen children also experience stress. These stresses arise from a variety of primary sources.

- School performance
- Too little playtime
- Parental unemployment
- Minimal contact with grandparents and extended family
- Peer pressure
- Too much responsibility too soon
- Lack of discipline
- Excessive television viewing

These stresses frequently affect children's health.

Warning signs of stress in children are similar to many normal ailments. However, physicians agree that when at least five of the symptoms listed below persist for an extended period, a child is showing high levels of stress.[3]

- Bed-wetting
- Chronic complaining
- Compulsive ear tugging or hair pulling
- Cruel behavior toward people or pets
- Poor grades
- Feeling afraid or upset without being able to identify the source
- Depression
- Aches or pains
- Sudden crying
- Extreme nervousness and worrying
- Listlessness or loss of interest
- Poor eating and sleeping habits
- Difficulty getting along with friends, siblings
- Alcohol or drug use
- Nightmares
- Nervous tics, twitches, or muscles spasms
- Lying

Steps can be taken to help your family cope with its stressors.

- Talk about pressures. After all, two (or more) heads are better than one when families face their stresses.
- Escape for a while. Everyone needs a break from togetherness occasionally, particularly when family relationships are already strained and nerves frayed. Give each other some space and read a book or take a walk.
- Exercise away some pent-up energy and frustration. Jog, swim, or enjoy a family outing.
- Talk to someone outside the family circle. Friends, fellow ministers, or a counselor can help put pressures into healthier perspective.
- Serve others. Get your mind off yourself.
- Create a private place for yourself. Prayer and meditation are recognized methods for reducing stress.
- Use Figure 2 from later in this chapter as a measuring stick to see how much change and stress have accumulated.

Charting Your Career Span

Just as your marriage and family move through stages, so your calling of ministry can be charted and examined as a developmental process.[4] Think of ministry as a career span of five steps.

1. *Entrance into ministry.* The secular work world claims that a worker's first professional job is crucial. It helps shape the worker's outlook about that particular vocation, about success and failure, and about his or her fit with that type of job. The same is apparently true for ministry as vocation too. For some, the work is exciting. For others, it is overwhelming and bewildering. The first three or four years of full-time ministry mold our feelings about working with people.

2. *Advancement and stablization.* Now committed to ministry, the still-young minister faces the "make or break" element of career spans. Identity and skills begin to mesh comfortably.

3. *Maintenance.* Thoroughly into the career of ministry by this time, ministers might begin to feel some pressure not to rock the career boat.

4. *Decline.* The point of no return in work has likely been reached by now. The minister must resist the attitude of "a job is a job is a job."

5. *Retirement.* Giving up work is difficult for most workers. But this transition is even more traumatic for many ministers who lose professional identity as well as vocational status.

Planning for Career Growth

The calling of ministry is a dynamic career; it grows and stretches the minister as God opens new frontiers to us. Some of the new opportunities are positive and exciting. Other situations are more uncomfortable and crisis oriented.

Three predictable crises in a minister's career[5] have been identified. The first predictable crisis in ministry tends to occur about three to five years out of seminary. In this crisis the realities of congregational leadership collide with the idealism of youth and academic life. To overstate the issue, the young minister feels the internal tension between a headful of theology and a bellyful of people. Application of biblical insights to the real world of caring for people is the challenge facing the young minister.

A second crisis emerges about mid life. Typically, young adults invest their energies in a variety of enterprises: work, family, advancement, and individual concerns. Life and ministry begin to feel frazzled around the edges. The challenge of mid life is to put all of our career eggs into one basket and regain a focus in our professional lives. As the apostle Paul said at mid life, "This one thing I do" (Phil. 3:13).

Predictably, a third crisis develops as retirement nears. Many ministers find laying down the mantle of pastoral ministry as difficult as it was to take up at our experience of calling. Older ministers are overlooked for new ministry opportunities. As an energetic minister friend reported to me, "A Pastor Search Committee visited my church, heard me preach, and enjoyed an animated luncheon conversation with my wife and me. They spoke of a visit to their church field, so we could get acquainted with their ministry opportunities. Then, they asked me how old I am. When I replied, '62,' the conversation tailed off. They said their good-byes. I haven't heard a word from them since." Preretirement and retirement are a difficult emotional, financial, and leadership transition to face.

These crises are prime times to consider career assessment. Various denominational agencies, such as the Baptist Sunday School Board in Nashville, and the network of career assessment centers across the United States coordinated by the Career Development Council headquarters in Lancaster, Pennsylvania, provide counseling support for ministers.

Discovering the Stages in a Minister's Career Cycle

Life and our careers move through a series of important stages. Each new stage builds on the former stages, profiting from the lessons learned earlier or being blocked by other lessons that haven't been incorporated. These stages, while natural and fairly predictable, are fueled primarily by our decisions.[6]

Novice adults enter the work world from their late teens to about age thirty. Novices experience some suspension of expectations. Five basic issues confront the novice. (1) What dream or life goal will I structure my life around? (2) Which career will I pursue? (3) Who will become my mate? (4) Who will become my mentor? (5) Who will become my lasting friends? Vocational issues underlie and color all five of these concerns.

Novice adults in ministry can take several positive steps to meet the challenge of this stage of ministry.

• Study the life of Christ as a model—especially His vision of the kingdom of God.

• Allow your sense of calling to grow. Ministry directions often require some time and experience before they emerge clearly and finally. Jesus, Paul, Luther, and Wesley were all mature persons before they launched the ministries we remember them for.

• Recognize that ministry involves "paying the rent" of varied expectations. Some members will expect what's within your power to perform. Others will expect the magical and unrealistic of you.

• Accept the guidance of experienced adults. Mentors can often sense our best potential even before we see it ourselves.

• Cultivate professional relationships from seminary and early ministry experiences. These friendships are apt to sustain you personally and professionally during the rest of your ministry.

• Choose a ministry style that's comfortable to you. Let your own unique approach emerge over time rather than adopting someone else's style wholesale.

Junior adults settle down as they enter their thirties. Junior adults begin to stand on their own two feet; they aren't still novices, but they aren't senior adults either. They are junior adults—in between.

Junior adults face four challenges. (1) Junior adults put down roots. During the late twenties or about thirty, adults examine their life structure and, if it has served well, they get serious about life. (2) Junior adults focus on career advancement. They pursue a dream and try to become craftsmen. (3) Junior adults recognize and concentrate on meeting real needs. They begin to take some time to cultivate emotional and spiritual gardens. (4) Junior adults grow more independent. They put away the childish ways of earlier days (1 Cor. 13:11) and ready themselves to become mentors in their own right.

A number of actions can be taken by junior adults to move them purposefully forward.

• Develop a strong ministry-support system. You can find several strategies to consider in strengthening your support network later in this chapter.

• Renew your marriage and family relationships. Keep in mind that no relationship flourishes on autopilot. Don't neglect these precious relationships; heed the suggestions mentioned earlier in this chapter.

• Plan for continuing education. Reading plans, seminars, and similar resources help us keep our ministry skills sharp.

• Cultivate your devotional life.

• Guard your physical and mental health. Discipline in diet, exercise, and stress management are wise actions.

• Establish family financial planning practices now. Saving now for college and retirement keeps more of your options open for the future.

Mid-life adults slow down for a major life and career evaluation sometime after age thirty-five. They sense they are "old" for the first time. They discover that aging is rarely fun—especially in a youth-worshiping culture.

1. Mid-life adults examine the structures of their lives. This "time out" to review life's progress is often referred to as a mid-life crisis.

2. Mid-life adults often revise their life dream. "Middlescence," mid-life's echo of adolescence, raises two old questions again: Who am I? What will I do with my life? These issues are raised when we feel plateaued and stuck, feel that we peaked too soon, or feel that we've failed in some significant way.

3. Mid-life adults are threatened by obsolescence. The deadline decade, ages thirty-five to forty-five, causes them to feel a sense of urgency and to ask, "If not now, when?"

4. Mid-life adults try to create a personal and professional legacy. Symbolically, they work to make themselves immortal by living on through children, church building programs, and books.

5. Mid-life adults watch the home nest empty.

6. Mid-life adults face obvious physical and emotional changes.

7. Mid-life adults move toward senior status.

Numerous possibilities are open to ministers at the mid-life stage.

• Create and maintain supportive relationships. Our friends often sustain us during difficult days.

• Continue to be involved in marriage and family enrichment activities.

• Research mid-life issues to lessen the anxiety of the unknown.

• Consider career assessment if you seriously question your fitness or ability to serve effectively in ministry posts.

• Stay fresh devotionally.

• Get regular exercise.

• Become a mentor for the next generation of ministers.

• Clarify your ministry priorities.

• Recommit yourself to lifelong learning. Many mid-life ministers investigate Doctor of Ministry programs as a structured approach to continuing education.

Senior adults approach their fifties and sixties feeling the double-edged nature of aging: mellowing because purpose and meaning in life have been discovered or becoming more brittle, bitter, and angry about growing older. Senior adults are approaching membership in America's largest minority—retirees.

Senior adults deal with several basic life and career transitions. (1) Senior adults transfer hope to the younger generation. To illustrate, aged Elijah gave his mantle to the younger Elisha. (2) Senior adults cope with fixed income. This situation is made even more difficult because fewer than one half of Americans under fifty-five have made any financial plans for retirement. (3) Senior adults face the erosion of health and vigor. (4) Senior adults accept followership. They may find freedom in an elder statesman role. (5) Senior adults may accept an expanded mission in life.

Numerous strategies are available to senior adults for moving through the transition to retirement.

• Plan for retirement. Some psychologists claim that vacations are miniretirements; our reactions to vacationing provide clues to how we'll retire.

• Stay green above the ears. Keep on learning.

• Exercise. Medical doctors prescribe walking because they describe our thigh muscles as substitute hearts.

• Take the risks of new ministries. Now may be the time in your life to start a new church or write a book. You've done so much else that the risks are low.

• Don't become angry that churches tend to value energy more than experience. The greying of America is working in the direction of raising the status of older ministers.

• Work smarter, not harder. You know some shortcuts now. Use them and save energy.

• Remember the difference between self-concern, a necessity for us as we age, and self-absorption, an unattractive trait in persons of any generation.

• Keep in perspective that ministry is an attitude as well as a role. Caleb at eighty-five asked for the toughest task in the conquest of the Promised Land; he was aging, but he retained an exciting "can do" attitude about life and work (Josh. 14).

Families and career opportunities are important aspects of managing our personal lives. Basic to guiding our own lives, additionally, is the strength of our support network.

Balancing Your Support Network

Support networks generally contain at least five ingredients: soul mates, lifelong learning, spiritual coaching, mentoring, and physical fitness. Each of these five ingredients suggests ways ministers have arranged for ministry support. Each ingredient is crucial; none is complete by itself. Some ministers, however, rely on one or two ingredients to the virtual exclusion of the others. All five ingredients, when balanced according to personal and professional needs, provide resourceful support for your ministry.[7]

Ingredient 1 in an effective support system is your network of friends. Ministry support is people-to-people relating. That's where our friends in Christ fit in. Friendly soul mates believe in us, pray for us, provide listening ears, share objective feedback amid our questions and struggles, and lend us a shoulder to cry on. Soul mates help us repair the frazzled edges of our lives. Intimate encouragers from our family and friendship circle help us recharge our spiritual and emotional batteries after we drain ourselves by constant caring for others, helping in crisis situations, and standing with others amid the general wear and tear of ministry.

Jesus, our Savior and model, chose twelve persons to minister with Him and *to be with Him* (Mark 3:14). Our network of friends provides us with similar vital assistance.

• Offsetting isolation
• Learning to be a helpee
• Encouraging us
• Exploring problems
• Helping face our weaknesses and owning our gifts.

Ingredient 2 in your support network is a portable seminary. Support for ministry is fresh ideas and lifelong learning.

Some ministers take a "union card" approach to education and assume that a seminary degree provides all of the information and training the minister will ever need. That mind-set cuts the minister off from new insights and overlooks what professional education means. The term *seminary* literally means seedbed. Seminaries are greenhouses where seeds are sprouted before they are transplanted into the world. A seminary is a starting point, not a finishing school. A plan of continuing education and ongoing growth, therefore, keeps us "green above the ears."

Our portable seminary lends us support in deepening our convictions and expanding our ideas. Book clubs, loan libraries of theological books and tapes, and idea-sharing groups are basic learning resources. Idea groups help us trade, test, and organize our thoughts. Some groups structure themselves to review books and read formal papers on topics of mutual interest. Most are less formal in their organization.

Because two (or more) heads are better than one, our portable seminary allows us several possibilities.

- Brainstorming ideas
- Exchanging newsletters, clippings, and resource lists
- Evaluating new approaches
- Analyzing books, literature, and programs

Ingredient 3 in your balanced support system is your spiritual coach. Ministry calls for the constant growth of our faith. One way many Christian groups have traditionally encouraged spiritual development is through the enlistment of a spiritual coach.

A spiritual coach is a person who helps you set, evaluate, and celebrate the milestones in your spiritual development. Almost always a one-to-one relationship, spiritual coaching requires maturity from the coach and commitment by the novice.

Disciplined spiritual growth takes advantage of a variety of resources. A spiritual coach helps us use all the avenues of development available to us.

- Studying the Bible
- Praying and confessing our sins
- Contemplating and using silence
- Reading the devotional classics and biographies of spiritual giants
- Fasting and other forms of self-discipline
- Fellowshipping with other Christian pilgrims

Ingredient 4 in your support network is mentoring. A mentor in ministry is a model, sponsor, advisor, and ally. Our mentors believe in us. They are ordinarily older ministers who have already reached some goal in ministry to which we still aspire. Our mentors see our potential and nurture the promise they see in us.

Mentor relationships are common in the pages of the Bible. Abraham for Lot. Elijah for Elisha. Saul for David. Barnabas for Paul and John Mark. Paul for Silas and Timothy. These biblical mentorships, like modern instances of mentoring, are intense and sometimes, therefore, end painfully. Being effectively mentored strengthens us for solid ministry now and for becoming a mentor for others in the future.

Mentoring brings a range of valuable resources to us.
- Apprenticing in our craft
- Evaluating professional progress
- "Learning the ropes" of ministry
- Modeling how-to-do acts of ministry
- Mapping a route of advancement

Ministry is an "on-the-job-training" vocation, for the most part. A mentor provides a key link in our ministry-support network by placing a mantle of confidence on us.

Ingredient 5 in your support system is our physical health. The apostle Paul described our bodies as temples of God (1 Cor. 3:16). Public speaking is considered the most fearsome activity humans indulge in. Someone has estimated that a twenty-minute sermon is as physically taxing as eight hours of moderate labor. Vigorous health provides us the energy reserve to engage in strenuous ministry.

Regular exercise and dietary discipline yields several important dividends.
- Maintaining health
- Looking fit
- Feeling good
- Increasing energy levels

Checking for Balance

Balanced support is necessary for healthy and effective ministry. Emotional support is aided by our network of friends. Practical ideas for ministry grow out of our portable seminary. Development of our religious life is assisted by our spiritual coach. Professional growth is encouraged by our mentors. Physical fitness occurs when we treat our bodies like God's temples.

When one or two elements of support are stressed primarily or exclusively, our support network becomes somewhat unbalanced. A complete system of support can be visualized as a wheel (Figure 1). Like a wheel, symmetry is essential for balance in our ministry-support resources. And balance is a critical clue to the strength of our support networks.

Figure 1

Balanced Support System

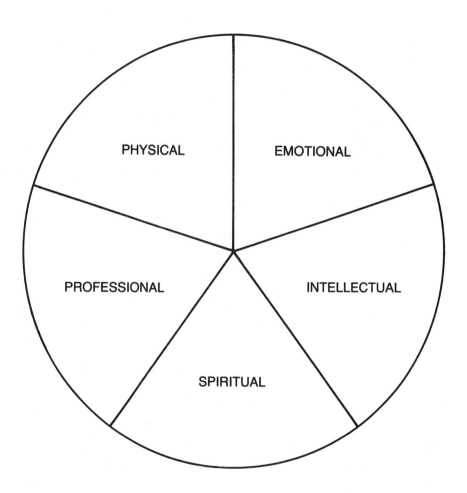

Managing Personal and Professional Stress

Stress accounts for the three best-selling prescription drugs in the United States: Tagamet (for ulcers and digestive tract upsets), Inderal (for high blood pressure), and Valium (for anxiety). According to family physicians, two of every three office visits are stress related. Ironically, our life-styles are making us sick.[8]

Stress is the "wear and tear of life,"[9] according to Hans Selye, the father of stress research. Stress is triggered by life changes that demand we adapt. A "ready response" is created by stress: adrenaline pumps, blood sugar levels soar, circulation to our extremities lessens to reduce blood loss in case of injury. (The last fact explains why our hands and feet feel cold and clammy when we get nervous.) The ready response is vital when we're in a real emergency situation. But if our life-style keeps us revved up too much of the time, and we catch "hurry up sickness," we wear out too fast. Then stress becomes distress, or bad stress. Interestingly, some folks react especially well to stress and are described as "hardy personalities."

Stress-free living is both impossible and unattractive. The complete lack of stress is death. Studies suggest that life needs some stress to spice it up. Moderate stress, then, becomes eustress, or good stress.

Several clues serve as early warnings of stress. This range of detection symptoms provide helpful signals for our self-care.

• Physical—fatigue, headaches, backaches, sleep disorders, chronic illness, hypertension, ulcers

• Psychological—boredom, irritability, defensive behaviors, anxiety, depression

• Behavioral—overeating, compulsive use of prescription or illicit drugs, drinking and/or smoking too much, temper tantrums, withdrawal from social contacts, escapist behaviors

• Occupational—job dissatisfaction, decreased work productivity, tardiness and absenteeism, sloppy decision making, sense of helplessness

Our natural "fight-flight" response, when constantly switched on, supercharges us and keeps us stuck in overdrive. The powerful chemicals triggered by stress combine to place unrelenting strain on our weakest organs. Our "reward" may be heart attacks, ulcers, diabetes, cancer, high blood pressure, suicide, and other physical or emotional breakdowns.

Some jobs are more stressful than others. Traditionally, we've thought policemen, surgeons, coaches, and air traffic controllers occupied the most stressing work positions. However, two factors combine in the most stressful jobs: high demands from people and low control over those demands. In reality, the toughest jobs belong to cooks, waiters, cashiers, telephone operators, and assembly-line workers. And ministers? Yes—when high demand and low control factors become prominent in our work.

Two mental health researchers, Thomas H. Holmes and Richard H. Rahe, have devised and refined a now widely used instrument, the social readjustment rating scale, to measure stress. These men have listed and ranked the forty-two common life changes they discovered to be precursors of illness. Strangely enough, an outstanding achievement was found to be as stressful as some dreaded catastrophe. Their basic finding was clear: change causes stress. For an indication of your personal level of accumulated stress, see Figure 2.

Stress management has grown into a multimillion-dollar-a-year industry in America. Professional help, while useful, isn't always required. Some personal strategies for coping with stress make our lives more manageable.

• Read up on stress and stress management. Understand the problem.

• Exercise. Change pace. Rest.

• Adjust diet. Eat balanced meals. Stop drinking caffeine and other stimulants. Lose weight. Reduce sugar and salt intake.

• Slow the pace of change. Approach decisions, career moves, and major projects deliberately. When large-scale events are completed, don't stop all activity abruptly. Live life as a process, not a series of sudden starts and stops.

• Cultivate your social support network. All of us need encouragers. Families and friends are particularly crucial in managing stress.

Figure 2

Holmes-Rahe Stress Test

Think back over the past year. How many of the events have occurred in your life? Check them on the list below.

RANK EVENT   VALUE YOUR SCORE

1. Death of spouse .... 100_____
2. Divorce .... 73_____
3. Marital separation .... 65_____
4. Jail term .... 63_____
5. Death of close family member .... 63_____
6. Personal injury or illness .... 53_____
7. Marriage .... 50_____
8. Fired from work .... 47_____
9. Marital reconcillation .... 45_____
10. Retirement .... 45_____
11. Change in family member's health .... 44_____
12. Pregnancy .... 40_____
13. Sex difficulties .... 39_____
14. Addition to family .... 39_____
15. Business readjustment .... 39_____
16. Change in financial status .... 38_____
17. Death of close friend .... 37_____
18. Change in number of marital arguments .... 35_____
19. Morgage or loan over $10,000 .... 31_____
20. Foreclosure of mortgage or loan .... 30_____
21. Change in work responsibilities .... 29_____
22. Son or daughter leaving home .... 29_____

23. Trouble with in-laws .... 29 _____

24. Outstanding personal achievement .... 28 _____

25. Spouse begins or starts work .... 26 _____

26. Starting or finishing school .... 26 _____

27. Change in living conditions .... 25 _____

28. Revision of personal habits .... 24 _____

29. Trouble with boss .... 23 _____

30. Change in work hours, conditions .... 20 _____

31. Change in residence .... 20 _____

32. Change in schools .... 20 _____

33. Change in recreational habits .... 19 _____

34. Change in church activities .... 19 _____

35. Change in social activities .... 18 _____

36. Mortgage or loan under $10,000 .... 18 _____

37. Change in sleeping habits .... 16 _____

38. Change in number of family gatherings .... 15 _____

39. Change in eating habits .... 15 _____

40. Vacation .... 13 _____

41. Christmas season .... 12 _____

42. Minor violation of the law .... 11 _____

TOTAL _____

Add up your total score. (Be sure to multiply individual event values by the number of their occurrences.)

Here's how to understand your score. A total of 150 or less gives you a 37 percent susceptibility to disease during the next two years, 150 to 300 points a 51 percent change, and over 300 points an 80 percent possibility of health difficulties.

Practicing preventive or management measures can help you deal with your stress level.

Avoiding Burnout

When ministers worship their work, work at their play, and play at their worship, they burn out personally and professionally. Misplaced priorities trigger burnout.[10] Satisfaction in ministry wanes when we become messianic. Inflexible overresponsibleness opens the door to disillusionment in ministry.

The minister who's "most likely to succeed" in the burnout process is the idealist who pursues an unattainable goal, like setting out to single-handedly bring in the Kingdom by Thursday. Their good intentions, verve, and extreme optimism can consume them and leave them spiritually arid and psychologically depleted. Godly persons don't have to carry their burdens alone like the godless do.

The most likely candidates for burning out (1) work with people and (2) have a low degree of control over their jobs. As a career, ministry may be more stressful than medicine, law enforcement, coaching, and air traffic control. Why? Because ministers deal with many situations in which their degree of control is low.

Four career stages indicate the process of dampening idealism. The burnout cycle repeats itself but can be recognized and successfully confronted.[11]

1. Enthusiasm is state one. Most ministers zero in on new tasks with fervor, hope, and tunnel vision. Typically, we overinvest in the new—jobs, relationships, and challenges. When idealism collides with reality, we may find ourselves blue, disillusioned, and unsure of our resources for coping.

2. Stagnation is stage two. The thrill of the job is dulled. Idealism tilts toward concern for days off, income, and evaluating performance. Dealing with isolation and intangible results wears on us. We still do the job, but the job does less for us.

3. Frustration is stage three. Powerlessness, red tape, and little leverage for change causes us to feel fatigued, irritable, and pessimistic. Because we wonder if we have any say in our own life's direction, we allow our frustration to set off a cycle of questioning our own effectiveness.

4. Apathy is stage four. We feel trapped. We must work, so we adopt "a-job-is-a-job-is-a-job" attitude. We withdraw from our tasks emotionally and do only what's absolutely necessary. Security becomes our goal. Otherwise, we just go through the motions. Apa-

thy is the bottom of the barrel but isn't the end of the story. We can light the fire again after burning out.

Self-care for the caregiver is the key to recovering from burnout. While churches and other Christian institutions help ministers cope with depletion and disillusionment, the recovery and preventive processes are set in motion by ministers themselves. Four families of growth strategies are available.

1. *Boundary marking.* Creating clear boundaries deflects burnout in ministry. Several boundaries need to be marked off and contrasted: call to ministry and basic identity, personal life and professional life, self and others, work and play, and possible goals and unrealistic expectations.

2. *Monitoring.* Tracking our feelings, patterns of ailments, and sense of spiritual depletion helps us confront the burnout process. Ministry is a vocation of attrition. When we give, give, give without renewal, we may give out and give up. Keeping tabs on where we are helps us avoid burnout.

3. *Replenishing.* Ministers need a backlog of encouraging relationships and accessible resources to offset burnout. Visualize your support system for replenishment as a cube. The cube's front face is your devotional disciplines and sense of relationship to God. The back face of the cube represents your family's encouragement. The cube's top face is your denomination's available relationships and continuing education resources. The bottom face of the cube symbolizes your congregation or institution's atmosphere of encouragement. The cube's right face points to your network of peers in ministry. Finally, the left face of the support cube notes the link ministers have with other helping professionals in the community and their insights into and resources for refreshing our vocational batteries. All six aspects of encouragement are needed for full and balanced support.

4. *Providing safety valves.* In spite of our best efforts, burnout can still sneak up on us. Real friends, spiritual revitalization, a healthy sense of humor, physical exercise routines, and medical assistance provide primary backup resources for recouping from burnout.

When response and reward remain at a minimum after idealism and effort have been kept at a maximum, burnout is a likely possibility. Ministers can begin the rebuilding process by taking some self-care actions. Then, with our batteries recharged again, we can minister effectively and give freely.

Self-Management: A Key Issue

Managing your personal life is crucial. In fact, it's commanded for the Christian. Jesus' great commandment reminds us to love God totally and to love our neighbor like we love ourselves (Matt. 22:36-40). By implication, if we're to care for others, we must take care of ourselves.

Notes

1. Robert and Carrie L. Dale, *Marriage: Partnership of the Committed* (Nashville: Sunday School Board of the Southern Baptist Convention, 1983).

2. "Teens' Private Moments Studied" (Raleigh, NC) *News and Observer,* 17 June 1984, p. 7C.

3. Steven Findlay and Gina Rogers-Gould, "The Pressure Is Starting to Get to Our Children," *USA Today,* 8 July 1983, p. 4D.

4. Charles William Stewart, *Person and Profession* (Nashville: Abingdon Press, 1974), pp. 75-78.

5. James D. Glasse, *Putting It Together in the Parish* (Nashville: Abingdon Press, 1972), pp. 40-42.

6. There are a variety of helpful resources available on career development. A basic beginning book is Daniel J. Levinson, et al, *The Seasons of a Man's Life* (New York: Alfred A. Knopf, Inc., 1978). The career framework used in this chapter draws heavily on Levinson's research.

7. For a complete discussion of this ministry support model, see Robert D. Dale, "The Minister of Youth: Developing a System of Support," in *The Work of the Minister of Youth,* comp. Bob R. Taylor (Nashville: Convention Press, 1982), pp. 95-107.

8. "Stress: Can We Cope?" *Time,* June 6, 1983, p. 48.

9. Hans Selye, *Stress Without Distress* (New York: Signet Book, 1974), pp. 11-51.

10. For a variety of definitions of burnout, see Jerry Edelwich with Archie Brodsky, *Burnout: Stages of Disillusionment in the Helping Professions* (New York: Human Sciences Press, 1980), p. 10; Herbert J. Freudenberger with Geraldine Richelson, *Burnout: The High Cost of High Achievement* (Garden City: Anchor Press, 1980), p. 13, Beverly A. Potter, *Beating Job Burnout* (San Francisco: Harbor Publishing, Inc., 1980, p. 10; and Robert L. Veninga and James P. Spradley, *The Work/Stress Connection: How to Cope with Job Burnout* (Boston: Little, Brown and Co., 1981), pp. 6-7.

11. For a brief overview of the burnout process, see Edelwich, *Burnout,* pp. 28-29. For a broader discussion of five phases of burnout, see Veninga and Spradley, *Work/Stress Connection,* pp. 36-73.

18

Perspective on Ministry

J. Ralph Hardee

In forming one's perspective on ministry, it should be remembered that act *follows* attitude. In other words, one's concept of ministry, to a large degree, determines one's approach to ministry. Thus, it is appropriate to examine one's attitude toward ministry prior to considering an approach to ministry.

Attitude Toward Ministry

Before one attempts to *do* ministry, some carefully considered decisions need to be made regarding *who* the ministers of a church are and *what* the role of staff ministers is.

Who Are the Ministers?

I once overheard a visitor ask the pastor after a worship service, "How many ministers do you have at this church?" Without hesitation, the pastor responded exuberantly, "Forty-five hundred!" This pastor knows what many clergy need desperately to learn! He has made a decision on who the ministers are in a church that is worthy of emulation by all staff ministers.

The church too often has reserved the term *minister* only for the clergy. But ministry is not the prerogative of a few; it is the calling of all of God's people—laity and clergy—into service. God's call is not for salvation alone but also to service for Christ among people. Baptism is, in essence, a Christian's ordination to ministry. The ministry should be seen *first* as the calling of the whole people of God into ministry—and *then* into *specialized functions* in ministry, that is, the enabling and equipping of ministers for ministry.

The difference in the ministry of the clergy and the ministry of the laity is primarily in form, not in importance or significance. Only chronologically is the ministry of clergy first. Of necessity, the ministry of training must *precede* the community of believers in the world. Unless this training is faithfully carried out, the ministry in the world will not have the necessary wholeness, vitality, and relevance. The task of "equipping the saints" is not a *higher* but a *prior* order of ministry.

The concept of a ministry of equal importance and equal validity for all Christians needs more converts among clergy and laity! Findley Edge, longtime professor at Southern Baptist Theological Seminary, frequently reminded students in his "renewal" classes that the work of the church is being done primarily by the wrong people and primarily in the wrong place. He admonished and pleaded with us aspiring clergy persons to commit ourselves to equipping the laity so they could be the *primary* ministers *primarily* in the world. Such a significant change in prevalent *approaches to ministry* in the church are not likely to happen, however, until (and if!) some changes in *attitude toward ministry* occur first.

What Is the Role of the Staff Ministers?

Another important attitudinal decision of ministry which needs to be made by every staff minister centers around the issue of the purpose of a church's staff. Two radically different views of the purpose of the church staff are portrayed in the following diagrams.

The view represented in Figure 1[1] conceives of the church as the arena for the staff ministers to do their ministry. The role of the laity, therefore, becomes to provide help and give support to the staff's ministry. This view places the church staff in a position of ministering *over* laypersons and tends to set a pattern of ministering for—rather than *through, with,* and *to*—the laity.

The view represented in Figure 2[2] conceives of the church as the arena for the laity to learn to do their ministry. Thus, the role of staff ministers becomes to provide help and give support to the ministry of the laity. This view places the church staff in a position of ministering *under* laypersons and tends to set a pattern of equipping ministry *through, with,* and *to*—rather than *for* the laity.

I believe a new—and exciting—era in approaches to ministry in a church could begin if all the members of a church staff understood and were committed to the attitude toward staff ministry depicted in Figure 2.

FLOW OF SUPPORT
(help, encouragement)

Staff's
Ministry

Other Leaders

General Church Body

FLOW OF RESOURCES
(skills, energy, time, money)

CHURCH EXISTING TO SUPPORT
THE STAFF'S MINISTRY

Figure 1

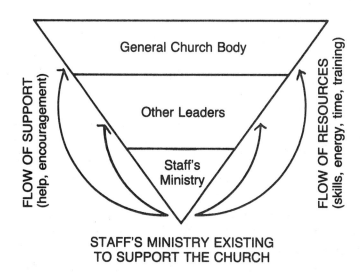

FLOW OF SUPPORT
(help, encouragement)

General Church Body

Other Leaders

Staff's
Ministry

FLOW OF RESOURCES
(skills, energy, time, training)

STAFF'S MINISTRY EXISTING
TO SUPPORT THE CHURCH

Figure 2

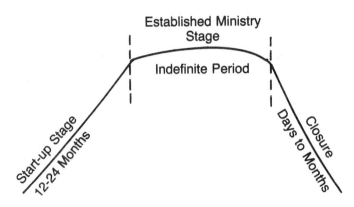

Figure 3

Approach to Ministry

Bruce Grubbs identifies three distinct stages of ministry in a local church, each of which falls in a natural sequence: start-up stage; established ministry stage; and closing.[3]

These stages are illustrated in Figure 3.[4]

Start-up Ministry

Frequently referred to as the "honeymoon" period of ministry, the first stage of ministry may extend over many months, but the first one-hundred days of this period will be the present focus. It is during these months that basic time-use priorities are set, and basic ministry patterns and habits are established. If the habits which one desires to practice later in ministry are not established during this period, the probability that they will become operable later is diminished considerably. In outline fashion, five "honeymoon habits" which should be established during the first three months of start-up ministry are suggested below.

Habit 1: Take Time to PLAN Together.—A staff that expects great things from God and attempts great things for God *must* pay the price of both short-range and long-range planning. The single most significant time for the staff to plan together is in the weekly church staff meeting. While planning is not the only activity during the staff meeting, it is a *necessary* activity. Many staff members I know feel that the greatest barrier to effective ministry by the staff is lack of adequate time for detailed and comprehensive planning in the staff meeting. The pastor must take responsibility for scheduling and conducting the weekly staff meeting. In addition to the staff meeting, another key opportunity for planning together by the staff is the monthly Church Council meeting. There are many excellent resources available to help a church staff in its planning endeavors—several are listed in the bibliography. Unless a staff gives priority to a time for planning together, however, the opportunity to use these resources seldom presents itself.

Habit 2: Take Time to PRAY Together.—Each staff member must see himself or herself as a spiritual leader with the responsibility for modeling all that is Christlike. One of the common interests which all staff members should have is the spiritual development of their colleagues on staff. Even if it is assumed that every staff member has a vital individual prayer life, it would still be a mistake to assume further that the need for prayer together is minimized. When a church staff as a group, and in one-on-one situations, intercedes for one another in earnest prayer, the sweet, sweet spirit so often sung about in the worship service but frequently unrealized among staff members will be developed. It should be as normal and as natural for church staff members to pray with and for each other as it is for them to pray with and for other members of the church!

Habit 3: Take Time to PLAY Together.—Staff members should genuinely enjoy being with each other—and should look for frequent opportunities to be together in play and relaxation. Some staff members will prefer less active activities than others. Every staff member won't be interested in golf, or bowling, or tennis, or Ping-Pong, but there is likely to be some common sports interest between any two staff members. This should be discussed and discovered. Play should not be limited to sports activities, however. Getting together in each others' homes and enjoying a meal together can also be a play activity. And every staff needs to have its own party occasionally!

Habit 4: Take Time to WORK Together.—There is a major difference between *independent* work and *interdependent* work by church staff members. Each member needs to do effective work independently, but all need also to be involved from time to time in participation and support of the work of others. It is important that staff members understand and affirm each others' ministries. Each staff member needs to be empathetic, sympathetic, and supportive of the work of all staff members. Get involved in the work of the other staff members. Look for areas of overlapping responsibilities with other staff members. Do some joint ministry. Taking time to work together contributes to a strong sense of "we-ness" among staff members and has a positive effect on staff morale. If churches could see a group of ministers who support each other and rejoice in the ministry of each other without the competition which sometimes emerges, it would do wonders for the church and everyone involved.

Habit 5: Take Time to GROW Together.—A climate should exist among staff members which encourages personal and professional growth. It is an exhilarating experience for several members of a church staff to attend a professional development event together. And they should . . . at least one annually. But personal and professional growth should not be limited to off-site activities. With a little ingenuity, an effective "at home" growth-producing plan can be developed among staff ministers. For example, all could read the same book and then discuss the issues, ideas, and so forth it addresses; or one could prepare a research paper related to some phase of ministry performance or issue in ministry which could be read and discussed by all. Some resources to assist in planning for personal and professional development are included at the end of this chapter.

Paying the Rent in Ministry

A staff member allocates a certain number of the 168 hours in a week to getting his or her work done—often giving 70 or more hours per week to the task. Every staff member, consciously or unconsciously, makes choices about *how* this time is used. Whatever one's position on a church staff, there are always numerous things that he or she *could do* and may even *want to do.* However, for a person to hold a position on a church staff requires that, because that position is held, certain things *must* be done. Until these *must do* functions of a staff member are performed satisfactorily, one has not "paid the rent," that is, met the minimal requirements expected by parishioners. And until the rent is paid, a staff member has not earned the right to engage in other equally desirable (and sometimes more desirable) activities.

The rent which must be paid varies according to the staff position held. Each staff member needs to calculate carefully what the rent is for him or her, then be sure that this "bill" is paid. In *Putting It Together in the Parish,* James D. Glasse says that most parishes want three things of their pastor: responsible (professional) performance in (1) preaching and worship; (2) teaching and pastoral care; and (3) organization and administration.[5] According to Glasse, when these basic services are delivered the rent has been paid, and the pastor is now free to do almost anything else he wants to do. Glasse cautions that a staff minister and the parish must understand that "paying the rent" should not be a full-time job: "There is a difference between devoting oneself *wholly* to the ministry of the gospel and devoting oneself *solely* to the service of a single parish!"[6] Glasse also contended that with good discipline and efficient management a minister can pay the rent in an average parish in from thirty to forty-five hours a week.

Closeout Ministry

This phase of ministry, under normal conditions, should not be less than two weeks nor more than six weeks. If staff relations have been as they should be, the resignation of a staff member will be a "trigger" event for both the church and the staff member in which emotions similar to the grief process experienced at death will be released. Adequate time should be allowed for "grieving," but once the resignation is submitted there should be visible evidence that one is departing, for example, packing of boxes, house-for-sale sign, moving van in yard, and other signs.

Although this is sometimes called the "lame duck" period of ministry, it need not be. It can be a very significant time in the life of the staff minister and the church if careful and deliberate attention is given to making a *graceful* exit. This period should be approached as an opportunity to *complete* one's ministry, rather than an occasion to simply *curtail* one's ministry.

Some of the elements involved in completing one's ministry are mentioned in A Code of Ethics for Changing Churches. This document is included here to provide some suggestions and guidelines for a staff member during the closeout period of ministry.

A Church Staff Member Code of Ethics
for Changing Churches

Guiding Principles

1. A staff member should be as certain as possible that any move is the result of the will of God for the individual and for *both* churches involved. Be sensitive to seek and abide by the will of God at every step in considering changing churches. In interpreting the call of God, one or more of the following factors may be involved:

   a. A feeling that one's work is finished.

   b. An awareness of overwhelming opposition. A degree of friction and opposition is to be expected, but sometimes the opposition is so great it is unwise to continue. To leave is not necessarily to surrender.

   c. The challenge of an inviting opportunity. The staff member need not feel that one's work is completed before another place of service is considered.

   d. A conviction apart from all of these. The call may come directly rather than through good or bad circumstances.

2. A staff member should understand that each move is unique. Different circumstances are involved and different considerations are necessary in each situation. The staff member should also realize that there is no perfect situation or perfect church.

Prestaff Relations with Prospective Church

1. A staff member should remain passive to all inquiries from a church whose staff counterpart has not yet resigned. It should be understood, however, that a church without a staff counterpart is justified in contacting any potential candidate whether or not that person is presently serving a church.

2. A staff member should not use flirtations with other churches to improve one's present position financially.

3. A staff member should not mislead a church into being considered if that person feels assured that he or she will not accept. One should not allow oneself to be recommended to a church that he or she is unwilling to accept.

4. A staff member should not allow oneself to be considered as a candidate by a church until there is positive assurance that no other candidate is being considered simultaneously. Care should be

taken to be sure that a church considers only one person at a time; each case should be closed before another person is considered.

5. A staff member is at liberty to use any dignified means to get oneself and his or her qualifications introduced to a church seeking to fill a position. The usual practice is not to apply directly to a church; rather, recommendations should come from one's circle of friends and from professional and educational sources.

6. A staff member should negotiate with only one church at a time. Never visit a prospective church if there is already involvement with another prospective church.

7. A staff member should relate to a key leader who can be taken into confidence when seriously considering a move. This confidant should be asked to keep it confidential and to pray with the staff member about the decision. One should also tell this confidant about any and all visits to be made to a prospective church *before* the visits are made.

8. The staff member should always take one's family—if married —into confidence when seriously considering a move. Any decision should be a family affair.

9. A staff member should always take into account the welfare of the church now being served, one's relationship to the present field, and the investment of the present church in one's ministry when deciding upon another field of work. If all relationships are happy, if the work is progressing, and if the opportunity is great, then the staff member should be patient, deliberative, and slow about moving.

10. A staff member should inform the key leader (see #7) as soon as the decision is made to resign; together they should decide on a timetable for the exiting process.

11. A staff member should request that the call by a church be upon the recommendation of the Personnel Committee or Pastor Selection Committee. This procedure helps to establish an initial wholesome understanding and working relationship with the church and its total staff.

12. A staff member, before going out to one's new work, should (1) write a formal letter of acceptance to the new church; (2) write individual letters of anticipation to the new staff members; and (3) write individual letters of anticipation to new key leaders.

Staff Relations with Present Church

1. A staff member should resign in such a way as to safeguard the interest of the work one leaves and to ensure the best possible continuance of the overall program up to the time one's successor arrives. Refuse to participate in critical evaluation of other staff members. Be as supportive as possible, still being honest. Affirming people, staff, leaders, and the position helps provide continuity and paves the way for a good beginning for one's successor.

2. A staff member should maintain relationships both in the church and in the community which would permit that person to return to any former church to serve again, and be able to look everybody straight in the eye without being ashamed.

3. A staff member should use finesse, discretion, and judgment in visiting former places of service. Relations with former members should be determined wholesomely by the nature of the relationships shared during one's service there. One should not return for a visit to the church most recently left without a specific invitation for at least six months. Under no circumstances should one return too frequently to visit. Nor should a visit be made before one's successor is on the job.

4. A staff member should allow the church to choose a successor without interference. Stay out of the selection process entirely. The church should select a committee or an interim worker without any involvement by the departing staff member.

5. A staff member should leave, if possible, when the work of the church is effective rather than when the tension is high.

6. A staff member, if asked to leave by the church and/or the pastor and the situation cannot be alleviated, should leave quietly. On the other hand if the pastor resigns, other staff members should plan to remain indefinitely, as long as the church needs their service.

Poststaff Relations with Present Church

1. A staff member, after arriving at one's new work, should (1) write a formal letter of appreciation to the former church; (2) write individual letters of appreciation to the former staff members; and (3) write individual letters of appreciation to former key leaders and friends.

2. When one's successor is selected, a letter of congratulations and encouragement should be written to that person.

Notes

1. Adapted from Bruce Grubbs, *The First Two Years: A Pastor's Guide to Getting Started in a Church* (Nashville: Convention Press, 1979), p. 6.
2. Ibid.
3. Ibid., p. 8.
4. Ibid.
5. James D. Glasse, *Putting It Together in the Parish* (Nashville: Abingdon, 1972), p. 56.
6. Ibid., p. 58.

Bibliography

Biersdorf, John, ed. *Creating an Intentional Ministry*. Nashville: Abingdon, 1976.
Glasse, James D. *Putting It Together in the Parish*. Nashville: Abingdon, 1972.
Grubbs, Bruce. *The First Two Years: A Pastor's Guide to Getting Started in a Church*. Nashville: Convention Press, 1979.
Wedel, Leonard E. *Church Staff Administration*. Nashville: Broadman Press, 1978.

Resources

The Seminary External Education Division (SEED), 901 Commerce Street, Nashville, Tennessee 37203-3620, is an outstanding resource for personal growth. Write for a free catalog of courses.

The Southern Baptist seminaries offer Continuing Theological Education Conferences on campus throughout the year. Request a listing of the conferences at these schools.

The Sunday School Board provides workshops, seminars, and conferences; write the Church Program Training Center, Sunday School Board, 127 Ninth Avenue North, Nashville, Tennessee 37234.

Week-long programs at Ridgecrest and Glorieta Conference Centers focus on personal and professional needs of ministers. For a schedule, write the Conference Center Division, 127 Ninth Avenue North, Nashville, Tennessee 37234.

The Career Guidance Section of the Church Administration Department, Sunday School Board offers eleven-day seminars on personal and professional growth and three-day personalized career assessments for ministers and their mates. Contact this section for complete details.

Some Baptist colleges and universities offer continuing education for ministers. Check with institutions in your area.

Contact the American Society of Training and Development, P. O. Box 8012, Madison, Wisconsin 53705 for leadership training courses and materials.

The Society for the Advancement of Continuing Education for Ministry

(SACEM). Write to SACEM, 3401 Brook Road, Richmond, Virginia 23227 to obtain a regional "Continuing Education Resource Guide."

The Academy of Parish Clergy. Write to APC, 3100 West Lake Street, Minneapolis, Minnesota 55416 for information about possible colleague groups in your area.

Action Training Centers. Write to Metropolitan Ecumenical Training Center (METC), 1419 V. Street, NW, Washington, DC 20009 to obtain a national listing of centers.

Association for Clinical Pastoral Education. Write to the association, 475 Riverside Drive, Room 450, New York, NY 10027 for information about accredited programs in your area.

Career Centers. Write to Career Development Council, 475 Riverside Drive, Room 760, New York, NY 10027 to obtain a list of accredited centers serving your region.

Hospitals are other sources of continuing education for personal growth, marriage enrichment, and improvement in caring skills.